# Love Songs

By the same author and compiler . . .

# AL BRYANT

# Love Songs

Daily Meditations for Married Couples

WORD BOOKS
PUBLISHER
WACO, TEXAS

Library of Congress Catalog Card Number: 78-59422

ISBN 0-8499-0306-8
Special Gift Edition—1982
Printed in the United States of America

Unless otherwise indicated, Scripture quotations are from the King James Version of the Bible. Scripture quotations marked RSV are from the Revised Standard Version of the Bible, copyright 1946, 1952, © 1971, 1973 by the Division of Christian Education of the National Council of the Churches of Christ in the U.S.A., and used by permission. Quotations marked TAB are from *The Amplified Bible,* copyright © 1965 by Zondervan Publishing House. Quotations marked ASV are from the American Standard Version of the Bible, published 1901. Quotations marked TLB are from the *The Living Bible, Paraphrased* (Wheaton: Tyndale House Publishers, 1971) and are used by permission. Scriptures marked MLB are from the New Berkeley Version in Modern English, Revised Edition: copyright 1945, 1959, © 1969 by Zondervan Publishing House; New Testament © 1945 by Gerrit Verkuyl; assigned 1958 to Zondervan Publishing House; used by permission.

*To my wife*
*JEANNE*
*the one with whom*
*I first learned these*
*lessons in love*

# Introduction

They tell me the institution of marriage is in trouble today. The meteoric rise in the national divorce rate, the multitudes of abused children, the proliferation of pornography would seem to indicate this is truly the case. And that is the reason for *LoveSongs:* In this day of "abbreviated" marriage and instant no-fault divorce, of crumbling homes and weakening marital ties, I have written *LoveSongs* to lift up God's lofty standard for the marriage relationship, and hopefully to set forth some practical as well as spiritual goals and guidelines for Christian couples.

When two people marry, the Bible says, they become as one person. From that biblical premise, I have prepared a book of devotionals specifically slanted and definitely designed for married couples. Each devotional is developed around a Scripture text, and frequently these verses use the pronoun "you." I have taken the liberty of applying that to the entity of you two in marriage, for the two of you have literally become one.

Many of the meditations in *LoveSongs* are my own; I have also drawn upon the devotional writers of a past generation for their insights on certain verses. The devotionals are loosely organized around the "fruits of the spirit" described by Paul in Galatians 5: 22–23; to these I have added the basic concept of salvation, and closed the book with the seasonal concepts of thankfulness and advent (Christmas).

Why base a book on marriage on the concept of "fruits of the spirit"? As I have written and researched these "lovesongs," I have been struck over and over again by the interrelationship of these "fruits"—love, joy, peace, longsuffering (patience), gentleness, goodness, faith (faithfulness), meekness, temperance (self-control). Really, the "fruits" of a truly Spirit-filled life cannot be separated from one another. They are a cluster of fruit on a branch, the Christian, stemming from the Vine, Jesus Christ. They are interwoven, overlapping one another in such richness and beauty that they become a massive cluster of Christlikeness as we contemplate the various facets of fruit-bearing and maturity in the growing Christian life.

The fruits of the spirit do not come all at once, instantaneously, at the moment of conversion. They come as a result of cultivation, pruning, weeding, watering, growing—they come as the Christian opens his life more and more to God, allowing Him to "squeeze out" the worldliness, the bitterness, the frustration of selfish and self-centered living, to fill the life instead with Himself, His blessed Holy Spirit, and the resulting richness of the Christ-life.

In the same way, the good marriage is not born full-blown at the moment of the wedding ceremony and exchanging of vows, meaningful as that moment may be. No, a marriage is a growing process as well, and as God is allowed to control, that marriage grows better and better. That is why there seems to be an aura almost of saintliness over those Christian couples who have survived (in more ways than one!) to celebrate a fiftieth, sixtieth, or even a seventy-fifth wedding anniversary. These beautiful marriages have been growing through the years, and like the stately and dignified giant redwood tree, the oldest of God's living creations, they reflect a grace and dignity, a selflessness that can come only with maturity in Christ.

I have dedicated *LoveSongs* to my wife, Jeanne, but in a sense it is also dedicated to our sons, Tom, Don and John, and to their wives, Gail, Mindy and Michele, with the prayer that these principles will help them avoid some of the pitfalls that could have swallowed up our marriage. In another sense, the book is dedicated to all Christian couples who have worked or are willing to work at making their marriages a monument to God's love and care. Marriage is a day-by-day, day-at-a-time growing process. There will be days when seemingly no progress is made—but other days in retrospect will turn out to be milestones in the mutuality of a growing marriage beautiful to behold.

Frankly, I don't think the concepts expressed in *Love-Songs* will work in any but Christian marriages, for they call for a common commitment to a Third Person, Christ, who must be the peak of the "divine triangle" at the heart of a successful marriage:

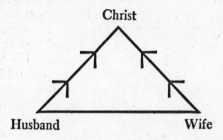

Notice how that triangle works; the closer husband and wife individually and together draw to Christ, the closer they grow toward one another.

If you are not Christians, or one of you is not a Christian, do not close this book, however. Rather, read it together, as it was designed to be read, and come to know the Christ it glorifies, and grow together into that exciting and adventurous discovery of what it means to become "lovers and friends" in this unique and God-given gift of marriage.

In His love and Mine
AL BRYANT

# January

*And Abraham said, My son, God will provide ...*
*[an] offering. .... And Abraham called the name of*
*that place Jehovah-jireh.* —Genesis 22:8–14

**1**

Write deep in your heart this New Year's day this word of sublime confidence, "Jehovah-jireh," "The Lord will provide!" It tells you that you can trust God always; that no promise of His ever fails; that He does all things well; that out of all seeming loss and destruction of human hope He brings blessing. You have not passed this way before. There will be sorrows and joys, failures and successes this year, just as there were last year. You cannot forecast individual experiences. You cannot see the next step before your feet. Yet Jehovah-jireh calls you to enter the new year with calm trust. He bids you put away all anxieties and fears, for "The Lord will provide!" —J. R. MILLER

*For Israel hath forgotten his Maker.* —Hosea 8:14

**2**

The phrase, "That marriage was made in heaven," is heard at many weddings. How often it is used to describe a particularly well-suited couple, only to be retracted later when the divorce is final. Even Christians, in unprecedented numbers, are experiencing the trauma and tragedy of divorce. What is the problem? Hosea, who himself survived and struggled through an unhappy marriage, gives us the answer in the words of our text: "Israel hath forgotten his Maker." The marriage has forgotten its Maker! George P. Weiss reminds us, "Marriages can be made in

# January

heaven, but they must be lived on earth." *Changing Times* says it another way: "Marriages may be made in heaven, but man is responsible for the maintenance work." If you are trying to maintain your marriage without recourse to its original Maker, that is your problem. Begin today to remember: "A good marriage is not a contract between two persons, but a sacred covenant between three. Too often Christ is never invited to the wedding and finds no room in the house" (DONALD T. KAUFFMAN). Did you invite Him to the wedding, but forget to invite Him to the home?

**3**

*And the Lord shall guide thee continually.*
*—Isaiah 58:11*
*My presence shall go with thee, and I will give thee rest.* *—Exodus 33:14*

The guidance of God is essential if we are to successfully reach our destination. Just as we do not set out on a journey (if we are wise) to a strange land without a road map, we should not start on the "marriage trip" without a map—the Word of God. But anyone going into unknown territory would be even wiser to hire a guide who was familiar with the area, in addition to the map. God is ready to guide you. Scores, even hundreds of times, He states that willingness to the children of Israel. Our passages for meditation today chronicle just two of those promises. The Psalms, in particular, are full of references to His guidance and His presence with His children. As you move through the "unknown territory" of married life, don't make the mistake of trying to go it on your own. Agree together on your need for guidance—and then go to the right Guide. He will guide you not just intermittently —but continually! And along with His constant guidance will come the "rest" of knowing you are on the right road, and the great privilege of His presence on your daily path!

*The Lord he is God; there is none else beside him.* —Deuteronomy 4:35

**4**

Allow God to take His place in your heart and life. Luther often said to people who came to him about difficulties, "Do let God be God." Let God be all in all, every day in your life, from morning to evening. No more say, "I am God"; let it be, "God and I"—God first, and I second; God to lead, and I to follow; God to work all in me, and I to work out only what God works; God to rule, and I to obey. Even in that order there is a danger, for the flesh is so subtle, and one might begin to think, "It is God and I. Oh, what a privilege that I have such a partner!" There might be a secret temptation to self-exaltation in associating God with myself. There is a more precious word still —"God and not I; not God first, and I second: God is all, and I am nothing." Paul said, "I labored more abundantly than they all, though I be nothing." —ANDREW MURRAY

*Certainly I will be with thee [Moses].*
—Exodus 3:12

**5**

*I . . . will keep thee [Jacob] in all places whither thou goest.* —Genesis 28:15

One of the greatest blessings of a good marriage is the companionship two like-minded people can enjoy. Companionship is friendship, and one of the most moving tributes I can give my marriage partner is to realize that this one with whom I share my life is more than just my lover; she is my best friend as well! But there is another Friend without whom no marriage is complete, and that is the One who spoke the words of our text addressed to Moses when he was watching over his father-in-law's flocks. He also spoke the words to Jacob when that complex man was struggling with Him at the time of the vision of the heavenly ladder. These two great men of God needed the assurance of God's companionship in the way. As you begin married life together, or continue on your way, you too need His companionship and friendship. Just as He promised Moses and Jacob His presence with them, He will be with you. So make Him your "companion on the way" as you take your journey into life!

**6** *The beloved of the Lord shall dwell in safety by him.* —Deuteronomy 33:12

God is *love*—what a word that is!—*Love*—and wherever God is, there is love; and surely God is everywhere with us, whether we perceive it or not. Love encircles, it encompasses us on every side, it pervades our whole being, even love, the love of the Most High.

"I have loved thee with an everlasting love" (Jer. 31:3). God did not wait till we had done something before He loved us. Before all ages He thought of us, and thought of us only to do us good. . . . O, unmeasured love which has given me what I possess, and promised me infinitely more! O, uninterrupted and unfading love! Where is my heart, O my God, if I am not filled with gratitude and affection for Thee? —FENELON

**7** *For God so loved the world that he gave. . . .* —John 3:16

The story is told of a child in Luther's time who had been taught to think of God only with dread, as of a terrible judge. In her stern home the name of God had been mentioned only to terrify and frighten her. But one day in her father's printing office she picked up a scrap of paper, and found on it the first words of our text, "God so loved the world that he gave—" The remaining words were torn off, but even in this mere fragment there was a new revelation to her. It told her that God loved the world, loved it well enough to give something. What He gave she did not know, but it was a great deal for her to know that He loved the world enough to give anything to it. The new thought brought great joy to her heart. It completely changed her conception of God. She learned to think of Him as one who loved her, as her Friend, ready to give her rich gifts and all good, and this concept brightened and transformed her life.   —J. R. MILLER

*God loved. . . .*   —2 Chronicles 9:8

# 8

Love is the great channel through which God pours His mercy upon mankind. Let our love be firm, constant and inseparable, not coming and returning like the tide, but descending like a never-failing river, ever running into the ocean of divine excellency, passing on in the channels of duty and in constant obedience, and never ceasing to be what it is.   —JEREMY TAYLOR

> As long as time is
> Love loveth . . . Time is but a span,
>   Love loves forever,
> And finds a sort of joy in pain,
> And gives with naught to take again,
> And loves too well to end in vain.
>   Is the gain small then?
>   Love laughs at never,
> Outlives our life, exceeds the span
> Appointed to mere mortal man;
> That which love is and does and can,
>   Is all in all then.
>           —CHRISTINA G. ROSETTI

*God is love.*   —1 John 4:8

# 9

There are questions which nothing can answer but God's love, which nothing can meet but God's promises, which nothing can calm but a perfect trust in His goodness. There is a shadow and a mystery upon all creation till we see God in it; there is trouble and fear till we see God's love.   —DEWEY

In any family circle the gentle influence of one loving soul is sufficient to breathe around it an unspeakable calm. It has a soothing power like the shining of sunlight, or the voice of doves heard at evening. How can you gain such an influence? Seek and you will know how, for to seek God is to find, and to listen is to hear, and to hear is to know and love.   —F. W. FARRAR

If your heart yearns for love, be loving; if you would free mankind, be free yourself; if you would have a brother be frank with you, be frank to him. This is the true atmosphere of love.

# 10

*Love never ends.*   —1 Corinthians 13:8, RSV

He who can say, "Nothing shall separate me from the love of God in Christ," will be able to triumph in the midst of the greatest troubles. The soul who lives under the assurance of divine favor cannot but bear up patiently and quietly under the greatest sufferings that can possibly befall it in the world.   —THOMAS BROOKS

Life is full of opportunities for learning love. Every man and every woman has a thousand of them every day. The world is not a playground—it is a schoolroom; and the great lesson we are always to learn is the lesson of love in all its parts. . . . "Character is the stream of life." That is where you are to learn love.   —HENRY DRUMMOND

Love does not mean one thing in man and another in God. . . . The divine heart is human in its sympathies.
                                              —F. W. ROBERTSON

*The love of Christ constraineth us. . . .*
—2 Corinthians 5:14

If God loves you, you need not fear what man can do unto you; and the Lord's love is as free as the air, full as the ocean, boundless as eternity, immutable as His throne, and unchangeable as His nature; then let nothing satisfy you but a heartfelt assurance of participation in the love of God. —UNKNOWN

We are apt to forget, amid the pressure of life's burdens, that the divine love is personal, individual, discriminating, and unchanging, and that through ways we know not, the Lord is leading us on. When we seem the most deserted, He may be drawing us nearer to Himself.

—UNKNOWN

God never changes, however circumstances may vary. He is *always* love. And,

> Eye hath not seen, ear hath not heard,
>    Nor heart of man can tell,
> The store of joys God has prepared
>    For those who love Him well.
> —*F. W. FABER*

*Workers together with him.*   —2 Corinthians 6:1

**12**

Here is an excellent creed on which to build a Christian marriage. Let's face it! A good marriage doesn't just happen automatically. It takes work—real work. But what a lofty concept to think of ourselves as co-workers with God. The apostle Paul shared a similar thought in his first letter to the Corinthians: "For we are labourers together

with God: ye are God's husbandry, ye are God's building"
(1 Cor. 3:9). If we begin our married life from this foundation of laboring together with God, our "building" will indeed be God's, and He will strengthen and sustain it. "Together"—what a beautiful word when considered in this
light. Charles Wesley, in his *Short Hymns on Select Passages of the Holy Scriptures,* had this insight:

> Not from his head was woman took,
> As made her husband to overlook;
> Not from his feet, as one designed
> The footstool of the stronger kind;
> But fashioned for himself a bride;
> An equal, taken from his side.

A marriage based on this kind of "equal rights" with God
at the helm will succeed—make "workers together with
Him" your creed.

**13**

*As thy days, so shall thy strength be.*
—Deuteronomy 33:25

There is in the Bible no promise of grace in advance of
the soul's need. God does not say He will put strength into
our arm for the battle while we are in quiet peace and the
battle is yet far off. When the conflict is at hand the
strength will be given. He does not open the gates for us,
nor roll away the stones, until we have come up to them.
He did not divide the Jordan's waters while the people
were yet in their camps, nor even as they began their
march toward the river. The wild stream continued to
flow as the host moved down the banks, even until the
feet of the priests had been dipped in the water. This is
the constant law of divine help. It is not given in advance.

As we come up to the need the supply is ready, but not before. Yet many Christians worry because they cannot see the way opened and the needs supplied far in advance of their steps. Shall we not let God provide and have faith in Him? —J. R. MILLER

*Trust in the Lord with all thine heart; and lean not unto thine own understanding. In all thy ways acknowledge him, and he shall direct thy paths.*
—Proverbs 3:5-6

**14**

Former President Gerald R. Ford claimed these verses as his guideline for living before, during, and after his years in the White House. And they are good verses on which to build a solid and growing marriage relationship as well. Someone has said, "You may trust the Lord too little, but you can never trust Him too much." Hammer William Peploe adds another dimension to our understanding of the concept of trust: "Don't try to hold God's hand; let Him hold yours. Let Him do the holding, and you do the trusting." Our place is to "acknowledge him," admit our own inner weaknesses and failures, and He will do the rest. "He shall direct thy paths." A marriage built on this premise of divine priority will mature and grow stronger with every passing day, no matter what that day may bring.

*For whosoever shall do the will of God, the same is my brother, and my sister, and mother.*
—Mark 3:35

**15**

There are many, very many Christians who are afraid to make an unreserved surrender to God. They are afraid that God will ask some hard thing of them, or some absurd thing. They fear sometimes that it will upset all their life

# January

plans. In a word, they are afraid to surrender unreservedly to the will of God, for Him to do all He wishes for them and whatsoever He wills with them. Fellow Christians, the will of God concerning us is not only the wisest and best thing in the world; it is also the tenderest and the sweetest. God's will for us is not only more loving than a father's; it is more tender than a mother's. It is true that God does oftentimes revolutionize utterly our life plans when we surrender ourselves to His will. It is true that He does sometimes require of us things that to others seem hard. But when the will is once surrendered, the revolutionized life plans become just the plans that are most pleasant, and the things that to others seem hard, are just the things that are easiest and most delightful. Do not let Satan deceive you into being afraid of God's plans for your life. —R. A. TORREY

**16** *Now to Him Who, by (in consequence of) the [action of His] power that is at work within us, is able to [carry out His purpose and] do superabundantly, far over and above all that we [dare] ask or think— infinitely beyond our highest prayers, desires, thoughts, hopes or dreams.* —Ephesians 3:20, TAB

Every marriage needs a dream. This verse tells us there is absolutely nothing God cannot do for His children—in fact, He is "superabundantly" able, unlimited in His power to do anything we might ask or think, "infinitely beyond our highest prayers, desires, thoughts, hopes or dreams." Do you have an "impossible dream"? Don't be afraid to dream—and to share that dream with the heavenly Father in prayer. After all, a dream is a perfectly respectable means of communication. God used dreams to speak to Jacob, Joseph, and Daniel in the Old Testament —and with Joseph, the husband of Mary, in the New

Testament. In these and other instances, dreams seem to be closely related to the attitude of prayer, and if your dreams are bathed in prayer . . . ? Thomas Benton Brooks said centuries ago: "God hears no more than the heart speaks; and if the heart be dumb, God will certainly be deaf." Don't be "dumb" about your dreams—dare to dream!

*Lord, show us the Father.* —John 14:8

# 17

A word is the manifestation of a thought. If I wish to communicate a thought to you, that thought must take shape into words. You cannot see my thought, but what is there comes through the channels of speech, and so travels through your ear to your mind. Thus, my thought becomes part of your thought.

Now Christ became the Word to take the thought out of the mind and heart of God, and translate that thought so that we could understand it, so that what was before invisible and inaudible, and beyond the reach of our senses, comes into our minds and hearts as something that was in God's mind and heart, but now is in ours. Beautiful indeed is this as an expression of what Christ is to us. You want to know God; well, then, study Christ, and you will know all about Him. "He that hath seen me hath seen the Father," said Jesus (v. 9). —ARTHUR T. PIERSON

*He loved us, and sent his Son to be the propitiation for our sins.* —1 John 4:10

# 18

Thy name is Love! I hear it from yon cross;
Thy name is love, I read it in yon tomb,
All murmur love. . . .

# January

It is Thy perfect love, that casts out fear,
  I know the voice that speaks the "It is I."
And in those well-known words of heavenly cheer
  I hear the voice that bids all sorrow fly.
                              —HORATIUS BONAR

Notice how a study of Scripture rewards us by revealing the counsel of God. Into the counsel chamber of love it guides us—verily the Word of God takes us, and shows us that according to this purpose of love God created the world, and sent His Son, that thus His grace should be seen. Who could have imagined this? A plan so vast, so grand, so beautiful could only emanate from Him who is Love, God Himself.   —SAPHIR

**19**  *[Christ said:] As the Father hath loved me, so have I loved you.*  —John 15:9

God is the Home both of the mind and the heart.
                              —FABER

If we will make a response worthy of His Love, first listen to what He says; "Give me thine heart." If we make the true and satisfying response we say, with generous love, "I will give it." But weigh well what the gift means—your very self! What a gift it is!   —H. MONSELL

God is love, and God is faithful because He loves. . . . He puts His love into promises to give our dull minds something to look at, and our unready hands something to hold.   —ALEXANDER RALEIGH

**20**  *And if children, then heirs; heirs of God, and joint-heirs with Christ.*  —Romans 8:17

Whatever makes us forget ourselves and think of others lifts us heavenward. This is one reason God permits suffering. We would never know the best and richest of human love if there were no pain, no distress, no appeal of grief or of need. The best and holiest of mother-love would never be brought out if the child never suffered. The same is true of God's love. God would have loved His children unfallen just as much as He loves them fallen, but the world would never have known so much of God's love had not man fallen. Our sore need called out all that was richest, holiest, and divinest in our Father's heart. If no night came, we should never know there are stars. Darkness is a revealer of blessing.  —J. R. MILLER

*By this we know that we love the children of God, when we love God and keep his commandments.* **21**
—1 John 5:2

Love does everything it can to please the *beloved* person; it performs all commandments. This is one of the greatest instances and arguments of our love that God requires of us, for it is by love that we keep His commandments—love is obedient.  —JEREMY TAYLOR

The reward of a life of faithful, loyal obedience comes at once to the individual himself in growth of character, according to the will of God and by His grace. To grow in faith, in *love*, in humility, in courage, cheerfulness, and consecration, that is surely to succeed—to have a perfected harvest.  —ALEXANDER RALEIGH

Love can lighten the weight of the suffering it cannot remove. It can transform what it cannot destroy. The divine love lifts us out of ourselves, above ourselves, so that we may find our truest selves in Him who has come to us that we may come to Him.  —B. F. WESTCOTT

*God hath . . . given us the spirit of . . . love and of a sound mind.*  —2 Timothy 1:7 **22**

Each day, each week, each month, each year is a new chance given you by God. A new chance, a new leaf, a

# January

new life—this the golden, the unspeakable gift which each new day offers you. . . . Advantage of position, power of mind; He gives them to us, for what purpose? To bury or hide? No! They are His, not ours—lent to us for His service, to be used for His glory with industry, with love.

—F. W. FARRAR

It is the verdict of the Lord Jesus that it is better not to live than not to love. —HENRY DRUMMOND

Love God and He will dwell with you. Obey God and He will reveal the truths of His deepest teachings to your soul. —F. W. ROBERTSON

**23** *But speaking the truth in love, may grow up into him in all things.* —Ephesians 4:15

Don't be satisfied with a mere feeble measure of spiritual life. Strive to have the abundant life and to be well-rounded Christians. Seek to have every power of your life developed to its utmost possibility of beauty and usefulness. Find out whatsoever things are pure, whatsoever things are lovely, and strive to have every mark and line of beauty in your own life. Grow toward God in all upward, heavenward reaching. Grow toward men on earth in all unselfishness and loving service. Grow in your own soul into the fulness of the stature of Christ. And all this you will gain by becoming filled more and more with Christ Himself. It was the daily prayer of one saintly man, "O God, make me an uncommon Christian." Let it be our prayer as well. —J. R. MILLER

*Many waters cannot quench love.*
—Song of Solomon 8:7

God is love. He loves with a love many waters cannot quench. Joy for us is in the thought! While we believe not, or even deny, He abideth faithful; while we forget, He remembers; He leads us; His knowledge of us is not general, but specific. He knows us not in mass, but soul by soul.   —UNKNOWN

What is it that glorifies God? *Love,* faith, gentleness, and obedience; where these are and are exercised, God is greatly honored. God loves simplicity and sincerity, even though it may be mixed up with ignorance and weakness, and grace never leaves a man where it finds him, nor as it finds him.   —UNKNOWN

*I will heal their backsliding, I will love them freely.*   —Hosea 14:4

There is nothing in the world so real and substantial as the love of God. An act of divine love is a more finished thing than anything man can accomplish. It is more firm than the foundation of the Alps. It is more enduring than the round world which God has made so strong. Everything else is as a bubble to it.   —F. W. FABER

Rest in the quiet confidence that through the love of God all is well. Murmur at nothing which brings thee nearer His own loving presence. Be thankful for your every care, because you can confidingly cast them all on Him. Commit, therefore, all that concerns you to His keeping and leave it there.   —MACDUFF

# January

## 26

*The Lord loveth ... and forsaketh not his saints.*
—Psalm 37:28

In the Savior's heart you will always find a refuge for your loneliness. Earthly love may fail you, but in Him you will find an unfailing Friend. You will discover that after all you are not alone, that as you travel along the path of life One is with you in the way—One is standing by your side, and His form is like the Son of God!
—S. W. Skeffington

God is able to make all grace abound! Let us not question the appointments of infinite wisdom. Let us lean on Him in little things as well as great. After the pledge of His love in Jesus, nothing can come wrong that comes from His hands:

> Lord, though Thou bend my spirit low,
>     Love only will I see!
> The very Hand that strikes the blow
>     Was wounded once for me.
> —MacDuff

## 27

*God hath also given us his Holy Spirit.*
—1 Thessalonians 4:8

Remember, the Holy Spirit is God, and God is love. And no man ever asks God to come into his heart, and holds his heart open to God, without God's entering. Children, pray the dear God, the blessed Holy Spirit, to come and live in your heart and show you Jesus, and make you love to do what is right for His sake. Old men, aspire to taste already here what is to be the life and joy of your eternity. Men and women in the thick of life, do not go away helpless when there is such help at hand; do not go on struggling by yourselves for truth and toiling at your work, when the Holy Spirit is waiting to show you Christ, and to give you in Him the profoundness of faith and the delightfulness of deference to God.   —PHILLIPS BROOKS

*For the eyes of the Lord are over the righteous and his ears are open to their prayers; but the face of the Lord is against them that do evil.*   —1 Peter 3:12
*For the Lord knoweth the way of the righteous . . . but the way of the ungodly shall perish.*   —Psalm 1:6

**28**

There is an exciting parallelism in these two passages which reflects the unity of the Scriptures. Peter expresses the same scriptural certainty in his Epistle that David expressed centuries before in his first Psalm. David repeats the same truth in Psalm 37:18: "The Lord knoweth the days of the upright: and their inheritance shall be for ever." On which side of these verses do you want to reside —with the righteous amid their blessings, or with the ungodly in their gloom? Later in Psalm 37 (v. 25), David says, "I have been young, and now am old; yet have I not seen the righteous forsaken, nor his seed [children] begging bread." Righteousness is a solid foundation on which to build a lasting and healthy marriage. And it brings with it blessings without number. David mentions one in our Psalm verse for the day: God's listening ear as we open our hearts to Him in prayer. Other blessings are listed earlier in the Psalm (1:3): fruitfulness and prosperity. No wonder Joshua declared when faced with a choice of gods, "As for me and my house, we will serve the Lord!" What will be your choice?

*The salvation of the righteous is of the Lord: he is their strength in the time of trouble.*
—Psalm 37:39

**29**

Would you be saved? The question of salvation is a moral one; it hinges on the will, and if the trembling soul says, "I would, but I cannot believe; I would, but I cannot repent," then with great joy the Shepherd takes the lost sheep upon His shoulders and says, "It is enough." "I will work in you what you lack; I will enter through the unlatched door of your heart—laden with gifts. I will cleanse you from all that grieves me, and I will produce in you all those holy habits you lack. They are the gifts of God to the recipient spirit through the agency of the Holy Spirit." The initial step of salvation is our willingness to be saved. If that is assured, tell Christ so, and look to Him to begin in you His greatest work. Thus there is in you a transformation, which starts with forgiveness, and ends in perfect conformity to the Son of God.  —F. B. MEYER

**30** *Nevertheless he saved them for his name's sake, that he might make his mighty power to be known.*
—Psalm 106:8

God's love is not only redemptive. It also shows His power. Here the psalmist, giving Israel a brief history lesson, reminds his readers: "We have sinned with our fathers, we have committed iniquity, we have done wickedly. Our fathers understood not thy wonders in Egypt; they remembered not the multitude of thy mercies; but provoked him at the sea, even the Red sea. *Nevertheless* he saved them for his name's sake, that he might make his mighty power to be known" (vv. 6-8). This same mighty power is available to the sinner today! God's love as evidenced by His salvation is not one bit less powerful than it was when He parted the Red Sea, or sent the plagues on Egypt. Exodus 9:16 quotes God's word to Pharaoh through Moses: "And in very deed for this cause have I raised thee up, for to shew in thee my power; and that my name may be declared throughout all the earth." We all remember how God rained mercy down on His people, but destruction down upon the Egyptians who refused to acknowledge His power. His salvation is just as available today to the repentant sinner who realizes his need!

*With long life will I satisfy him, and shew him my salvation.* —Psalm 91:16

**31**

During this first month of "LoveSong" meditations, we have been looking at the theme of God's love in two dimensions: the earthly and the eternal. We not only receive God's love in the here and now—we can look forward to living in it throughout eternity! David dwelt on this theme throughout the Psalms, and it is prominent in this passage. In Psalm 21:4, in the midst of thanking God for past victories, David says of himself, "He [the king] asked life of thee [God], and thou gavest it to him, even length of days for ever and ever." Asaph, David's contemporary and fellow psalmist, spelled out the rules: "Whoso offereth praise glorifieth me: and to him that ordereth his conversation aright will I shew the salvation of God" (Ps. 50:23). The supply of eternal salvation is just one evidence of God's love. God's love is not the shallow sentiment touted abroad in modern love songs. No, His love is redemptive. It cost Him something—His Son! As an anonymous writer has said, "Salvation is free to you because someone else paid." He is the God we worship!

# February

*The fruit of the spirit is love....* —Galatians 5:22

## 1

We may have the Spirit within us, and yet there may be a sad lack of fruit in our lives. The Holy Spirit may be grieved. And when He is grieved He ceases to fill us with His fruit. It is not by strain and effort that we become fruitful. As with growth, so with fruitfulness, it is not energy that is needed so much as a healthy condition of soul. Then we must keep clearly before us, it is not the fruit of the Christian but the fruit of the Holy Spirit which is being considered here. The Christian *bears* the fruit, but the Spirit *produces* it.

The fruit of the Spirit consists of one cluster of nine different virtues. In no sense have we to manufacture them.

What, then, is the secret of divine fruitfulness? The indwelling and fellowship of the Holy Spirit. Let Christ be recognized as Lord within the soul; let Him be honored and obeyed, and the Holy Spirit will not fail to shed abroad in our hearts the love of God (Romans 5:5). He will not fail to fill us "with all joy and peace in believing" (Romans 15:13).

Fruitfulness is brought about not by *imitation* so much as by *manifestation*. It is the outcome of that which dwells within.   —EVAN H. HOPKINS

*Husbands, love your wives, even as Christ has also loved the church.* —Ephesians 5:25

## 2

The true Christian is to be such a husband as Christ was to His church. The love of a husband is *special*. The

# February

Lord Jesus cherishes for His church a special affection, which is set upon her above the rest of mankind: "I pray for them, I pray not for the world." The elect church is the favorite of heaven, a treasure of Christ, the crown of His head, the bracelet of His arm, the breastplate of His heart, the very center and core of His love. A husband should love his wife with a *constant* love, for so Jesus loves His church. He does not vary in His affection. He may change in His display of affection, but the affection itself is still the same. A husband should love his wife with an *enduring* love, for nothing "shall be able to separate us from the love of God, which is in Christ Jesus our Lord." (Rom. 8: 39) A true husband loves his wife with a *hearty* love, fervent and intense, not just paying her lip service. Ah! what more could Christ have done to prove His love than He has done? Jesus has a *delighted* love toward His spouse: He prizes her affection and delights in her. Believer, you wonder at Christ's love; you admire it—*are you imitating it?* In your relationships with your loved one, is the rule and measure of your love—"*even as Christ loved the church*"?

—C. H. Spurgeon

**3**   *See that ye love one another with a pure heart fervently.* —1 Peter 1:22

The spirit of Christian love, if allowed to work deeply and thoroughly in all hearts and lives, will prevent disagreement and dissension among Christians. It will lead us to forget ourselves and think of others, not pushing our own interests unduly or demanding first place, but in honor preferring one another. It will make us willing to serve, to minister, even to stoop down to unloose a brother's shoes. It will make us thoughtful, too, in all our acts, in our manners, in our words. It will make us gentle, kindly, patient, teaching us to be all that Christ would be if He were in our place. —J. R. Miller

# February

*Let not the sun go down upon your wrath.*
*—Ephesians 4:26*

## 4

Here is a command of the apostle Paul that might well be the "eleventh commandment" for a happy home life. One of the closest human relationships is that of a husband with his wife. When God instituted the marriage relationship, He meant for it to be the most intimate of human ties. Yet this tie can be severed—or frayed—by the primitive emotion of anger. Anger is human—and marriage is human. Unquestionably, anger can enter the most idyllic marriage. And when it does so, it must be dealt with. Paul has given us the answer in this practical, workable solution: "Let not the sun go down upon your wrath." Whatever happens, make up before dark! If your relationship is threatened by this very human emotion, ask God to help you apply Paul's prescription for a happy married life.

*Speaking the truth in love.* *—Ephesians 4:15*

## 5

A husband and wife would do well to put this Pauline premise to work in their marriage. As Christians, we are admonished, indeed we are commanded, to be truthful, according to the Scriptures. On the other hand, some wag has said truthfully, "The truth hurts." The dilemma for the Christian marriage partner is to obey the scriptural command without hurting his loved one. The secret ingredient is love! Sometimes the truth bluntly stated can cause heartache and anguish. But mix in a liberal amount of love —and that same criticism or correction can create a positive response in the partner on the receiving end. One of Christ's commands was, "Do unto others as you would have them do unto you." If you speak the truth in that spirit, you'll find your relationship a growing and vital one. So "speak the truth in love" and watch your marriage grow!

# February

**6**
*The traditional fasts and times of mourning you have kept in July, August, October, and January are ended. They will be changed to joyous festivals if you love truth and peace.* —Zechariah 8:19, TLB

Love shall be purified by pain,
And pain shall be soothed by love;
So let us take heart and go again
Cheerfully on, through joy and woe.
Remember, "the love of God lives through eternity
And conquers all!"

—ADELAIDE A. PROCTOR

A realization of the anguish of the children of men sometimes wraps around one like sudden darkness. . . . Infinite Love is suffering too—yes, in the fullness of knowledge God suffers, yearns, mourns; and it is blind self-seeking which wants to be freed from the sorrow in which the whole creation groans and travails. Surely it is not true blessedness to be free from sorrow while there is sorrow and sin in the world. Sorrow is then a part of love, and love does not seek to throw it off. —GEORGE ELIOT

**7**
*Return to thine own house, and shew how great things God hath done unto thee.* —Luke 8:39

Friendships in the family require most gentle care and cultivation. We must win each other's love within our homes just as we win the love of those outside—by the gentleness and grace of our attitudes. We must prove ourselves worthy of being loved by those who are nearest; they will not truly love us unless we do, merely because we are of the same household. We must show ourselves unselfish, thoughtful, gentle, helpful. Home friendships must be formed as all friendships are formed—by the patient knitting of soul to soul and the slow growing of life into life. Then we must retain home-friends after winning just as we retain other friends—by a thousand little winning expressions of love. We cannot depend upon relationship to keep us loved and loving. We must live for each other. We must give as well as receive. We must be watchful of our acts and words.    —J. R. MILLER

*Beloved, if God so loved us, we ought also to love one another.*   —1 John 4:11

**8**

To know that long before I cared for Him, He cared for me; that while I wandered up and down in carelessness, perhaps while I was plunging deep in flagrant sin, God's eye was never off me for a moment, He was always watching for the instant when His hand might touch me and His voice speak to me—there is nothing which can appeal to one like that. The individual is made of stone who cannot be touched by the tenderness of that thought. When, touched by the knowledge of that untiring love, a man gives himself at last to God, every act of loving service which he does afterward is fired and colored by the power of gratitude, out of which it springs. How shall he overtake this love, which has such a head start on him?

—PHILLIPS BROOKS

*Love unfeigned . . .*   —2 Corinthians 6:6

**9**

There are few prophets in the world—few heroes. I can't afford to give all my love and reverence to such rarities. I want a great deal of these feelings for my everyday fellow-man, especially for the select few in the foreground of the great multitude, whose faces I know, whose hands I touch. It is far more important that my heart should swell with pride and loving admiration at some trait of gentle goodness in those ordinary people who share my hearth,

# February

than at the deeds of heroes whom I shall never know except by reputation. —GEORGE ELIOT

"Love is the fulfilling of the law"; and surely we cannot care too tenderly for our dear ones since God's Word bids us love one another as He has loved us. Such love indeed we cannot strive for, but we can let it operate in us through the divine Love-giver, Jesus Christ, our Savior and Lord. —UNKNOWN

**10**  *Can two walk together, except they be agreed?*
*—Amos 3:3*

I think this verse has lost a certain flavor in its more recent translations. Indeed, it spoke deeply to my own heart when I looked at it in the light of what love means in marriage. Though I've never heard it quoted in a wedding ceremony, I think it should be used in that context just as often and just as emphatically as we use Ruth's immortal words to Naomi, "Whither thou goest I will go." What does it mean to "agree"? It means to travel together (as later translations of this verse bring out), to have a common goal. What better description could we have of what marriage is all about? As partners in the home, my wife and I know the blessed unity of oneness of spirit at every level of life. This doesn't mean we are no longer individuals—it means we have surrendered our rights to ourselves to one another. What emerges from that surrender is a "walk together" that culminates in joy and fulfillment.

**11**  *Set a watch, O Lord, before my mouth; keep the*
*door of my lips. —Psalm 141:3*

No prayer should be spoken more often by us than this prayer of David: "Keep the door of my lips." There is nothing in all of life to which most of us give less attention than to our words. We let them fly from our lips as the leaves fly from the trees when the autumn winds blow. Many people seem to think that words are not important. They watch their acts, their conduct, and then give full license to their tongues. This is not right. A true Christian should have a Christian tongue. James 1 makes that clear. Words have terrific power for harm if they are wrong words, and blessed, immortal power for good if they are holy words. We need to pray continually that God would keep the door of our lips and set a watch before our mouths. Only love should be permitted to interpret itself in speech. Bitterness and all evil should be restrained.

—J. R. MILLER

*What doth the Lord thy God require of thee but to fear the Lord thy God, to walk in all his ways, and to love Him and to serve [Him] with all thy heart.*
—Deuteronomy 10:12

**12**

The character of God's goodness is to be communicative. He is always communicating Himself to His creatures in nature, in grace and in glory. We must copy this example. There is no such thing as selfish goodness, thinking only about ourselves and our own souls. This example is easy, for everything comes easy to love.   —F. W. FABER

Christ came to love as none had ever loved. He was the protector of children, the Healer of the sick, the Friend of the sinful, the Teacher of the ignorant, the Seeker of the wandering, and the Savior of the lost.   —F. W. FARRAR

The Savior is acquainted with our domestic ties, and takes an interest in each one. Oh, there lives not a being who can enter into our bereavement with the sympathy, the succor, and soothing of Christ, and into our joys as well.   —WINSLOW

# February

## 13

*Follow after love....* —1 Corinthians 14:1, ASV

Christ said, "He that keepeth my commandments, he it is that loveth me." Obey Him and you must love Him. Abide in Him and you must obey Him. Cultivate His friendship. Live after Christ in His spirit as in His presence.....If you cannot at once and always feel the play of His life upon yours, watch for it also indirectly. The whole earth is full of the character of God.   —Henry Drummond

The law of Christ is the law of *love*, and to love is not merely to wish well to one another, but to bear one another's burdens, that is to bear those things which are grievous, and which you would not willingly bear.

When the heart is filled with the Savior's presence and a sense of the Savior's love, how natural and how easy it is to speak of Him. Had we more experience of what the Scripture recommends as the communing of saints, the path of the Christian would be luminous with light, and we would find strength in the sweet relationship.....And we know, too, that our Heavenly Father looks down with a smile upon those who thus *love* to talk of Him.

—Theodore Irving

## 14

*This is my commandment, That ye love one another, as I have loved you.* —John 15:12

"Love one another as I have loved you." How did Christ love His followers? How did Christ love His disciples? How did He show His love to them? Was it not, among other ways, in wondrous patience with them, with their faults, their ignorance, their unfaithfulness? Was it not in considerate kindness, in ever-watchful thoughtfulness, in compassionate gentleness? Was it not in ministering to them in all possible ways? What is it, then, to love one another as He loves us? Is it not to take His example for our pattern? But how slowly we learn it! How hard it is to be gentle, patient, kind, thoughtful, even perfectly true and just to one another! Still, there the lesson stands and waits for us, and we must never falter in learning it.

—J. R. MILLER

*Then saith he to the disciple, Behold thy mother! And from that hour that disciple took her unto his own home.* —John 19:27

**15**

Heaven is the Father's house. A father's house is a home; and can you think for one moment of a home in which the members of the household do not know each other? The sweetest, best, happiest, and most perfect earthly home is but a dim picture of the love and gladness of the home in heaven. Heaven is like a holy home, only infinitely sweeter, truer, and better. Home has been called "heaven's fallen sister." If in the imperfect homes of this world we find so much gladness in the ties that bind heart to heart and knit life to life, may we not be confident that in the perfect home of our heavenly Father all this gladness will be infinitely deepened and enriched? Love will not be different in heaven; it will be wondrously purified and exalted, but earthly love will live on through death into eternity. —J. R. MILLER

*And now I beseech thee, not as though I wrote a new commandment unto thee, but that which we had from the beginning that we love one another.*
—2 John 5

**16**

The greatest thing a man can do for his Heavenly Father is to be kind to some of His other children. I wonder how it is that we are not all kinder than we are. How

# February

much the world needs it! How easily it is done. How instantaneously it acts. How infallibly it is remembered. How abundantly it pays itself back. For there is no debt in the world so honorable as love.   —Henry Drummond

The love revealed in the ascension of Christ is, in a word, His going to the Father—to His Father and our Father, the invisible pledge and symbol of the exaltation of the earthly into the heavenly. It is a revelation of heavenly life, the open fulfillment of man's destiny made possible by divine love for all men.   —B. F. Westcott

**17**   *They say unto him, We have here but five loaves.... —Matthew 14:17*

God does not like to give out His blessings where they will be hoarded, but He loves to put them into the hands of those who will do the most with them to bless their fellows. The central object of true Christian living is to be helpful to others. The true life is one devoted to Christ, to be used then by Him in blessing others. Lay every gift at the Master's feet, and then, when it has been blessed by Him, carry it out to bless others. Bring your barley loaves to Christ, and then, with the spell of His touch upon them, you may feed the hungry lives around you with His love.   —J. R. Miller

An old Persian proverb: What I kept, I lost; What I spent, I had; What I gave, I have.

**18**   *This is my commandment, that ye love one another, as I have loved you.  —John 15:12*

"Love makes drudgery divine." Love cannot help itself; it outruns and leaves law far behind. The question is not what *must* I do, but what *may* I do? Love will stop at nothing. It takes up its cross and travels after its object over every hill and mountain of difficulty. Love desires all to share its bliss; it runs on with unceasing cry: "What shall I render for such benefits?"  —POWERSCOURT

> Can I with loveless heart receive
>   Tokens of love that never cease?
> Can I be thankless still, and grieve
>   Him who is all my joy and peace?
>
> Could I but honor Thee aright,
>   Noble and sweet my song should be,
> That earth and heaven should learn Thy might,
>   And what my God hath done for me.
>                              —J. G. HERMANN

*So faith, hope and love abide, these three; but the greatest of these is love.*
                              —1 Corinthians 13:13, ASV

# 19

Love springs out of faith and is supported by it. Faith enables us to enter on the unseen, to give reality to the fabrics of hope. And love, born of and by faith, dimly sensible of its power under the limitations of earth, rises into the spiritual realm, and knows that all things are possible to the love of God.  —B. F. WESTCOTT

We hear much of love to God; Christ spoke much of love to man. We make a great deal of peace with heaven; Christ made much of peace on earth. Christianity is not a strange or added thing, but the inspiration of the secular life, the breathing of an eternal spirit through this temporal world.  —HENRY DRUMMOND

# February

**20**
*What doth the Lord require of thee, but to do justly, and to love mercy, and to walk humbly with thy God?* —Micah 6:8

Hold fast to Love. If men wound your heart, let them not sour or embitter it; let them not shut up or narrow it; let them only expand it more and more, and be always able to say, with St. Paul, "My heart is enlarged."

Love is universal. It is interested in all that is human, not merely in the concerns of its own family, nation, sect or circle of association. Humanity is the sphere of its activity. —F. W. Robertson

All things are vain save only to love and serve God. He who loves God with all his heart fears neither death, nor pain, nor judgment. Perfect love gives a man boldness to appear before God. —Thomas à Kempis

**21**
*There is no fear in love.* —1 John 4:18

Intellectually God can never be known. He must be known by *love*, for if any man love God the same is known of Him. —F. W. Robertson

It is an exceeding weight of glory to feel on us the touch of the divine hand, the being called by name. We surrender our own individuality, because God in His *love* has individualized us, and called us with a special call. And God's love is so real, and so true with us as to oblige us to be true to Him. —H. Monsell

# February

All that Jesus has done for us has been done with such an out-pouring of love. He not only pardons, but at the same time adopts us as sons. He at the same time makes us heirs of heaven. Every gift of love is double and pays eternal dividends. —F. W. Faber

*Beloved, let us love one another: for love is of God.* —1 John 4:7

## 22

Love is unselfishness; it is the power of sympathy; it is to feel that all powers are given us to make others happy; and to be contriving happiness for others; that is like God, and God is *love*. —F. W. Robertson

Love is the greatest thing that God can give us; for He Himself is Love; and it is the greatest thing we can give to God! For it will give ourselves, and carry with it all that is ours. —Jeremy Taylor

> His Love of us may teach us how
> To love Him in return.
> Love cannot help but grow more free
> The more its raptures burn.
> —Faber

*Love be with you all in Christ Jesus.*
—1 Corinthians 16:24

## 23

Love never contracts itself in circles; they who love widen their horizons by as fixed and sure a law as those around a pebble cast into still water. —Thomas à Kempis

The love of Christ was the spirit of giving all He had to give—Christ's love was not a sentiment, it was self-giving. Love gives itself. —F. W. Robertson

# February

A man's duty is wider than a care for the salvation of his individual soul; even in matters of religion selfishness must be excluded. Love of our neighbor is ever mingled with, and is the appointed way of manifesting, our love to God.   —F. W. Farrar

Love is as communicative as fire.   —Jeremy Taylor

## 24
*His love is perfected in us.*   —1 John 4:12

Love, if you would be beloved; serve, if you would be served; and humble yourself if you would be exalted. The more you feel your weakness, the more you should cling to Jesus, who is your strength. Let the ivy be your example, and as that clings to the oak, so do you cling to Christ. He that does this is always safe.   —Unknown

The noble, blessed model of self-forgetting love— Christ who came into the world, not to be ministered to, but to minister. Love Him until you learn to love your family and friends with a love that is self-forgetting and selfless.   —Tholuck

## 25
*Thou shalt love thy neighbor as thyself.*
—Matthew 22:39

Love—"thou shalt love thy neighbor as thyself." Love is the test and condition of discipleship. Love is greater than our faith or hope, love is the fulfilling of the law.
—F. W. Farrar

God's love gives in such a way that it flows from a father's heart, the well-spring of all good. The heart of the Giver makes the gift dear and precious, so among ourselves we say, "It comes from the hand of love! We look not so much at the gift as at the Heart."

—MARTIN LUTHER

Let Christ's love flow into our souls and fill them. Then struggles and sacrifices will lose their bitterness, even if they must keep some of their pain. God's work begun within is a pledge of His work finished. Until the day of the Lord Jesus, then, let us look up, rejoice and hope and love.   —UNKNOWN

## 26

*When Jesus therefore saw his mother and the disciple standing by whom he loved, he said unto his mother: Woman, behold thy son! Then saith he to that disciple: Behold thy mother.*   —John 19:26

On the cross the Lord established family relationships in the Spirit. He points all who love Him, and whom He loves, to each other, and thus confirms the great law of love from the cross, and draws believers together through the cross; but the care in this love is its specific point: He remembers everyone.   —STIER

All things work together for good to those who love God. Have patience, have faith, have hope, have love as you stand at the foot of Christ's cross, and hold fast to it—the anchor of the soul and reason as well as of the heart.

—CHARLES KINGSLEY

## 27

*She hath done what she could. . . . this also that she hath done shall be spoken of for a memorial of her.*   —Mark 14:8-9

Love in its supreme moments does not stop at a little. It does not weigh and measure and calculate and restrain its impulses and check its budget. They know nothing of love who think strange of Mary's costly action, who try to explain why she acted so generously, so lavishly, so wastefully, when she put upon her Lord the highest honor she could bestow upon Him. If our love for Christ were only stronger, deeper, richer, we would not need to have Mary's deed explained; we would not calculate so closely how much we can afford to give or do.   —J. R. MILLER

**28**   *He that loveth not knoweth not God; for God is love. In this was manifested the love of God toward us, because that God sent his only begotten Son into the world, that we might live through him.*
                                                              *—1 John 4:8-9*

The practical evidence of the new birth is love for the children of God. He has manifested His perfect love toward us in the gift of His only-begotten Son. Now we manifest our love to Him by our care for and interest in His own. Christ was sent that He might give life to those who were dead in trespasses and sins. That life is divine and he who possesses it loves others because God has so loved him. The next verse tells us that Christ also came to be the propitiation for our sins. On the basis of this we are justified freely by His grace. When one is converted to God the two things are true. He is both regenerated and justified. The child of God stands before His Father as free from guilt as if he had never sinned at all. Such is the fulness of God's salvation which calls forth our adoring gratitude shown in unselfish love.   —H. A. IRONSIDE

**29**   *If we love one another, God dwelleth in us, and his love is perfected in us.*   —1 John 4:12

After the terrible earthquakes and fire in San Francisco, some children far out in the country were gathering up

# February

pieces of charred paper which had been carried for miles by the currents of air. Among the fragments they found a partly burned leaf of the Bible. A boy found it and took it home to his father, who smoothed it out and read for the first time the immortal words, "Now abideth faith, hope, love, these three, and the greatest of these is love." It was a strange message to come out of the great upheaval—strange, but wonderfully fitting. Everything else of beauty and power had gone down in dust and ashes, but love remained—that was imperishable, and faith and hope remained. Nothing is worth living for but love—God's love and the love that it inspires.   —J. R. MILLER

# March

*The fruit of the Spirit is ... joy ...*   —Galatians 5:22

**1**

Joy does not come alone. It comes between "love" and "peace." Those are three things we cannot bring about in ourselves by any direct efforts of our own, however earnestly and feverishly we may try. We cannot make ourselves love, or rejoice, or be peaceful. These are the fruit of the Spirit.

In relation to these inner conditions of mind we are to be passive. It is the Holy Spirit who produces this fruit and fills our hearts with such emotions. The active virtues follow as the necessary outcome of this inner condition. It is when divine "love, joy, and peace" are graciously filling our hearts that our actions will be characterized by long-suffering, gentleness, goodness, faithfulness, etc.

Let us recognize the Holy Spirit's personality and presence, as One dwelling within us. If we are grieving Him, how can He comfort us? He is then our Reprover. But it is emphatically His office or capacity to comfort. When we honor Him, and yield to His gracious sovereign sway, then He not only ceases to reprove—He begins at once to fill our hearts with His fruit.   —Evan H. Hopkins

*Paul, filled with the Holy Spirit. ...*   —Acts 13:9

**2**

We talk about being "filled with the Spirit," yet Paul goes beyond that in Ephesians 3 where he says, "For this cause I bow my knees unto the Father ... that Christ may

# March

dwell in your hearts by faith; that ye, being rooted and grounded in love, may be able to comprehend with all saints what is the breadth, and length, and depth, and height; and to know the love of Christ . . . that ye might be filled with all the fulness of God" (vv. 14, 17–19). Do you see the distinction? Here are empty vessels. You say, "First get yourself empty and then full." I may dip out and fill these vessels; but put an empty vessel into the ocean, and it quickly fills itself. This seems to be Paul's thought. Archbishop Leighton makes a beautiful comment on the words of Christ: "Enter thou into the joy of thy Lord." Lifting his eyes to heaven, He said, "Lord Jesus, it is only a little joy that now enters us; but by-and-by we shall enter into joy as vessels put into a sea of happiness." Cast yourself into the great deeps of the Spirit; then there will be no trouble in getting filled!   —A. J. GORDON

**3**   *Rejoice before the Lord thy God in all that thou puttest thine hands unto.*   —Deuteronomy 12:18

"Rejoice in work," Moses is telling the Israelites here, a good suggestion for modern marrieds as well. This admonition is a repetition of what he has told them earlier in the chapter, in verses 7 and 12. Anyone who has been forced into a "life of leisure" by illness or circumstances will recognize the value of work in a well-rounded life. And a balanced marriage will require periods of genuine work as well. I remember how my wife and I started our married life—I was still in college and in debt—no furniture except the bare essentials, cheap student housing. But what a challenge to build upon! When you start out at the bottom there's no way to go but up! And we did discover the joy in working together toward common goals. I still remember the thrill of buying our first refrigerator! And our first new car! We accomplished these material goals together—and those early years were difficult but rewarding. We wouldn't exchange them for easier, more luxurious years even if we had the opportunity. And there were spiritual goals as well, for which we thank God together. "Rejoice before the Lord your God in all that you undertake," reads the Revised Standard Version. A motto like that will make your marriage a delight, helping you through the difficult days, sustaining you in the dark moments, and developing a strong structure for the future. "Real joy comes not from ease or riches or from the praise of men, but from doing something worthwhile"

(SIR WILFRED GRENFELL).

*Truly our fellowship is with the Father, and with his Son Jesus Christ.* —1 John 1:3

**4**

How it would bless and brighten our lives if we were to carry always in our hearts the image and conception of God as our Father! When we can look up into God's face and say out of warm and responding hearts, "Our Father," all our world and all life take on new aspects for our eyes. Duty is no longer hard and a drudgery, but becomes a joy. Keeping the commandments is hard if we think of God merely as a king; but if we look up to Him and conceive of Him as our Father, all is changed, and our love for Him, and our desire to please Him, make obedience a gladness. We can say then, "I *delight* to do thy will, O my God."

—J. R. MILLER

*That day they offered great sacrifices, and rejoiced: for God had made them rejoice with great joy: the wives also and the children rejoiced: so that the joy of Jerusalem was heard even afar off.*
—Nehemiah 12:43

**5**

"Rejoicing" and family life belong together. This striking verse is found in the very heart of Nehemiah's account of the rebuilding of Jerusalem, as part of the ceremony

# March

dedicating the rebuilt wall of Jerusalem to the glory of God. True rejoicing comes from dedication of lives and families to the One who made them. As Augustine says, "There is a God-shaped vacuum" in each one of us which is not content until it is in fellowship with God. This is true of families as well as individuals. When a family is out of fellowship with the One who ordained the family as the basic unit of society, it is out of harmony with itself and headed for destruction and disintegration. The great preacher, Charles Haddon Spurgeon, once said, "It is not how much we have, but how much we enjoy, that makes happiness." In this day of affluence, too many mistakenly think possessions assure joy. On the contrary, as we center our family life, whether just husband and wife or the more extended family, around the spiritual rather than the material, we will find true joy and lasting happiness.

## 6

*Brethren, rejoice in the Lord.* —Philippians 3:1

It is the law of God that wherever there is duty to be done, there is also possible joy to be found in doing it. Just as the man who sees foliage knows that somewhere there must be water (although his eyes or ears cannot discern it, and the trees seem to grow out of the sand), so he can know that there is a happiness for him somewhere in doing that duty, even though for the moment it seems nothing but drudgery. In the expectation of that joy he works. The expectation of joy *is* joy; and so the man who in doing God's will surrenders some delight or privilege, finds that there is a subtler mastery of happiness to be gained only by giving it up for something higher, though for a time it may seem to separate him from the present happiness he has come to love. —Phillips Brooks

# March

*And Hannah prayed, and said, My heart rejoiceth
in the Lord, mine horn [strength] is exalted in the
Lord . . . because I rejoice in thy salvation.*
—1 Samuel 2:1

Hannah is one of my favorite people. Her song of praise
here recorded reminds me of Mary's as she exulted in the
thought of bearing the Savior of the world (see Luke 1:
46–56). Hannah also reminds me of Isaiah's thankful expression of praise for God's salvation: "Behold, God is my
salvation; I will trust, and not be afraid: for the Lord Je-
hovah is my strength and my song; he is also become my
salvation. Therefore with joy shall ye draw water out of
the wells of salvation" (Is. 12:2,3). "Rejoice in . . . salvation." What cause for rejoicing this is. "The Lord is my
light and my salvation; whom shall I fear? the Lord is the
strength of my life; of whom shall I be afraid?" (Ps. 27:1).
Say it with Billy Sunday, the Billy Graham of a past generation: "If you have no joy in your religion, there's a leak in
your Christianity somewhere."

*Acquaint now thyself with him, and be at peace:
thereby good shall come unto thee. . . . For then
shalt thou have thy delight in the Almighty, and
shalt lift up thy face unto God.* —Job 22:21–26

This interesting insight into the relationship of joy and
peace is found in the midst of Eliphaz's third speech to
Job. You will recall that Job's "friends" gathered around
him in his despair, and "comforted" him by castigating
him for his so-called sins, those actions in his life which
had resulted in what they considered to be his punishment
for breaking God's laws. Despite his mistaken analysis of

# March

Job's problems, Eliphaz has hit upon a real spiritual truth here. Jeremiah agrees with Eliphaz when he says: "But let him that glorieth glory in this, that he understandeth and knoweth me, that I am the Lord which exercise loving-kindness, judgment, and righteousness, in the earth: for in these things I delight, saith the Lord" (9:24). And Job himself later asks, "Will he [the hypocrite] delight himself in the Almighty? will he always call upon God?" (27:10). And Paul asks, "But now, after that ye have known God, . . . how turn ye again to the weak and beggarly elements?" (Gal. 4:9). Isaiah exults, "Delight thyself in the Lord; and I will cause thee to ride upon the high places of the earth" (58:14). Joy and peace, those two blessed aspects of the Spirit-filled life, do indeed walk hand in hand in the life of the surrendered Christian, rightly related to his heavenly Father.

**9** *My soul shall be joyful in the Lord: it shall rejoice in his salvation.* —Psalm 35:9

We need Christ just as much in our bright, prosperous, exalted hours as in the days of darkness, adversity, and depression. We are quite in danger of thinking that the Christian faith is only for sickrooms and funerals, and for times of great trial and great sorrow—a lamp to shine at night, help when the road is rough, a friendly hand to hold us up when we are stumbling. This is not true. Jesus went to the marriage feast as well as to the home of sorrow. The Christian faith is just as much for the hours of joy as for our days of grief. There are just as many stars in the sky at noon as at midnight, although we cannot see them in the sun's bright glare. And there are just as many comforts, divine encouragements, and blessings above us when we are in the noons of our human gladness and earthly success, as when we are in our nights of pain and shadow. We may not see them in the brightness about us, but they are there, and their benedictions fall upon us as perpetually, in a gentle rain of grace.   —J. R. MILLER

*Let all those who put their trust in thee rejoice: let them ever shout for joy, because thou defendest them: let them also that love thy name be joyful in thee.* —Psalm 5:11

**10**

Our great God is the Defender of them who love Him. What a cause for rejoicing this should be! Do you need defending? The world is too much with us, said William Wordsworth. What would he think of our complex modern society? The enemy surrounds us on every side, looking for a chink in our armor, a weakness in our defense. Let us rejoice in the fact of God's defense of His children. Does your marriage face dangers, temptations, perhaps? I can guarantee you that if you will "exult" in the Lord, you won't have cause for despair because of a dissolved marriage bond. This assurance isn't a man-made guarantee. It's based on the word of God Himself, in His Word. Those couples who together worship and adore the Father will find Him their defense against the enemy. Isaiah contrasted the lot of the obedient and the disobedient: "Behold, my servants shall eat, but ye (the disobedient) will be hungry; my servants shall drink, but ye will be thirsty, my servants shall rejoice, but ye shall be ashamed" (65:13). Choose for God today and enjoy the Christian life, reaping the benefits of a right relationship to God and one another.

*Be glad in the Lord, and rejoice, ye righteous: and shout for joy, all ye that are upright in heart.*
—Psalm 32:11

**11**

I love the Psalms! If I could have only one Book from the Old Testament, I think I would choose this collection

# March

of "songs to the Lord." They reflect every aspect and mood of the Christian life for me, and I particularly appreciate the note of "joy in the Lord" which pervades the psalms of David. He sounds this note again in Psalm 64:10 ("the righteous shall be glad in the Lord, and shall trust in him; and all the upright in heart shall glory"), thanking God for the refuge to be found in Him, a further reflection on yesterday's meditation on Psalm 5:11. David strikes the same note again in Psalm 25:20, "O keep my soul, and deliver me: let me not be ashamed; for I put my trust in thee." How often David reminds us of the blessings of the righteous by contrasting our lot with the fate of the wicked: "Many sorrows shall be to the wicked: but he that trusteth in the Lord, mercy shall compass him about" (Ps. 32:10). The Revised Standard Version renders this verse: "Many are the pangs of the wicked; but *steadfast love* surrounds him who trusts in the Lord." In the light of this blessed truth, truly let us *"Be glad in the Lord"!*

**12**     *Weeping may endure for a night, but joy cometh in the morning.* —Psalm 30:5

How strange to put weeping together with joy—weeping at night, but joy in the morning. Humanly speaking, this is an unacceptable combination. But from the divine perspective, these two experiences can be the opposite sides of a coin. Joy is a "morning experience," true, but it sometimes seems greater against the dark background of sorrow. Weeping does seem to be a nighttime affliction. But remember this: true joy does not depend upon circumstances. An old Chinese proverb says, "You cannot prevent the birds of sorrow from flying over your head, but you *can* prevent them from building nests in your hair." This is an interesting concept and illustrates to a degree, at least, what that fruit of the Spirit, "joy," can mean in a growing marriage relationship. Some of us are so constituted psychologically that we just naturally "look on the bright side." We are the eternal optimists. Others cannot seem to help dwelling on the dark side. They are the eternal pessimists. Personally, I think a marriage is enriched when the partners meet somewhere in between. They face the reality of life, which has its share of both joy and sorrow. If we accept both as a gift from an all-knowing Father, both kinds of experience will bear fruit in our lives!

*I went with them to the house of God, with the voice of joy and praise....* —Psalm 42:4

**13**

Joy and praise are inseparable companions, and in the Psalms they seem to have been an integral part of the worship service in the temple. In Psalm 100:4, David tells us: "Enter into his gates with thanksgiving, and into his courts with praise; be thankful unto him, and bless his name." Isaiah, too, coupled joy with praise in the worship experience: "Ye shall have a song . . . and gladness of heart, as when one goeth with a pipe to come into the mountain of the Lord, to the mighty One of Israel" (30: 29). But do we need to wait 'til the Lord's Day to bring our joy and praise into the presence of Him whom we worship? No, the truly Christ-centered marriage and home will be strengthened even more if this praise and worship is part of the daily practice. As Jesus said in Matthew 18: 20, "For where two or three are gathered together in my name, there am I in the midst of them." Robert Louis Stevenson wrote: "Do not forget that even as 'to work is to worship, so to be cheery is to worship also, and to be happy is the first step to being pious." Join joy and praise together in your life and marriage—and let them worship the Lord together.

# March

**14**

*Let the righteous be joyful; let them exult before God; let them be jubilant with joy!*
—Psalm 68:3 RSV

Joy and righteousness belong together, says David in this Psalm, in which he later chronicles the exodus of the children of Israel from Egypt. I particularly like the Revised Standard Version's rendering of this verse, which properly conveys the ectasy, the sheer exuberance, that should be the experience of the child of God as he thinks upon the greatness of his Father. Indeed, David goes on in verse 4 to instruct us to "Sing to God, sing praises to his name; lift up a song to him who rides upon the clouds; his name is the Lord, exult before him!" This passage, too, reflects the same joy expressed in Psalm 32:11, the meditation verse for March 11. Job 36:7 also echoes the exaltation of the righteous: "He withdraweth not his eyes from the righteous: but with kings are they on the throne; yea, he doth establish them for ever, and they are exalted." The Chronicler, probably Ezra, says of gladness in 2 Chronicles 30:21 that "the children of Israel that were present at Jerusalem kept the feast of unleavened bread seven days with great *gladness:* and the Levites and the priests praised the Lord day by day, singing with loud instruments unto the Lord" (italics added). As Proverbs 14:34 so graphically points out: "Righteousness exalteth a nation: but sin is a reproach to any people." Let righteousness and joy be companions in your home!

**15**

*Speak, Lord; for thy servant heareth.*
—1 Samuel 3:9

"And whosoever will be chief [great] among you, let him be your servant" (Matt. 20:27). As a mere boy, Samuel learned to listen: first, to Eli's advice, and second, to God Himself. Jesus, too, was obedient to His Father, and He advised the same kind of obedient, listening attitude in His followers (see Matt. 20:27). In that closest of earthly relationships, the marriage bond, this "you first" kind of attitude will do much to get you over those first months (even years) of adjustment to one another. If each partner in the relationship will consider himself servant of the other, you will discover a thrilling secret: there is real joy in serving the one who is dearest on earth to you (and I don't mean yourself!). Jesus also said: "It is more blessed to give than to receive," and that sums it up. In a relationship of love, it is more blessed to give than to receive. In fact, if you want to measure your love, gauge it by your willingness to give and joy in doing so. If you begrudge your marriage partner, perhaps you don't know what love really is. In your marriage, assume the listening attitude of the boy Samuel, and you will find real joy in serving. "It is possible to give without loving, but it is impossible to love without giving," says Richard Braunstein.

*A merry heart doeth good like a medicine.*
　　　　—Proverbs 17:22

# 16

The world needs nothing more than it needs happiness-makers. There is a great deal of sadness everywhere. The Bible is a book meant to make people happy. Joy-bells ring all through it. The mission of the gospel is to make happiness. The angel's announcement of good tidings of great joy is going forth yet on every breeze. The story of the love of Christ is changing darkness to light, despair to hope, tears to laughter, sorrow to rejoicing, in all lands. It is the mission of every Christian to be a happiness-maker. Each one of us has power, too, to add something at least to the world's gladness. We can do this in a thousand ways—by being joyful Christians ourselves, making our lives a sweet song; by telling others the joyful things of the Word of God; by doing kindnesses to all we meet; by comforting

# March

sorrow, lifting burdens away, cheering sadness and weariness, and scattering blessings wherever we go.

—J. R. MILLER

**17** *The meek also shall increase their joy in the Lord, and the poor among men shall rejoice in the Holy One of Israel.* —Isaiah 29:19

In one of the Beatitudes Jesus tells us, "Blessed are the meek: for they shall inherit the earth." I wonder if He had read this passage in Isaiah—or if Isaiah was looking ahead to His teaching. Regardless, the two passages agree in joining meekness to joy. In that Psalm in which he foretells the suffering and glory of the Messiah, David, too, couples meekness with blessing: "The meek shall eat and be satisfied: they shall praise the Lord that seek him: your heart shall live for ever" (22:26). And in Psalm 37:11, David promises that "the meek shall inherit the earth." Meekness is spiritual fruit number eight and joy is number two in the Galatians listing set forth by Paul—and I don't think it's any accident that the two are juxtaposed by David and Isaiah here in the Old Testament as well. These spiritual attributes are designed to go together—and this is just another proof or instance of that truth. Put on meekness and you "will increase [your] joy in the Lord!"

**18** *For ye shall go out with joy, and be led forth with peace: the mountains and the hills shall break forth before you into singing, and all the trees . . . shall clap their hands.* —Isaiah 55:12

Here again joy is joined to one of the other fruits of the Spirit, peace, in an Old Testament context—another proof and confirmation of the divine unity of the Scriptures. Earlier, in a predictive prayer recorded by Isaiah, joy and singing are coupled and expressed: "Therefore the redeemed of the Lord shall return, and come with singing unto Zion; and everlasting joy shall be upon their head: and they shall obtain gladness and joy; and sorrow and mourning shall flee away" (51:11). In 1 Chronicles 16:32-33, Ezra also informs us that even "the fields rejoice, and all that is therein. . . . the trees of the wood sing out at the presence of the Lord. . . ." Such joy is hard to contain, even for the trees, fields, mountains, and hills. As Jesus once said, "If these [people] should hold their peace, the stones would immediately cry out" (Luke 19:40). In the face of such joy from inanimate nature, how should the Christian react when he contemplates the greatness of God? Back in the nineteenth century, Maltbie D. Babcock answered that question for us: "The Christian life that is joyless is a discredit to God and a disgrace to itself." Let the companionship of joy and peace be the Christian's portion day by day.

*Behold, my servants shall sing for joy of heart, but ye shall . . . sorrow. . . . But be ye [Christians] glad and rejoice for ever in that which I create: for behold, I create Jerusalem a rejoicing, and her people a joy.* —Isaiah 65:14-18

**19**

God's people are to be a glad, a joyous people. Notice again how the sacred writer contrasts the gladness of the godly with the wailing of the wicked. Ours is not an empty, shallow joy emanating from an unrealistic view of life, but a serenity of soul stemming from a right relationship to the great God of the universe. "The ungodly are not so: but are like the chaff which the wind driveth away" (Ps. 1:4). Thomas à Kempis once said: "All men de-

# March

sire peace, but very few desire those things that make for peace." The secret of soul serenity is a Christ-centered personality as one of God's people. The secret of a truly happy home does not lie in its exterior beauty or interior luxuriousness; the secret lies in the "desires of the hearts" of those living in that home. If the Spirit is supreme, the joy will be there, regardless of material accomplishments.

**20**   *Thy words were found and I did eat them; and thy word was unto me the joy and rejoicing of my heart: for I am called by thy name, O Lord of hosts.*
—Jeremiah 15:16

Another wellspring of joy for the child of God is the Word of God, as Jeremiah so exultantly proclaims in this passage. The Psalmist, too, found the Word "better unto me than thousands of gold and silver" (119:72). The famous testimony of the prophet Ezekiel tells us what the Word of God meant to him, how it was the joy of his heart to eat, to own, and to proclaim it: "Moreover he said unto me, Son of man, eat that thou findest; eat this roll, and go speak unto the house of Israel. . . . Then did I eat it; and it was in my mouth as honey for sweetness" (3:1–3). The New Testament, too, underlines the Word's importance to the Christian. John tells us: "In the beginning was the Word, and the Word was with God, and the Word was God" (1:1). And Peter tells us it is our sustenance: "As newborn babes, desire the sincere milk of the word, that ye may grow thereby" (1 Peter 2:2). The famous itinerant evangelist of a past generation, Gipsy Smith, perceptively analyzed the Christian's vital relationship to the Word: "What makes the difference is not how many times you have been through the Bible, but how many times and how thoroughly the Bible has been through you." Are you "eating" the Word today?

*Thy words were found, and I did eat them; and thy
word was unto me the joy and rejoicing of mine
heart: for I am called by thy name, O Lord God of
hosts.* —Jeremiah 15:16

**21**

Jeremiah is not a joyful book. This verse lies like an
oasis in a desert of doom. The bulk of Jeremiah's writing is
devoted to dire predictions concerning the fall of Jerusalem, judgment unless the people mend their ways, prophe-
cies against the heathen nations surrounding Israel, and
similar matters. Yet, lying here like a sparkling jewel
against a black velvet background, is this beautiful note of
joy, this heartfelt expression of happiness in the Lord. It
arrests the reader's attention and stirs his emotions. The
Word of God is the source and secret of Jeremiah's joy—
and it is to be ours as well. Back in the sixteenth century
Lady Jane Grey, a descendant of Henry VII of England,
wrote: "The highest earthly enjoyments are but a shadow
of the joy I find in reading God's Word." She was later executed to remove her as a potential rival to the throne, but
one does not need to wonder where she is—nor whether
she is enjoying eternity. I wonder what would happen in
our spiritual lives if we would put Lady Jane's precept into
practice, or if we joined Jeremiah in his devotions, "eating
the word of God."

*Sing and rejoice, O daughter of Zion: for lo, I come,
and I will dwell in the midst of thee, saith the
Lord.* —Zechariah 2:10

**22**

Singing and rejoicing go naturally together. This quality
is what sets the Christian religion apart from all others—
the joy in Christ which verbalizes itself in the sheer jubi-
lance of singing. What other religion has given birth to

# March

such a vast body of hymnody, our heritage as Christians? Think of the exultant, exuberant anthems with which we Christians praise our heavenly Father! Isaiah, too, proclaims this truth: "Sing unto the Lord; for he hath done excellent things: this is known in all the earth. Cry out and shout, . . . . for great is the Holy One of Israel" (12:5-6). Zephaniah, Zechariah's neighbor in the Old Testament canon, also cites this aspect of the Christian faith: "Sing, O daughter of Zion; shout, O Israel; be glad and rejoice with all the heart, O daughter of Jerusalem" (3:14). Why are we Christians a happy people? Because God is in our midst, says Zechariah. What greater cause for rejoicing can we have than that? "The Lord is my strength and song, and is become my salvation" (Ps. 118:14; Isa. 12:2).

## 23

*Rejoice that your names are written in heaven.*
—Luke 10:20

This must be the ultimate height of joy this side of heaven itself—to know that your name is written down in the Lamb's book of life: "And there shall in no wise enter into it anything that defileth . . . or maketh a lie: but they which are written in the Lamb's book of life" (Rev. 21:27). David, too, referred to this book: "Let them be blotted out of the book of the living, and not be written with the righteous" (Ps. 69:28). In his description of the end of the tribulation and the resurrection of the dead, Daniel prophesied: "At that time . . . there shall be a time of trouble . . . and at that time thy people shall be delivered, every one that shall be found written in the book" (12:1). Paul, too, knew of its existence: "Help those women which laboured with me in the gospel, with Clement also, and with other my fellow-labourers, whose names are in the book of life" (Phil. 4:3). The writer to the Hebrews referred to those in this book as "the assembly of the firstborn who are enrolled in heaven" (12:23 RSV). *Rejoice that your name is written in heaven!* But don't forget your responsibility to those whose names are not yet there.

> When Christ ascended
> Triumphantly from star to star,
> He left the gates of heaven ajar!
> HENRY WADSWORTH
> LONGFELLOW

*And of his fulness have all we received, and grace for grace.* —John 1:16

**24**

There is no favoritism with God; just as the spring flowers, the sunshine, and the pure air are for all, as free to the beggar as to the king, so God's abundant grace is for every man and woman, and there is nothing anyone has ever had which you may not have if you will. The same stream is passing your door, though you may not utilize the power to drive your machinery; the same electricity is in the air, though you may not have learned to make it flash your messages or light your home. The same grace that made a Luther, a Calvin, a Knox, a Spurgeon, is for you today. If you are living a defeated life, beaten and thwarted, frustrated and constantly compelled to admit shortcomings and failure, understand it is not because there is any favoritism on God's part; because all the Holy Spirit's power, and everything which is stored in Jesus Christ, is waiting to make you a saint, and to lift you to the level which you long for in your best moments. It makes a great difference when the Christian understands this—and taps into the power that awaits him. —F. B. MEYER

# March

**25** *I am come that they might have life, and that they might have it more abundantly.* —John 10:10

This often memorized and frequently quoted verse speaks to me of God's grace, that added dimension to earthly life that makes it truly "abundant." Another word comes to mind as I look at this blessed promise—and that word is *joy*. Apparently the concept of joy is included here; the Amplified New Testament translates this verse: ". . . that they may have and enjoy life, and have it in abundance—to the full, till it overflows." As the word "grace" means "unmerited favor and love of God," so joy, too, cannot be earned or merited. In fact, Alexander MacLaren says: "To pursue joy is to lose it. The only way to get it is to follow steadily the path of duty, without thinking of joy, and then, like sheep, it comes most surely, unsought, and we 'being in the way' the angel of God, bright-haired Joy, is sure to meet us." It is comforting to know that as we turn our lives over to God, He has this abundant life waiting for us. If we open our emptiness to Him for His filling, we will discover that "the half has not been told" of the blessing awaiting those who yield their lives to Him.

**26** *These things have I spoken unto you, that my joy might remain in you, and that your joy might be full.* —John 15:11

"My joy . . . your joy." True joy cannot be known apart from the Source and Giver of every good and perfect gift, Jesus Christ Himself. This is the second in the catalog of Christian virtues listed in Galatians 5:22, and without joy any marriage would end up with the "blahs." But true joy does not depend, indeed cannot depend, on outward circumstances. If it did, it would be mere happiness which fluctuates with the tide. True joy must come from within, from an attitude of heart instilled by the Savior Himself. Robert Browning said it well: "Desire joy and thank God for it. Renounce it, if need be, for other's sake. That's joy beyond joy." Samuel Dickey Gordon puts joy into perspective for us when he says: "Joy is distinctly a Christian word and a Christian thing. It is the reverse of happiness. Happiness is the result of what happens of an agreeable sort. Joy has its springs down inside. And that spring never runs dry, no matter what happens. Only Jesus gives that joy. He had joy, singing its music within, even under the shadow of the cross. It is an unknown word and thing except as He has sway within."

*And the disciples were filled with joy, and with the Holy Ghost.* —Acts 13:52

**27**

This brief sentence sums up the relationship of our joy as followers of Christ to our infilling by the Holy Spirit. It comes at the conclusion of part of the story of Paul's first missionary journey and his ministry at Antioch, where believers were first identified with the distinctive name of "Christians." Remember that at the advent of the Holy Spirit on the day of Pentecost, reported in Acts 2:4, the believers were "filled with the Holy Spirit." But this new outbreak of heavenly power occurred far from the center of early church activity. As Anders Nygren has so perceptively pointed out, "The church is not man's work; it is God's work, the work of the Holy Ghost who 'calls, gathers, enlightens, and sanctifies the whole Christian church on earth, and preserves it in union with Jesus Christ in the one true faith.' " The infilling of joy and the infilling of the Holy Spirit are companion works in the life of the Christian. Have they happened to you?

# March

**28** *Be not drunk with wine . . . but be filled with the Spirit; speaking to yourselves in psalms and hymns and spiritual songs, singing and making melody in your heart to the Lord.* —Ephesians 5:18–19

What a pageant of praise Paul is calling for here as he urges Christians to be, first of all, filled with the Spirit. Then Paul tells Christians they are to go on expressing their joy "in psalms and hymns and spiritual songs, singing. . . ." This is another reminder of our "singing faith" as Christians. Think of it: each one of us, no matter how humble, can experience this infilling. While the Scriptures seem to indicate that this experience comes in concert with fellow-Christians, it is also possible for the experience to come when we are alone, or perhaps together with our spouse, in quiet contemplation and meditation upon the greatness of our God. As Martin Luther used to say, "Even a humble straw, lying flat on the surface of the waters, can feel the boundless power of the ocean surging through it." Have you felt the Spirit's surging power? The secret of joy is the filling of the Spirit, the Imparter of all spiritual gifts!

**29** *And ye became followers of us, and of the Lord, having received the word in much affliction, with joy of the Holy Ghost.* —1 Thessalonians 1:6

Being a follower of Christ does not immunize the believer from affliction and trouble. Paul, of all people, knew this from experience. What afflictions he faced for his uncompromising stand for Christ! His former friends became his bitterest enemies. He ended his life, so far as we know, a martyr for Christ, as did so many of the other early disciples. And often he stood alone, or nearly so, as he faced the buffetings handed out to him by both man and nature: "In journeyings often, in perils of waters, . . . in perils of mine own countrymen . . . the heathen . . . in the city . . . the wilderness . . . the sea . . . among false brethren. . . ." (2 Cor. 11:26). As another great follower of the Lord, George Müller, once put it: "Enjoyment in the Lord does not depend upon the multitude of believers by whom we are surrounded." No, our joy depends upon the Holy Spirit!

*Whom having not seen, ye love; in whom, though now ye see him not, yet believing, we rejoice with joy unspeakable and full of glory.* —1 Peter 1:8

**30**

"Love is more than a characteristic of God; it *is* His character." The Bible says that God is love, and that love itself is "of God." The two great commandments which Jesus left with His disciples encompass every dimension of love, so far as humanity is capable of expressing it: "Love God" and "love others as yourself." This love lies at the heart of the Christian life—but it is even more basic to a good marriage relationship. In your marriage put God first, others second, and yourself last, and you will be amazed at how all aspects of life will find their proper level. Martin Luther said, "Love is an image of God, and not a lifeless image, but the living essence of the divine nature which beams full of all goodness." It is interesting that Peter couples two of the fruits of the Spirit in this passage: love and joy. All these fruits do go together—and all stem from God's divine storehouse of spiritual treasures. As St. Augustine perceptively said, "Love God, and do what you like!" Do you dare live like that?

# March

**31**

*But rejoice, inasmuch as ye are partakers of Christ's sufferings; that when his glory shall be revealed, ye may be glad also with exceeding joy.*

—1 Peter 4:13

Peter, like Paul, could speak first-hand of the suffering that can come to Christ's servants. History tells us that he, too, went to a martyr's death, probably being crucified upside-down on a cross. Paul had told the Philippians: "That I may know him, and the power of his resurrection, and the fellowship of his sufferings, being made conformable unto his death" (3:10), and the Romans: ". . . heirs of God, and joint-heirs with Christ; if so be that we suffer with him, that we may be also glorified together" (8:17). So Peter, too, told the early Christians that pain and suffering bring praise and glory to God. The key to profiting from suffering and pain is to remember to rejoice in it. Henry Ward Beecher once said: "Of all the lights you carry in your face, joy will reach the farthest out to sea." How far does your joy reach—as far as your spouse?

# April

*But the fruit of the Spirit is . . . peace. . . .*
—Galatians 5:22

**1**

The presence of peace in a marriage relationship could easily become an overlooked blessing. By very definition, peace cannot come by striving. It is a sense of serenity that must arise from within a person and spread to those around him. Peace is a spirit or an attitude that can pervade a home to make it a place of blessing. Brother Lawrence in his *Practice of the Presence of God* said, "The time of business does not differ from the time of prayer; and in the noise and clutter of my kitchen, while several persons are at the same time calling for different things, I possess God in as great tranquility as if I were upon my knees at the Blessed Sacrament." He lived in the presence of the Peacegiver Himself, and even the most mundane of pursuits had a sacred sense. Two centuries earlier Thomas à Kempis, another Christian mystic, had advised in *The Imitation of Christ*: "My son, now will I teach thee the way of peace and inward liberty. Be desirous to do the will of another rather than thine own. Choose always to have less rather than more. Seek always the lowest place, and to be inferior to everyone. Wish always, and pray, that the will of God may be wholly fulfilled in thee." What Christlike counsel for Christian marriages!

John Ruskin once made the interesting observation: "People are always expecting to get peace in heaven: but you know whatever peace they get there will be readymade. Whatever making of peace *they* can be blest for, must be on earth here."

# April

## 2

*And Abraham said unto Lot, Let there be no strife, I pray thee, between me and thee. . . .*
—Genesis 13:8

In this passage we see the spiritual fruit of peace being exemplified by and evidenced in that giant of the faith and father of the faithful, Abraham. Abraham, however, is working out the wisdom of Proverbs 15:18—"A wrathful man stirreth up strife: but he that is slow to anger appeaseth strife" ("quiets contention," RSV)—and 20:3—"It is an honor for a man to keep aloof from strife; but every fool will be quarreling" (RSV). In Ecclesiastes 10:4 the "Preacher" tells us that "deference will make amends for great offenses" (RSV). Peace is not free! It takes work and willingness sometimes to defer to the wishes of others. Nowhere is this more true than in the intimate relationship of marriage. Marriage is not, as some would have us believe, necessarily a 50-50 proposition. Sometimes it's 60-40, and you may have to be on the short end! But if both spouses are willing to be "on the short end," you'll be surprised at how seldom you are called upon to take that position.

## 3

*The Lord will give strength to his people; the Lord will bless his people with peace.* —Psalm 29:11

The people in all lines of endeavor who do the most work, who accomplish the most, are the calmest, most unhurried people in the community. Duties never wildly chase each other in their lives. One task never crowds another out, nor ever compels hurried, and therefore imperfect, doing. The calm spirit works methodically, doing one thing at a time, and doing it well; and it therefore works swiftly, though never appearing to be in haste.

We need the peace of God in our hearts just as really for the doing of the little things of our secular life as for the doing of the greatest duties of Christ's kingdom. Our faces ought to shine, and our spirits ought to be tranquil, and our eyes ought to be clear, and our nerves ought to be steady, as we press through the tasks of our routine day. Then we shall do them all well, slurring nothing, marring nothing. We want heart-peace before we begin any day's duties, and we should wait at Christ's feet before we go forth. —J. R. MILLER

*Depart from evil, and do good; seek peace, and pursue it.* —Psalm 34:14

**4**

We have already pointed out in the meditation on Abraham that the spiritual fruit of peace does not come easily. We have also previously looked at David's attitude toward peace, and here he expands upon the subject and calls upon us to "pursue" peace. The Living Bible tells us to "try to live in peace with everyone; work hard at it." Peter quotes this passage directly when he tells the early Christians to "Turn away from evil and do good. Try to live in peace even if you must run after it to catch and hold it!"( 1 Peter 3:11 TLB). Peace is worth pursuing; in fact, it does not come without hard work. In Job 22:21, that false friend, Eliphaz, urges Job to "acquaint now thyself with [God] and be at peace: thereby good shall come unto thee." Good advice, even though mistakenly motivated. Christian husband and wife, don't be afraid to "pursue peace." It's worth the work!

*Great peace have they which love thy law.* —Psalm 119:165

**5**

"When a man's ways please the Lord, he maketh even his enemies to be at peace with him. Better is a little with righteousness than great revenues without right" (Prov. 16:7–8). "Acquaint now thyself with him, and be at peace"

# April

(Job 22:21). The first step toward universal peace is an adjusted relationship with God. Let every man make peace with God, on God's terms, and peace will come. Men of good will must be the instruments and agents of Him who yearns over all the families of the earth. When man is out of fellowship with his God, he is distrustful, fearful, and filled with revenge. "There is no peace, saith the Lord, unto the wicked" (Isa. 48:22).

When the soul surrenders to Christ, and the inner drives are purified, man is at peace—with himself, and with God. There is a promised future state of peace and prosperity for the world: "They shall beat their swords into plowshares; and their spears into pruninghooks; nation shall not lift up a sword against nation, neither shall they learn war any more" (Micah 4:3). This golden age, this yearning hope, is to be brought in by the Christ. It may be entered now in personal experience, and it will spread over the whole earth when the Lord Jesus Christ establishes His everlasting kingdom over all earthly kingdoms.   —O. G. Wilson

**6**   *I am for peace: but when I speak, they are for war.*
*—Psalm 120:7*

What a strange claim for a man of war like David to make! He referred to this problem before: "Draw me not away with the wicked, and with the workers of iniquity, which speak peace to their neighbors, but mischief is in their hearts. . . . The words of his mouth were smoother than butter, but war was in his heart: his words were softer than oil, yet were they drawn swords" (Psalms 28:3; 55:21). As we look at his warlike life, we wonder if David would have preferred the modern-day motto, "Make love —not war" to the life style he was forced by circumstances to live. In Psalm 140:1–2, David prays for deliverance from those who would make war: "Deliver me, O Lord, from the evil man ... the violent man; which imagine mischiefs in their heart; continually are they gathered together for war." This is not the spirit of contentiousness Abraham tried to avoid in our meditation for April 2. Contentiousness is the opposite of the spirit Jesus was calling for in Mark 9:50, "Have salt in yourselves, and have peace with one another." Tagore, Hindu priest and Nobel Peace Prize-winner, once wrote: "The mountain-fir, in its rustling, modulates the memory of its fights with the storm into a hymn of peace." This is the attitude the Christian should have toward his problems and "fights with the storms." He can buckle under to them, or he can ride the storm to the heights of peace.

*Behold, how good and pleasant it is when brothers dwell in unity!* —Psalm 133:1, ASV

7

I'd like to paraphrase this verse slightly: "Behold, how good and pleasant it is when husband and wife dwell in unity!" Unity speaks of peace and harmony. In fact, the Living Bible translates this word "unity" as "harmony." What a happy marriage that will be that makes "unity" its motto. Unity is oneness, and in a Christian marriage, two become one, in the deepest sense of the word. This truth reminds me of the action of Abraham already mentioned in the meditation for April 2, based on Genesis 13:8, in which Abraham says to Lot: "Let there be no strife, I pray thee, between thee .... and me" and Abraham subsequently expresses his willingness to go the "extra mile" to avoid that strife. The writer to the Hebrews was thinking of this attitude when he wrote: "Let brotherly love continue" (13:1). Here again a slight paraphrase is in order: "Let marital love continue." Just as brotherly love is but a weak reflection of the godly affection God has for His children, so the love of husband and wife is but a likeness, an echo, of the divine love that lies at the root of all love.

# April

George Granville, English playwright who died in 1835, has one of his characters say to the other: "There is no heaven like mutual love." What a picture of marital happiness that conjures up for us!

**8**     *I know that whatever God does endures for ever; nothing can be added to it, nor anything taken from it; God has made it so, in order that men should fear before him.* —Ecclesiastes 3:14 RSV

There is a perfection and a permanency about God's planning and program that cannot possibly be compared to the imperfection and uncertainty of man's scheming. And yet our human tendency is to emphasize and follow our own program, virtually ignoring God so far as our daily practice is concerned. Earthbound as we are, we neglect the access we might have daily right into the throne room of glory where we could receive from our Father His plans for our day. Rather, we follow our own narrow paths to temporal satisfaction and material gain, deluding ourselves into thinking this, too, is God's will for us. How often do we honestly ask, "Lord, what would You have me to do?" If we really believed what "The Preacher" (the meaning of the title, "Ecclesiastes") was saying here, wouldn't our orientation be God-ward rather than manward? Before the turn of the century, Joseph Parker wrote: "Have no fear for the unsettlement or the disturbance of the Kingdom of heaven. It began in eternity, it will go on through everlasting; there is no panic in the divine personality. God is peace, God gives peace, God gives rest."

**9**     *Better is an handful with quietness, than both the hands full with travail [toil] and vexation of spirit.* —Ecclesiastes 4:6

Paul put it this way: "Godliness with contentment is great gain" (1 Tim. 6:6). A wise man who lived barely past his fortieth birthday (he died in 1719) made this insightful observation: "A contented mind is the greatest blessing a man can enjoy in this world; and if, in the present life, his happiness arises from the subduing of his desires, it will rise to the next from the gratification of them" (JOSEPH ADDISON). In Proverbs 15:16–17, Solomon saw it this way: "Better is little with the fear of the Lord than great treasure and trouble therewith. Better is a dinner with herbs where love is, than a stalled ox and hatred therewith." Almost Solomon persuades me to become a vegetarian! In Proverbs 17:1 Solomon wisely opined, "Better is a dry morsel, and quietness therewith, than an house full of sacrifices with strife." And in Psalm 39:6, Solomon's father, David, equally wise, declared: "Surely man goes about as a shadow! Surely for nought are they in turmoil; man heaps up, and knows not who will gather!" (RSV) Quietness comes from the presence of peace in the life, not from material gain. Sow the seed of peace and reap the harvest of quiet. Isn't this a blessed picture of the heavenly haven a home can be when God reigns in it?

*When a man's ways please the Lord, he maketh even his enemies to be at peace with him.*
—Proverbs 16:7

**10**

What a remarkable statement—"Even his enemies to be at peace with him"! Solomon makes it clear here that this just doesn't *happen*—no, the prerequisite for peace is that "a man's ways please the Lord." Reminds you of the New Testament admonition from the lips of Jesus, doesn't it? "Seek ye first the kingdom of God, . . . and all these things shall be added unto you." In 2 Chronicles 17:10, this very thing happened to King Jehoshaphat because the godly king rediscovered the Word of God and ordered that it be taught, thus "pleasing" the Lord: "And the fear of the Lord fell upon all the kingdoms of the lands that

# April

were round about Judah, so that they made no war against Jehoshaphat." T. T. Faichney says: "With God in charge of our defenses, there will be peace within." Let me paraphrase this excellent observation: "With God in charge of our marriage, there will be peace within!"

**11** *And he shall judge among the nations, and shall rebuke many people; and they shall beat their swords into plowshares, and their spears into pruninghooks; nation shall not lift up sword against nation, neither shall they learn war any more.* —Isaiah 2:4

*War and peace!* Eternal enemies. This classic description of the outbreak of messianic peace in the midst of a world at war has been quoted many times, in these last days, as well as down through the centuries—but probably never before in a book on marriage! Nevertheless, it is appropriate to our theme of peace being traced through the Scriptures during this month. And its truths apply equally to homes as well as nations. For example, look at Isaiah's later comments: "The work of righteousness shall be peace; and the effect of righteousness quietness and assurance for ever. And my people shall dwell in a peaceable habitation, and in sure dwellings, and in quiet resting places" (32:17–18). I'd like a home like that, wouldn't you? And look at Hosea, that expert on broken homes, who said: "I will make a covenant for them with the beasts of the field, and with the fowls of heaven, and with the creeping things . . . and I will break the bow and the sword and the battle out of the earth, and will make them to lie down safely" (2:18) There is a formula for peace—it comes only when we give God preeminence in our lives. William Cowper, English poet and hymnologist, wrote:

> Those Christians best deserve the name
> Who studiously make peace their aim;
> Peace, both the duty and the prize
> Of him that creeps and him that flies.

*I form the light, and create darkness: I make peace,
and create evil: I the Lord do all these things.*
                                        —Isaiah 45:7

**12**

This one *is* a puzzler! How can a good God be the
Author of both peace and evil? I don't have much trouble
conceding His creation of light and darkness, even though
they are opposites. But peace and evil? I asked Matthew
Henry about it and he said: "Not the evil of sin (God is
not the author of that), but the evil of punishment. Light
and darkness are opposite to each other. . . . The selfsame
cause of both is He that is first Cause of all. He who
formed the natural light (see Gen. 1:3) still forms the
providential light. He also who at first made peace among
the jarring principles of nature makes peace in the affairs
of men. He who allowed the natural darkness which was
mere privation, creates the providential darkness." Then I
looked elsewhere in the Old Testament for enlightenment
and found Job saying to God, "I know that thou canst do
everything, and that no thought can be withholden from
thee" (42:2). After that I consulted David, who told me:
"But our God is in the heavens: he hath done whatsoever
he hath pleased" (Ps. 115:3). For one last comment I con-
ferred with Amos, who pointed out: "Shall a trumpet be
blown in the city, and the people not be afraid? shall there
be evil in a city, and the Lord hath not done it?" (3:6). I
cannot understand it, but I can accept it: My God is Creator and Ruler of all—"I the Lord do all these things."

*Seek the peace of the city whither I have caused you
to be carried away captives, and pray unto the Lord
for it: for in the peace thereof shall ye have peace.*
                                        —Jeremiah 29:7

**13**

This quote from Jeremiah proves to me that I can have
peace in spite of my circumstances. The secret of peace,
for one thing, is in prayer, which puts me in direct contact

# April

with the Prince of Peace. This passage also points out to me another responsibility of the Christian citizen—to pray for those in authority over me. Ezra had much to say on this matter of civic responsibility: "Pray for the life of the king, and of his sons" (6:10); "And whosoever will not do the law of thy God, and the law of the king, let judgment be executed speedily upon him" (7:26). In the New Testament, Paul urged Timothy to pray "For kings, and for all that are in authority; that we may lead a quiet and peaceable life in all godliness and honesty" (1 Tim. 2:2). As Daniel Webster said more than a century ago "Whatever makes men good Christians makes them good citizens." How do you measure up in that area of life?

**14**  *Thus saith the Lord of hosts: The fast ... shall be to the house of Judah joy and gladness, and cheerful feasts; therefore love the truth and peace.*
—Zechariah 8:19

Truth is another fellow traveler with the produce of peace. The idea of truth and peace traveling together is also conveyed in verse 16 of this same chapter of Zechariah: "These are the things that ye shall do; Speak ye every man the truth to his neighbour, execute the judgment of truth and peace in your gates. ... and love no false oath." Jesus' words in Mark 9:50 also apply here as in other places where we have looked at peace: "Salt is good: but if salt have lost his saltness, wherewith will ye season it? Have salt in yourselves, and have peace one with another." Seen in this light, truth becomes just as much a sign of Christian character as do the more frequently listed traits of Galatians 5:22, 23. Indeed, F. W. Robertson, eminent divine of another century, saw this as vital to Christian living: "Truth lies in character. Christ did not simply speak the truth; He was Truth—Truth through and through, for truth is a thing not of words but a life and being." This man, who died before his fortieth birthday, had the spiritual insight to put truth in divine perspective. If you want to live as Christ would have you live, *love the truth and peace.*

*Blessed are the peacemakers: for they shall be called the children of God.* —Matthew 5:9

# 15

In Paul's list of Christian virtues given in Galatians 5: 22, he gives a place of prominence to "peace." Jesus, too, emphasized this attribute of peaceableness in His ministry. Every Christian is to be a peacemaker! On this subject, J. R. Miller writes: "It is very easy, if you are talking to one who has a little distrust of another or a little bitterness against another, to say a word which will increase the distrust or add to the bitterness. We like to approve and justify the one with whom we are speaking, and in doing so we are apt to confirm him in his bitterness or sense of wrong. Let us be on our guard that we do not unintentionally widen little rifts into great breaches. Let us seek ever to be peacemakers. There is no beatitude whose blessing is more radiant than that of the peacemakers—"they shall be called sons of God." As Matthew Henry once said, "Peace is such a precious jewel that I would give anything for it but truth."

*Glory to God in the highest, and on earth peace, good will toward men.* —Luke 2:14

# 16

True peace is found nowhere else but in the Person of Jesus Christ. Indeed, one of the names Isaiah gave Him

# April

centuries before His birth was that striking title, "Prince of Peace." No other man can bring peace into the world; on the contrary, sometimes well-meaning men who have tried to bring peace have more often ended up bringing a "sword." There is no peace for the wicked, says Isaiah, but "Peace, peace, to the far and to the near, says the Lord; and I will heal him [the repentant who recognizes who Jesus is]" (Isa. 57:19). Indeed, Luke has already made it clear that the Messiah came "to guide our feet into the way of peace" (1:79). As we have said before, peace connotes harmony and reconciliation between Creator and created. As Frederic W. Farrar once said: "Jesus came not to hush the natural music of men's lives, nor to fill it with storm and agitation, but to retune every silver chord in that 'harp of a thousand strings' and to make it echo with the harmonies of heaven." We shout with the angels, "Glory to God in the highest, and on earth peace, good will toward men."

**17**     *Jesus saith . . . I am the way, the truth, and the life: no man cometh unto the Father but by me.*
—John 14:6

In this familiar yet ringing declaration of His identity, Jesus gives us facts to count on:
  (1) A sense of direction, a *way* to go.
  (2) A sense of purpose, something and Someone to believe in—*truth.*
  (3) A sense of spontaneity, something to live for right now, in the present—*life.*

So much is wrapped up in these three words, bursting as they are with eternal meaning: the past, present, and future tenses of the Christian life. The poet has said it for us:

He is a path, if any be misled;
   He is a robe, if any naked be;
If any chance to hunger, he is bread;
   If any be a bondman, he is free;
   If any be but weak, how strong is he!
To dead men life is he, to sick men health;
To blind men sight, and to the needy wealth;
A pleasure without loss, a treasure without stealth.
              —GILES FLETCHER

If you are looking for a motto for life, let this be it. Ponder the truth Henry Drummond expressed: "Every character has an inward spring; let Christ be that spring. Every action has a keynote; let Christ be that note, to which your whole life is attuned."

*Peace I leave with you, my peace I give unto you....* —John 14:27

**18**

Of all the attributes or fruits of the Spirit that should characterize a good marriage, the gift of "peace" seems most basic. I am not talking about a passive "peace" that submits to all things, simply to "keep the peace." Rather, I'm thinking about a kind of peace that "is not the absence of conflict from life, but the ability to cope with it." Henry van Dyke said, "The Bible teaches us that there is no foundation for enduring peace on earth, except in righteousness; that it is our duty to suffer for that cause if need be; that we are bound to fight for it if we have the power; and that if God gives us the victory we must use it for the perpetuation of righteous peace." That definition is anything but passive, and it emphasizes that anything worth having is worth fighting for. Husband and wife must join forces in seeking this atmosphere of peace in the home. They are not to be in competition—they are to complement one another, to be two sides or halves of a unified whole, as they allow this divine peace to fill their hearts and home.

## 19

*Grace to you and peace from God our Father, and the Lord Jesus Christ.* —Romans 1:7

Perfect loyalty to Christ brings perfect peace into the heart. The secret of Christ's own peace was His absolute devotion to His Father's will. We can find peace in no other way. Any resistance to God's will, any disobedience of His law, any wrenching of our lives out of His hand, must break the peace of our hearts. No lesson that He gives ever mars our peace if we receive it with a willing, teachable spirit, and strive to learn it just as He has written it out for us. If we take the lessons just as our Master gives them to us, we shall make our life all music, and we shall find peace. —J. R. MILLER

"Thou wilt keep Him in perfect peace, whose mind is stayed on thee: because he trusteth in thee" (Isa. 26:3).

## 20

*To be spiritually minded is life and peace.* —Romans 8:6

If we really are Christ's, then back into the very bosom of the Father where Christ is hid, there He will carry us. We, too, shall look out and be as calm and as independent as He is. The needs of men shall touch us just as keenly as they touch Him, but the sneers and strife of men shall pass us by as they pass by Him and leave no mark on His unruffled life. For us, just as for Him, this will not mean a cold and selfish separation from our brethren. We shall be infinitely closer to real life when we separate ourselves from their outside strifes and superficial pride, and know and love them truly by knowing and loving them in God.

This is the power and progress of true Christianity. It leads us into, it abounds in peace. It is a brave, vigorous peace, full of life, full of interest and work. It is a peace that means thoroughness, that refuses to waste its force and time in little superficial tumults which come to nothing, while there is so much real work to be done, so much real help to be given, and such a real life to be lived with God. That peace, His peace, may Jesus give to us all.

—PHILLIPS BROOKS

*Be perfect, be of good comfort, be of one mind, live in peace; and the God of love and peace shall be with you.* —2 Corinthians 13:11

**21**

It is not unusual for a Christian to become despondent over the lack of spiritual progress he is making. What should be done in such a situation? Look up to the "God of peace," be reconciled in Christ. He carried out His holy will in Christ, and raised Him from the dead. He can raise you, too, from the spiritual deadness you deplore. He can make you "perfect in every good work"—not, perhaps, to do all you desire, but to do "His will." He can work within you what He approves, and all through the teaching, the example, the grace, the finished work of Jesus. Look away from self to Him. —JOHN HALL

*For he is our peace, who hath . . . broken down the middle wall of partition between us.*
—Ephesians 2:14

**22**

Christ, Himself, crucified, risen, now exalted to God's right hand in glory, is our peace. On the cross He made peace by the shedding of His blood. Before returning to heaven He said, "Peace be unto you." Now, "being justified by faith, we have peace with God through our Lord Jesus Christ" (Rom. 5:1). He undertook to settle the sin-

# April

question by making expiation for iniquity. God is satisfied with His finished work. When the Father raised His Son from the dead He bore witness to the perfection of His work. Now the troubled soul looks up to the Throne, by the eye of faith, and sees the Man who was once on the tree, forsaken of God, crowned with honor and glory. He could not be there if the sin-question had not been disposed of. So the believer can exultingly say, "He is my peace!" —H. A. IRONSIDE

**23** *These things I have spoken unto you, that in me ye might have peace.* —John 16:33

Serenity is distinctive and divine. There is a peace of God, a peace of Christ, a peace of the Spirit, all one divine peace. And this is communicated to us by the Holy Spirit. Jesus distinguishes His peace from every other kind and quality. "My peace I give unto you, not as the world giveth. . . ." He recognized that the world had a peace to offer. He does not ask us to be blind to the world's satisfactions, He asks us to look at them squarely, appraise their real worth, and then weigh them honestly against the gifts He offers.

This serenity is not idleness, nor stillness, nor is it the boon of a life remote from care, dwelling in some dream island to which the wings of a dove carry the wistful heart; it is peace in the midst of care, the fruit of the Spirit in an atmosphere that may be hostile rather than kind to such fruitfulness. Serenity is the result of confidence in God's control of all the forces and events of our experience. It is the distinctive bounty of Christ, not a gift we receive apart from Him, but a gift we receive in Him, sharing His implicit trust in the will of God, and being at rest in its wisdom and love. —JOHN MACBEATH

*And the peace of God, which passeth all under-
standing, shall keep your hearts and minds through
Christ Jesus.* —Philippians 4:7

**24**

How close to the real me am I getting when I talk about
my heart and mind? "Man looketh on the outward appearance, but God looketh on the heart" is a spiritual principle
and a fact of life that runs throughout the Scripture. It
reveals that only God truly knows me—I am a stranger,
really, even to those nearest and dearest to me. That is
why true peace can only come from Him who knows me
so well. When Paul writes here of the "inner island of
peace" that should characterize the Christian, he's not
thinking about a shallow, surface kind of serenity—but of
a deep-down permeation of every layer of my being by the
blessed angel of peace. Regardless of outward circumstances, this peaceful perspective belongs to the Christian
who is "kept by the power of God." In Colossians 3:15
Paul tells us we must "let" this peace prevail or rule in our
hearts, so our part is to yield our wills—but the peace
comes from God! On this subject F. B. Meyer wrote: "The
Apostle bids us think as Jesus thought; do not look exclu-
sively upon your own interests; do not count anything of
your own worthy to stand in the way, but always be prepared to deny yourself that through you God's redeeming
love may pass to those that need His help." This is the
path to peace laid out for us—"walk ye in it!"

*For it pleased the Father that in him should all ful-
ness dwell; and, having made peace through the
blood of his cross....* —Colossians 1:19–20

**25**

Peace and bloodshed! What strange companions! Yet
the Prince of Peace was a Person—Jesus Christ Himself.

# April

He came into the world, very God Himself, to purchase our peace at the cost of His own life. The Divine Son of God had to give His life to insure our ultimate peace. The gulf between us and our God was so vast that no other sacrifice would suffice. As Daniel Webster said of Him: "If I might comprehend Jesus Christ, I could not believe on Him. He would be no greater than myself. Such is my consciousness of sin and inability that I must have a super-human Savior." Paul in Ephesians 2:13-14 sums up this concept for us: "But now in Christ Jesus ye who sometimes were far off are made nigh by the blood of Christ. For he is our peace, who hath made both one, and hath broken down the middle wall of partition between us." O the peace of the cross!

## 26

*For ye are dead, and your life is hid with Christ in God.* —Colossians 3:3

There are three grades of Christian life. There is, first of all, the dissatisfied life—the life that knows there is something which it does not possess; the life that is perpetually discontented, and rightly so, with itself. There is, second, the life that is half and half, that now and then rises up to the Mount of Transfiguration, and then paces for long seasons in the lowlands of life. There is the third life of satisfaction and contentment, of peace and power and rest; the life that has made Jesus Christ its one object; the life that every man lives who is able to say with Paul, "For me to live *is* Christ!" The soul that has made Christ its one object has entered into rest, and has entered into power; it has entered into a life of activity which no foe can withstand, and of contentment which no storm can ruffle; for over all the seas where it voyages speaks that Voice which quieted the turbulent waves of Galilee: "Peace, be still." Nothing can overcome or disturb that soul hid with Christ in God, who has made Christ the one object of its life. —ROBERT E. SPEER

*And let the peace of God rule in your hearts. . . .*
—Colossians 3:15

In our verse for today, Paul is supplying the key that unlocks the door of peace—submission to the rule of God. In the very next verse he adds another key to the ring: "Let the word of Christ dwell in you richly in all wisdom. . . ." The Modern Language Bible adds a deeper dimension: "Let the enriching message of Christ have ample room in your lives. . . ." Herein lies the secret of inner peace that is the atmosphere of the happy home: submission to the will and Word of God. Centuries ago, a great Christian thinker, François de Salignac de La Mothe Fénelon, expressed it: "Peace does not dwell in outward things, but within the soul; we may preserve it in the midst of the bitterest pain, if our will remain firm and submissive. Peace in this life springs from acquiescence, not in an exemption from suffering." To put it another way, life is a cycle: First the blessing, then the testing. Over and over again as in the case of Job, until His final purpose is worked out in our lives.

*Now the Lord of peace himself give you peace always by all means. The Lord be with you all.*
—2 Thessalonians 3:16

Paul often wished for his fellow Christians that they would know peace. In fact, in Romans 15:33 he uses the warm expression: "Now the God of peace be with you all. Amen," a beautiful and meaningful benediction. But in writing to the Thessalonians, he adds an emphasis that is lacking in some of his shorter benedictions: "The Lord of peace *himself* give you peace always by all means. *The Lord be with you all.*" Peace is priceless—and the only Source of true peace is "the Lord . . . *himself.*" Here Paul is actually quoting the exact words of the greeting Boaz gave his reapers, "The Lord be with you" (Ruth 2:4). So the

# April

words come out of a Jewish tradition which has lived for centuries, making them that much more meaningful in our modern setting. Truly, the home where Christ is honored, where God is revered, will know the peace of God in rich measure. An old Chinese proverb rightly says: "If there is righteousness in the heart there will be beauty in the character. If there be beauty in the character, there is harmony in the home. If there is harmony in the home, there will be order in the nation. If there is order in the nation, there will be peace in the world." May the *peace of God* be our portion this day!

**29**     *Now may the God of peace who brought again from the dead our Lord Jesus . . . equip you with everything good that you may do his will, working in you that which is pleasing in his sight, through Jesus Christ.* —Hebrews 13:20-21

There is a Pauline ring to this benediction passage in Hebrews, the Epistle of unknown authorship. The author may be unnamed, but his advice is certainly biblical! Just as God is love, and the Source of love, He is also Peace personified. And who is the Agent of that peace? Our Lord and Savior, Jesus Christ. David wrote, "Mark the perfect ["blameless," RSV] man, and behold the upright: for the end of that man is peace" (Ps. 37:37). The path to peace lies in proper perspectives and priorities. If Jesus Christ is given His proper place in our lives and in our marriage, so "that you may do *his* will, working in you that which is pleasing in *his* sight," then every other area of your life will find its proper level. Edmund Burke once said, "The Christian religion, by confining marriage to pairs, and rendering the relation indissoluble, has by these two things done more toward the peace, happiness, settlement, and civilization of the world, than by any other part in this whole scheme of divine wisdom." Peace will be your portion, if Christ is your Center!

*I will hear what God the Lord will speak: for he will speak peace unto his people, and to his saints.*
—Psalm 85:8

Jesus came as the Prince of Peace. Why is it that our world today knows no peace? As our technology and scientific achievements have grown, our ability to destroy one another as individuals and nations has also grown. In Matthew 10 Jesus said: "And the brother shall deliver up the brother to death, and the father the child: and the children shall rise up against their parents, and cause them to be put to death. . . . Think not that I am come to send peace on earth: I came not to send peace, but a sword. For I am come to set a man at variance against his father, and the daughter against her mother. . . . And a man's foes shall be they of his own household" (vv. 21, 34–36). This certainly describes our present-day world to a "T"—and seems almost a contradiction coming from the "Prince of Peace." But bear with me:

In our verse for the day, the Psalmist zeroes in on our problem. The key word is "hear." The peace must come from the Prince of Peace, and if the world will not listen . . . . (Jesus described the result in Matthew 10!). But notice the comforting conclusion in today's verse: "He will speak peace unto his people, and to his saints." John Foster Dulles once said: "The world will never have lasting peace so long as men reserve for war the finest human qualities. Peace, no less than war, requires idealism and self-sacrifice and a righteous and dynamic faith." Peace must start with individuals and spread from the top down —or from the bottom up. As George Eliot said a hundred years ago: "I could not live in peace if I put the shadow of a wilful sin between myself and God." Peace is a personal matter. Thank God, He is our Peace—and He is our God!

# May

*The fruit of the spirit is . . . longsuffering. . . .*
                                    —Galatians 5:22

**1**

*Rest in the Lord; wait patiently for him to act. Don't be envious of evil men who prosper.*
                                    —Psalm 37:7, TLB

"Longsuffering," the fourth in Paul's catalog of Christian virtues listed in Galatians 5, has been translated *patience* by the Revised Standard Version and other modern versions. Patience has been defined as "the bearing of provocation, annoyance, misfortune, pain, etc. without complaint, loss of temper, or irritation." What a "plus" this virtue will add to any marriage! According to David, we are to "*wait* patiently" upon the Lord after we have committed our way to Him (v. 5). In Psalm 40:1 David says, "I waited patiently for the Lord; he inclined to me and heard my cry" (RSV). So patient waiting does not imply lack of communication with the heavenly Father. In fact, David says in Psalm 62:5, "For God alone my soul waits in silence, for my hope is in him"! It is apparent that words are not needed as we communicate with our Father God.

*A hot-tempered man stirs up strife, but he who is slow to anger quiets contention.*
                                    —Proverbs 15:18, RSV

**2**

Another aspect of the fruit of patience is seen in the control of anger. In Proverbs 26:20–21, wise old Solomon

# May

has another colorful comment on the effect of the hot-tempered man: "For lack of wood the fire goes out; and where there is no whisperer, quarreling ceases. As charcoal to hot embers and wood to fire, so is a quarrelsome man for kindling strife." In Proverbs 15:1 he gives us this jewel of wisdom which will work in every home: "A soft answer turneth away wrath: but grievous words stir up anger." In our home, my wife has learned that there are times when it is not best to spring new ideas or try to discuss touchy subjects—when the man of the house is either tired or hungry. Her motto is, "Feed the brute" before getting into these ticklish topics. As we live together, we learn to know one another's weaknesses and points of vulnerability. The wise wife or prudent husband will avoid those situations that cause strife, and will use his or her spirit to "quiet contention."

3

*Their fruit does not mature . . . [but] as for that in the good soil, they are those who, hearing the word, hold it fast in an honest and good heart, and bring forth fruit with patience.* —Luke 8:14–15, RSV

In this book we have emphasized the fruit of the Spirit in its many and varied aspects (see Paul's list in Galatians 5:22–23). Jesus, too, had His list of spiritual fruit, and one is mentioned in his parable of the sower. "Longsuffering," or "patience," is the fourth attribute mentioned by Paul. Here in Luke's Gospel, Jesus talks about fruit, too, and gives the secret of fruitbearing. It's the soil that makes the difference! In the case of the fruit that grew to maturity, He said, "As for that in the good soil, they are those who, hearing the word, hold it fast in an honest and good heart, and bring forth fruit with *patience*." He has gone right to the heart of the problem. It's not the Word, the seed, which is at fault. It's the unreceptive receiver of that seed. A receptive heart must have nothing else competing with the seed for sustenance. If the receiver's first concerns are "cares, riches, and pleasures" (not necessarily in that order), he will miss God's best. What kind of soil does the Sower find in your hearts? If patience is on your cluster of fruit, it will crown the blessings your home will enjoy—and complement every area of your life. "Let steadfastness have its full effect ["patience . . . have her perfect work," KJV], that you may be perfect and complete, lacking in nothing" (James 1:4, RSV).

*That on the good ground are they, which in an honest and good heart, having heard the word, keep it, and bring forth fruit with patience. —Luke 8:15*

**4**

There's even more wisdom to be found in this "parable of the soils." In the words of our text, Jesus is pointing out the results of sowing in good soil, those in whom the spiritual harvest will have its richest fruition. Matthew Henry has some fruitful thoughts on this aspect of fruit-bearing: "It is not enough that the fruit be brought forth, but it must be *brought to perfection*, it must be fully ripened. If it be not, it is as if there was no fruit at all. . . . the good ground; which brings forth *good fruit*, is an *honest* and *good heart*; a heart firmly fixed for God and duty, an upright heart, a tender heart, is an honest and good heart, which, having heard the word, *understands* it (see Matthew), *receives* it (Mark), and *keeps* it, as the soil not only receives, but keeps the seed." May we bring forth this fruit with patience!

*In your patience possess ye your souls. —Luke 21:19*

**5**

It is interesting to note the other words some translators have used in rendering the concept of "patience" expressed in this verse. The Revised Standard Version uses the word "endures." The Living Bible suggests the wording: "For if you *stand firm*, you will win your souls." Phillips uses the term, *"Hold on. . . ."* It is obvious that patience is not just a passive acceptance of whatever comes our way. In fact, the idea of action is expressed in Revelation 2:7, "To him that *overcometh* ["conquers," RSV] will I give to eat of the tree of life, which is in the midst of the paradise of God." Patience, as expressed here, is definitely not passive! As Matthew Henry says of the section in Luke: "It is by patience, Christian patience, that we keep possession of our own souls." Another way to express it: "*Possess your own souls*, be your own man!" Patience calls for complete commitment to the Christ of the cross. As Samuel Wilberforce so succinctly stated it some centuries ago, "Christianity can be condensed into four words: Admit, Submit, Commit, and Transmit." This is our calling!

**6**        *Love is patient and kind.*    —1 Corinthians 13:4

Here Paul intertwines three of the "fruits" of the Spirit in just five short words—emphasizing again the unity of the "fruit" of the Spirit listed for us in Galatians 5:22–23. This fruit comes from one branch, which in turn stems from one Vine, the Lord Jesus Christ. As we contemplate the various aspects of spiritual fruit, we sense the oneness of this Source, and realize that the true Christian will evidence *all* these supernatural characteristics in his life. Being human, he may show forth more of one than another. But in the growing process which marks the maturing Christian, he should display all these fruits to some degree. In the kinship of marriage, how important love is as the cornerstone of the home, as the root of patience.

Grudging patience is not patience at all, but is merely putting up with the partner. Often this kind of "patience" is merely overlooking a partner's shortcomings from a position of superiority. True patience is rooted in love, and is exercised not from an attitude of superiority, but from a spirit of oneness and equality. In his classic, *The Imitation of Christ*, Thomas à Kempis says, "Wheresoever a man seeketh his own, there he falleth from love." If our love as husband and wife has this quality of patience and kindness, our home will reflect the very happiness of heaven, and the brightness of an earthly paradise!

We glory in tribulations also: knowing that tribulation worketh patience.   —Romans 5:3

**7**

Patience, this all-pervading fruit of the Spirit, does not come easily, as Paul points out here in writing to the Romans. In fact, says Paul, it takes real tribulation ["trials and troubles," Phillips; "problems and trials," TLB; "suffering," RSV] to develop patience. In 2 Corinthians 12:10, Paul expands upon this list of "tribulations": "Therefore I take pleasure in infirmities, in reproaches, in necessities, in persecution, in distresses for Christ's sake: for *when I am weak, then am I strong*"! James agrees with Paul: "Knowing this, that the trial of your faith worketh patience" (1:3). In light of this constructive use of tribulation, we should, with James, "Count it all joy when ye fall into divers temptations" ["when you meet various trials," 1:2, RSV]. An anonymous writer has pointed out: "Temptations (trials) that find us dwelling in God are to our faith like winds that more firmly root the tree." Matthew Henry sums it up: "Tribulation worketh patience, the powerful grace of God working in and with the tribulation. It proves, and by proving improves, patience as steel is hardened by the fire. That which worketh patience is matter of joy; for patience does us more good than tribulation can do us hurt. Tribulation in itself worketh impatience, but as it is sanctified to the saints, it worketh *patience*." Let patience have her perfect work in me!

**8**
> To them who by patient endurance [continuance] in well-doing seek for glory and honor and immortality, eternal life.... —Romans 2:7

J. B. Phillips translates this verse: "... that means eternal life to those who, in patiently doing good, aim at the unseen (but real) glory and honor of the eternal world." In this verse, the concepts of patience and perseverance are joined. In another of his epistles, Paul rounds this out for us: "Let us not grow tired of doing good, for, unless we throw in our hand, the ultimate harvest is assured" (Gal. 6: 9, Phillips). Here again the idea of fruit is implied. We have already pointed out that patience is *not* passive, and here we see that it *is* to be persevering. The reward is immediate, but it is also eternal. Tertullian, who lived and wrote shortly after the apostle Paul, once said: "A man *becomes* a Christian; he is not born one." A Christian *becomes* patient as he attends Christ's school of discipleship!

**9**
> Whatsoever things were written aforetime were written for our learning, that we through patience and comfort of the scriptures might have hope. Now the God of patience and consolation grant you to be like-minded one toward another....
> —Romans 15:4-5

There is a direct relationship between patience and those important areas of comfort and consolation. Paul calls God "the God of patience" in this passage, and indeed He is the Source of all patience in this matter of fruitbearing. We don't dig down into ourselves and dredge up patience by gritting our teeth and trying. No, we *receive* patience as one of those beautiful fruits of the Spirit. Patience comes to us "through" the Scriptures "as the conduit pipe, but from God as the fountainhead," Matthew Henry tells us. Note that we are not only to be *recipients* of this rich comfort and consolation, but we are also to be *dispensers* of it to our brethren in Christ: "be like-minded one toward another according to Christ Jesus" (v. 5). If in my role as spouse I exercise this comforting spirit, will not my marriage be enriched by it?

*Patience in tribulation.* —Romans 12:12

# 10

We are not only to allow tribulation to work patience in us, but we are also to be patient *in* tribulation, Paul says. He is very explicit on this point. In 1 Thessalonians 5:14, he tells us clearly that we are to "be patient toward all men," even, I must assume, those who might be responsible for some of our troubles! The writer to the Hebrews also touches on this matter of patience under affliction: "You must never forget those past days when you had received the light and endured such a great and painful struggle" (Heb. 10:32, Phillips). Struggle is as natural in the growing Christian life as it is in the physical life. Physical growth entails struggle. Don't expect your marriage relationship to mature without accompanying struggle. Trials, said John Bunyan, "when we first meet them, are as the lion that roared upon Samson; but if we overcome them, the next time we see them we shall find a nest of honey within them."

*And let us not be weary in well doing, for in due season we shall reap if we faint not.*
—Galatians 6:9

# 11

Patience has many guises—and we have looked at the subject in the light of many of these aspects during this

# May

month's meditations. Today we see patience pictured as it relates to work and well-doing. Paul tells us here in Galatians not to become "weary in well doing," but to persevere patiently. In 1 Corinthians 15:58 he admonished the Corinthian Christians (and us!): "Therefore, my beloved brethren, be ye stedfast, unmoveable, always abounding in the work of the Lord, forasmuch as ye know that your labor is not in vain in the Lord." He tells his spiritual son, Timothy, and us as well: "Continue thou in the things which thou hast learned and hast been assured of, knowing of whom thou hast learned them" (2 Tim. 3:14), calling for perseverance in the Christian walk. He also told the Ephesian church: "Wherefore I desire that ye faint not. . . ." (3:13), calling for them, too, to keep plugging away at this matter of being a Christian to the very depths of one's being, allowing the Spirit of Christ to permeate every area of one's life. To me, this means that the Holy Spirit *must* influence my working life, since work makes up so much of my daily existence, whether it be in the home or in the profession I happen to follow. Of this aspect of our lives, John Ruskin wrote: "It is no man's business if he has genius or not. Work he must, whatever he is, but quietly and steadily; and the natural and enforced results of such work will always be the thing that God meant him to do, and will be his best." Let us not be weary in well doing, as we work in that spirit!

**12** *Thou shalt guide me with thy counsel, and afterward receive me to glory.* —Psalm 73:24

"Afterward." In the divine providence nothing comes a moment too soon or too late, but everything comes in its own true time. God's clock is never slow. Every link of the chain of God's providence fits into its own place. We do not see the providence at the time. Not until afterward will you see that your disappointments, hardships, trials, and the wrongs inflicted on you by others are parts of God's good providence toward you, full of blessing. Not until afterward will you see it, but the "afterward" is sure if you firmly and faithfully follow Christ and cleave to Him. The "Afterward" of every disappointment or sorrow is blessing and good. We need only to learn to wait in patience.  —J. R. MILLER

*If you love me, keep my commandments.*
                —John 14:15                          **13**

To believe and to love, these two commandments form the summary of all God's commandments, for one is the inward spirit of obedience, the other its outward form. He who thus keeps God's commandments abides in God, and God in him.  —F. W. FARRAR

Love is patience. . . . love understands, and therefore waits. Love is kindness. Have you ever noticed how much of Christ's life was spent in doing kind things for others? He spent a great proportion of His time simply in making people happy, in doing good turns to people. . . . God has put in our power the happiness of those about us, and that is largely to be accomplished by the way we treat them— kindly or otherwise.  —HENRY DRUMMOND

*Let patience have her perfect work, that ye may be*    **14**
*perfect and entire, wanting nothing.*  —James 1:4

The very idea of Christian perfection scares some Christians. And yet for our Lord's brother, James, traditionally considered the author of the Epistle that bears his name, it appears to be a natural outgrowth of allowing pa-

# May

tience to "have her perfect work." Later in his Epistle, James adds: "Be patient, therefore, brethren, unto the coming of the Lord. Behold, the husbandman [farmer] waiteth for the precious fruit of the earth, and hath long patience for it, until he receive the early and latter rain. Be ye also patient; stablish your hearts: for the coming of the Lord draweth nigh" (5:7-8). Thus he makes patience and Christian perfection prerequisites for Christians while they await the coming of the Lord. In all our relationships with others, we go one of two ways: patience or impatience. James calls on us to choose the path of patience, warning us to "Grudge not one against another, brethren," in verse 9. This warning applies equally to husbands and wives. Peter, too, calls for perfection: "But the God of all grace, who hath called us unto his eternal glory by Christ Jesus, after that ye have suffered awhile, make you *perfect*, stablish, strengthen, settle you" (1 Pet. 5:10). With these scriptural admonitions to patience and perfection, I look at work as did the great naturalist, Henry David Thoreau: "Good for the body is the work of the body, good for the soul the work of the soul, and good for either the work of the other." Let patience "have her perfect work"!

**15** *With all lowliness and meekness, with longsuffering, forbearing one another in love.* —Ephesians 4:2

Over and over I am impressed with the way the apostle Paul overlaps the "fruit of the Spirit" in his Epistles. Here again he groups several of the spiritual characteristics listed in Galatians 5:22 within the relatively small scope of this short verse addressed to the Ephesian Christians, and to us their spiritual descendants. Earlier in the same Epistle Paul had written: "According as he hath chosen us in him before the foundation of the world, that we should be holy and without blame before him in *love*" (1:4). He told the Colossian Christians: "Put on therefore, as the elect of God, holy and beloved, bowels of mercies, kindness, humbleness of mind, meekness, longsuffering [patience]" (3:12). So we see how love underlies every aspect of the Spirit-filled life, particularly in this area of "patience." How basic love is to all the other outworkings of the Spirit, as Paul so strongly emphasizes in 1 Corinthians 13. Indeed, without love none of the other spiritual attributes has any meaning or value. Thus patience must have her "perfect work" if any human relationship is to succeed— and this is particularly basic to the marriage bond, above all others. As Henry Drummond so perceptively points out, "Instead of allowing yourself to be so unhappy, just let your love grow as God wants it to grow: seek goodness in others, love more persons more; love them . . . unselfishly, without thought of return. The return, never fear, will take care of itself." Does love underlie my patience? It *must!*

*Thy word is a lamp unto my feet, and a light unto my path.* —Psalm 119:105

**16**

God's Word as a guiding light is a *lamp* unto our *feet*, not a sun flooding a hemisphere. It is not meant to shine upon miles of road, but in the darkest night it will always show us the one next step; then when we have taken that, carrying the lamp forward, it will show us another step, and on till it brings us out into the full, clear sunlight of coming day. It is a lamp, and it is designed to lighten only little steps, one by one. We need to learn well the lesson of patience if we would have God guide us. He does not lead us rapidly. Sometimes we must go very slowly if we wait for Him. Only pace by pace does He take us, and unless we wait, we must go in darkness. But if we wait for Him, and for His leading, it will always be light for one step. —J. R. Miller

# May

**17**

*Put on therefore, as the elect of God, holy and beloved, bowels of mercies, kindness, humbleness of mind, meekness, longsuffering; forbearing one another, and forgiving one another . . . even as Christ forgave you.* —Colossians 3:12,13

In this power-packed paragraph Paul again groups many of the "fruits" of the Spirit that are to characterize the lives of Spirit-filled Christians. What impresses me here is how Paul links "patience" and "forgiveness," as well as forbearance. How important a true spirit of forgiveness is to a good marriage! In Philippians 2:3 Paul gives us a good rule for any interpersonal relationship, particularly that of marriage: "Let nothing be done through strife or vainglory; but in lowliness of mind let each esteem other better than themselves." In 2 Corinthians 6:6 he shares with us how that Spirit pervaded his own life: "By pureness, by knowledge, by *longsuffering*, by *kindness* . . . "Paul was able to live a life which expressed "love unfeigned." He told the Ephesians to "be ye kind one to another, tenderhearted, *forgiving* one another, even as God for Christ's sake hath forgiven you," again connecting the two concepts of forgiveness and patience (Eph. 4:32). Thus Paul builds again on the foundation of love at work in the lives of Christians. As Jean Paul Richter said centuries ago: "Humanity is never so beautiful as when praying for forgiveness, or else forgiving another." May that sweet spirit mold our marriages!

**18**

*The patient in spirit is better than the proud in spirit.* —Ecclesiastes 7:8

What a striking juxtaposition of adjectives! While pride and patience are not diametrically opposite each other in meaning, still they do not seem likely to dwell in the same heart—or spirit. In Proverbs 14:29 Solomon says: "He that is slow to wrath [anger] is of great understanding: but he that is hasty of spirit exalteth folly." Moving into the New Testament, the apostle Paul says: "With all lowliness and meekness, with longsuffering, forbearing one another in love" (Eph. 4:2). A proud man will not be a patient man, and therefore he will not evidence the fruit of the Spirit. In fact, Emerson once said succinctly: "Pride ruined the angels." And another perceptive modern-day prophet warns us: "Though the Bible urges us on to perfection it gives no encouragement to suppose that perfection is achieved. ... *A man who thinks he is righteous is not righteous ... for the reason primarily that he is full of spiritual pride, the most deadly form that sin can take*" (D. ELTON TRUEBLOOD). Pride on the part of one or both partners in a marriage can ruin a marriage. Choose patience instead!

*Remembering without ceasing your work of faith, and labor of love, and patience of hope in our Lord Jesus Christ.* —1 Thessalonians 1:3

**19**

Here Paul is listing for us a trinity of traits that should characterize Christians: "work of *faith*, labor of *love*, and patience of *hope*. ... " He concludes the list with a plea for and praise for patience or steadfastness in hope—because that hope is based upon our relationship to Jesus Christ. The patience of hope is to be part of our character as Christians, and that hope is to be rooted in our Redeemer, Jesus Christ Himself. Every marriage must have hope in its foundation, or it will falter and reel under the onslaughts of life. The only solid foundation for a lasting life together lies in our relationship to Jesus Christ, not only individually, but also as husband and wife. 2 Thessalonians 1:3, 11 speaks of the power of God let loose in the life and the inevitable result of that power: "We are bound to thank God always for you, brethren [and sisters!], as it is meet, because that your faith groweth ex-

# May

ceedingly, and the charity of every one of you all toward each other aboundeth. . . . Wherefore also we pray always for you, that our God would count you worthy of this calling, and fulfill all the good pleasure of his goodness, and the work of faith with power." Growth spiritually comes when we are tied to the Source of our life together, the Lord Jesus, who is the Vine. May our tie-in to that divine power Source be healthy and constant!

## 20

*Order my steps in thy word.* —Psalm 119:133

"Order my steps" is a prayer that should ever be on our lips. We should get our orders from God, not only once in our lifetime (when we first give ourselves to Him); not only at the beginning of each day, as we go out to the day's task; not merely at the beginning of each new piece of work or of each fresh task—but every moment, for each step. That is what walking with God means. We may make this so real that we shall look up into God's face continually, asking, "What next, dear Lord? What shall I do now? Which course shall I take today? How shall I accomplish this duty You have for me to do?" If we can but have God's guidance for the little short steps, we need not fear for the long miles, the great stretches of road. If each step is of His ordering, the long miles will be paths of His choosing. —J. R. MILLER

## 21

*In all things approving ourselves as the ministers of God, in much patience, in afflictions, in necessities, in distresses. . . .* —2 Corinthians 6:4

In his Epistles Paul wrote much about patience—and indeed, he was in many ways the epitome of patience when it came to his own personal life and well-being. How often we read of his patience in suffering: "You [the Corinthians] are held in honor, but we in disrepute. To the present hour we hunger and thirst, we are ill-clad and buffeted and homeless, and we labor, working with our own hands. When reviled, we bless; when persecuted, we endure; when slandered, we try to conciliate . . . ."(1 Cor. 4: 10-13, RSV). This from a man with all the advanced degrees his age had to offer—a man who could have sat among the rulers of his people, but who chose instead to suffer for Christ's sake, even if it meant martyrdom! Yes, Paul offers us a real pattern in patience. One ancient commentator said: "Those who would approve themselves to God must approve themselves faithful in trouble as well as in peace, not only in doing the work of God diligently, but also in bearing the will of God patiently." If you and I were to exercise Paul's patience, how we would enrich the lives of those around us!

*The Lord direct your hearts into the love of God, and into the patient waiting for Christ.*
                        —2 Thessalonians 3:5

# 22

Jesus Christ is coming again! And we as Christians are admonished elsewhere by Paul to be alert to the imminence of that return. But in this verse Paul is calling for the Thessalonian Christians, and modern-day Christians as well, to live steadfastly and faithfully while they have the opportunity here in this world, showing by their faithful lives their allegiance to the living Christ. David had something like this in mind when he prayed: "O Lord, . . . . God of Abraham, Isaac, and Israel, our fathers, keep for ever such purposes and thoughts in the hearts of thy people, and direct their hearts toward thee" (1 Chron. 29: 18). Thus through his public prayer he urged the Israelites to live faithful lives. A New Testament writer, Jude, urged Christians, "Keep yourselves in the love of God, looking

# May

for the mercy of our Lord Jesus Christ unto eternal life" (v. 21).

This is the kind of faith-living that should characterize the Christian marriage. This "patient waiting for Christ" will shed such an aura around the home that its inhabitants will have a foretaste of heaven itself!

## 23

*Thou, O man of God, flee these things; and follow after righteousness, godliness, faith, love, patience, meekness.* —1 Timothy 6:11

This exhortation to patience is addressed by Paul to Timothy, his spiritual son and "candidate for the ministry." But it is equally applicable to all Christians who are striving for spiritual excellence. Note that Paul tells Timothy to flee "these things" (temptation, lust, love of money —vv. 9 and 10) and "follow after righteousness, godliness, faith, love, *patience*, meekness." Among other things, we are to make patience a way of life, just as we are to mirror the other fruits of the Spirit. To cultivate this fruit, we must turn our backs on the opposite fruits of an evil spirit. Patience, as has been said before, is not just a *passive* acceptance of everything life hands out to us; it is to be an *active* pursuit of spiritual excellence. As Paul says in 1 Thessalonians 5:14, "Now we exhort you, brethren [and sisters!], warn them that are unruly, comfort the feebleminded, support the weak, *be patient toward all men.*" Matthew Henry says of this admonition: "We must bear and forbear. And this duty must be exercised toward all men, good and bad, high and low. We must endeavor to make the best we can of everything, and think the best we can of everybody." As we show this kind of spirit to our marriage partner, and all we come into contact with, we will be fleeing the false and following the true.

*And the servant of the Lord must not strive (be quarrelsome, RSV); but be gentle unto all men ... patient.* —2 Timothy 2:24

These verses in 2 Timothy tie in closely with Paul's emphasis in 1 Timothy 6:11. In fact, Paul introduces the thought of this passage with the same admonition to *"flee also youthful lusts"* and *"follow righteousness, faith, charity, peace ..."* (vv. 22 and 23). In this case the apostle couples patience and gentleness, another of the catalog of Christian fruit he spelled out in Galatians 5:22. How can we combine gentleness and patience? Paul explained it thus to Titus: "Speak evil of no man ... be no brawlers, but gentle, shewing all meekness unto all men" (3:2; *meekness* is another spiritual fruit). He also told Titus the old men among the Christians are to be "sober, grave, temperate, sound in faith, in charity, in *patience*" (2:2). The epitome of gentleness was Jesus Christ, and of Him we read, "When he was reviled, he reviled not again; when he suffered, he threatened not. . . ." (1 Peter 2:23). There must be some significance in the fact that gentleness follows immediately upon the heels of patience in the list of Christian virtues. May this gentle spirit, growing out of patient submission to God's will for my life, be the fruit of His spirit in our lives as husband and wife!

*Be not slothful, but followers of them who through faith and patience inherit the promises.*
                                        —Hebrews 6:12

**25**

I once read an atheist's definition of faith which nearly broke my heart with its hopelessness, its glorification of an opinion opposite my own relative to my heavenly Father's ability to care for me. H. L. Mencken once said: "Faith may be defined briefly as an illogical belief in the occurrence of the improbable." How sad—and how different from the sacred writer's definition of faith elsewhere in Hebrews: "Now faith is the substance of things hoped for, the evidence [conviction] of things not seen" (11:1). Andrew Murray, writing on the subject of faith, and its fellow fruit, patience, said: "Faith always attaches itself to what God has said or promised. When an honorable man says anything, he also does it: on the back of the saying follows the doing. So also is it with God. . . . When I have a word of God in which He promises to do something I can always remain sure that He will do it. I have simply to take and hold fast the word, and therewith wait upon God: God will take care that He fulfills His word to me." May I have the same confidence in God's faithfulness—and in patience inherit His promise!

## 26

*Run with patience the race that is set before us.*
*—Hebrews 12:1*

In many ways, marriage can be compared to a footrace. Just as there are moments of stress and crisis in a race, there are stress-filled moments in a marriage. Just as there is competition in a race, there can be competition in a marriage. Also, runners in a race have to learn to "pace themselves," and not burn themselves out at the very outset of the competition. Isn't there a word of wisdom here for married couples as well? With the sacred writer, learn what it means to "run with *patience* the race that is set before (you)."

Patience seems a strange companion in a race, but patience is important in running—particularly those grueling long distance runs which require not only good physical condition and stamina—but wise strategy as well. In running, wisdom is important, as it is in marriage. As Solomon once said, "Happy is the man that findeth wisdom, and the man that getteth understanding" (Proverbs 3:13). Of wisdom, Thomas à Kempis said: "To have a low opinion of our own merits and to think highly of others is evidence of wisdom." That's a pretty good creed for Christian marriage.

*The trying of your faith worketh patience.*
—James 1:3

# 27

Way back in the fourth century, the early church father, St. John Chrysostom, defined faith as "love under pressure." We might even say that patience is the pressure gauge which measures the extent, the depth of our love for one another. How does your marriage withstand pressure? Do you "blow your cool" at the slightest provocation—or do you from your vantage point of maturity and quiet confidence in one another measure your love with God's gauge? Many centuries after Chrysostom wrote about "love under pressure" Jeremy Taylor wrote: "Love is the greatest thing that God can give us, for himself is love; and it is the greatest thing we can give to God, for it will also give ourselves, and carry with it all that is ours. The apostle calls it the bond of perfection; it is the old, the new, and the great commandment, and all the commandments, for it is the fulfilling of the law." Wise old James knew that anything worth building, takes work to build. Patience is worth our every effort for it must lie at the heart of every good relationship between human beings—and between us and our Holy God. Where would you and I be without the patience and love of God? As our faith is tried, says James, it develops in us the patient spirit so needed in marriage—and every interpersonal association.

*I John, who am also your brother, and companion in tribulation, and in the kingdom and patience of Jesus Christ. . . .* —Revelation 1:9

# 28

Of all the Scriptural patterns for patience which we could name, our Lord Jesus Christ is the greatest and most

# May

perfect, as John points out so clearly here. Yet John dares to claim companionship with Jesus in this very area of patience! In his holy boldness he reminds me of Paul, who told Timothy: "If we suffer, we shall also reign with him...." (2 Tim. 2:12), a daring declaration of our oneness with Christ. This attitude of patience was not limited to individual Christians either. In Revelation 2:2, 3, John quotes the words of the risen Christ to the church at Ephesus: "I know thy works, and thy labour, and thy patience, and how thou canst not bear them which are evil: and thou hast tried them which say they are apostles, and are not, and hast found them liars: and hast borne, and hast *patience*, and for my name's sake hast laboured, and hast not fainted." Churches, too, are to be noted and commended for their patience as a positive Christian virtue. And so should we commend a good marriage in a pattern of patience, as patience joins the other "fruits" of the Spirit in the garden of your life together.

**29**     *Ye have heard of the patience of Job....*
                                        —James 5:11

As we look at Job's life, what incentive do we see for the Christian to learn patience? And, says James in verse 10, "Take, my brethren, the prophets, who have spoken in the name of the Lord, for an example of suffering affliction, and of *patience*." Matthew Henry says, "We are encouraged to be patient by the example of the prophets. When we think that the best men have had the hardest usage in this world, we should [by this] be reconciled to affliction. Those who were the greatest examples of suffering affliction were also the best and greatest examples of patience. Job also is proposed as an example. Under all, he could bless God. And what came to him in the end? God accomplished those things for him which plainly prove that 'the Lord is very pitiful, and of tender mercy' (v. 11). The tender mercy of God is such that he will make his people an abundant amends for all their sufferings and afflictions. Let us serve our God, and endure our trials, as those who believe the end will crown all." As I contemplate "the patience of Job," I want to accept affliction as he did—rather than as his wife did, who counseled him to "curse God and die." What a blessed and happy marriage it will be that exercises the "patience of Job"—both husband and wife. Don't be satisfied with less than God's best —the marriage bathed in godly patience is but a foretaste of heaven itself!

*Here is the patience and the faith of the saints.*
—Revelation 13:10

## 30

Fellow Christians, whether we look like it—or act like it —we are saints! On the authority of the Word of God, I declare it. And as saints we have definite responsibilities —plus the divine strength necessary to carry them out. In this passage John combines two of the Christian virtues listed by Paul in Galatians—faith and patience, numbers 4 and 7 in the cluster. He then traces them back to their ultimate Source, the Lord Jesus Christ Himself! If you feel defeated and discouraged in your Christian life, in your marriage situation, looking in vain for the fruit of love, joy, peace, patience, and so on, perhaps it's because you've neglected the Source—and the soil of your own life as well. Faith must underlie the Christian life like the floor under the vast ocean. As Paul reminds us in Romans 12:3, "God hath dealt to every man the measure of faith." Let us join with Helen Keller, that blind saint of another day, in acknowledging that gift of faith: "A simple, childlike faith in a divine Friend solves all the problems that come to us by land or sea." "Here is the patience and the faith of the saints"!

# May

## 31

*That ye might walk worthy of the Lord unto all pleasing, being fruitful in every good work, and increasing in the knowledge of God; strengthened with all might, according to his glorious power, unto all patience and longsuffering with joyfulness.*

—Colossians 1:10,11

Walking in the Spirit and fruit-bearing are inextricably linked in the Scriptures, particularly in the writings of the apostle Paul. It is clear, too, from these verses, that growth must be the result of a healthy spiritual walk. Paul dared to cite himself as an example of this spiritual growing in 1 Thessalonians 4:1, "Furthermore then we beseech you, brethren, and exhort you by the Lord Jesus, that as ye have received of us how ye ought to walk and please God, so ye would abound more and more." In Ephesians 3:16 Paul pinpoints the Source of that inner spiritual strength: "That he would grant you, according to the riches of his glory, to be strengthened with might by his Spirit in the inner man." To Timothy, Paul revealed God's plan for His redeemed children: "That they do good, that they be rich in good works, ready to distribute, willing to communicate" (1 Tim. 6:18). Our works as Christians are to glorify our heavenly Father. One of the greatest Christian poets has shown us the relationship of work and growth in the Christian life:

> I stood up straight and worked
> My veritable work. And as the soul
> Which grows within a child makes the child grow,
> Or, as the fiery sap, the touch of God,
> Careering through a tree, dilates the bark
> And toughs with scale and knob, before it strikes
> The summer foliage out in a green flame—
> So life, in deepening within me, depended all
> The course I took, the work I did.
> —ELIZABETH BARRETT BROWNING

It is no quirk of faith that Mrs. Browning had deep insight into the meaning of God's love as well as the noble Christian love that can arise between husband and wife.

# June

*The fruit of the Spirit is . . . goodness . . .*
—Galatians 5:22–23

**1**

Goodness is not just a passive fruit of the Spirit, any more than are the other fruit of Paul's cluster in Galatians 5:22–23. No, we Christians must make a conscious choice of good over evil, if we expect to live a fruitful Christian life. In Joshua's day, the easy thing to do was to "go along with the crowd" and worship the idols of Canaan, and live like the godless Canaanites. But faithful Israelites like Joshua made a choice for good—and led their households in that decision to follow the good rather than the evil in the world around us: "As for me and my house, we will serve the Lord" (Josh. 24:15). Ruth made such a decision: "[Naomi] said, Behold, thy sister-in-law is gone back . . . unto her gods . . . And Ruth said, Entreat me not to leave thee, or to return from following after thee. . . ." (1:15–16). Goodness isn't natural, even to the Christian. It must result from a conscious choice of direction. As the great Dr. Samuel Johnson said in the eighteenth century: "The two great movers of the human mind are the desire of good, and the fear of evil." What is your choice today?

*And he said, I will make all my goodness pass before thee, and I will proclaim the name of the Lord before thee; and will be gracious to whom I will be gracious, and will shew mercy on whom I will shew mercy.* —Exodus 33:19

**2**

When I read this verse, I think of the caption, "God's goodness on parade." After all, *He* is the source of all

# June

goodness. Henry Ward Beecher once said, "We give God the name of good: it is only by shortening it that it becomes God." In ourselves, we are the very opposite of goodness—we, fallen humanity, are of our father, the devil, until we are redeemed and ransomed by the blood of the Lamb, Jesus Christ, the Son of God. And this renewal is not our accomplishment—it is entirely God's doing. Paul emphasizes that aspect of redemption in Romans 9: "For he saith to Moses, I will have mercy on whom I will have mercy, and I will have compassion on whom I will have compassion. So then it is not of him that willeth, nor of him that runneth, but of God that sheweth mercy. . . . Therefore hath he mercy on whom he will have mercy, and whom he will he hardeneth" (vv. 15, 16, 18). As Henry Ward Beecher also said: "The very word 'God' suggests care, kindness, goodness; and the idea of God in His infinity is infinite care, infinite kindness, infinite goodness." Goodness comes from God—and we Christians are to reflect His goodness every day of our lives!

**3** *And the Lord passed by before him, and proclaimed, The Lord, The Lord God, merciful and gracious, longsuffering, and abundant in goodness and truth.* —Exodus 34:6

If you or I were to describe ourselves in this way we would be considered boastful and proud. But when God describes Himself in these terms, He is merely stating facts. The Revised Standard Version translates the word "goodness" as "steadfast love," and that is so descriptive of God's nature. In Numbers 14:18 where Moses is interceding for Israel before the Lord, he prays, "The Lord is slow to anger, and abounding in steadfast love, forgiving iniquity and transgression. . . ." (RSV). The psalmist describes

God's nature: "But thou, O Lord, art a God merciful and gracious, slow to anger and abounding in steadfast love and faithfulness" (86:15; cp. 103:8). Knowing and experiencing God's goodness, love, and mercy, what kind of a life should I live—how can my life reflect His life which is in me? A servant of God from the nineteenth century has this strikingly up-to-date insight:

> Being all fashioned of the self-same dust,
> Let us be merciful as well as just.
> —HENRY WADSWORTH LONGFELLOW

*Let thy priests, O Lord God, be clothed with salvation, and let thy saints rejoice in goodness.*
—2 Chronicles 6:41

**4**

The wisest king the nation of Israel ever knew used these words at the conclusion of his prayer of dedication, reminding God of His steadfast love (mercy and goodness) for His people. Solomon's spiritual insight was a heritage from his father David, who had earlier stated: "And of all my sons ... he [God] hath chosen Solomon ... to sit upon the throne ... And thou, Solomon, my son, know thou the God of thy father, and serve him with a perfect heart and with a willing mind" (1 Chron. 28:5-9). In another prayer, the psalmist echoed the words of Solomon, "Arise, O Lord, into thy rest. . . . Let thy priests be clothed with righteousness; and let thy saints shout for joy" (Ps. 132: 8-9). As God's goodness is extolled, we, His children, living thousands of years after David and Solomon, are also to "rejoice in goodness." We are to follow James Hamilton's advice: "Goodness is love in action, love with its hand to the plow, love with the burden on its back, love following His footsteps who went about continually doing good." Let us show our salvation by living a life "rejoicing in goodness"!

# June

**5**

*Now the rest of the acts of Hezekiah, and his goodness, behold, they are written in the vision of Isaiah.... —2 Chronicles 32:32*

Why do we think of Hezekiah as "good King Hezekiah"? Because of his actions, his way of life. Dr. Herbert Lockyer says that "Hezekiah was one of the best kings who ever sat upon the throne of Judah, and is distinguished as the greatest in faith of all Judah's kings." 2 Kings 18:5-6 tells us "He trusted in the Lord God of Israel; so that after him was none like him among all the kings of Judah, nor any that were before him. For he clave to the Lord, and departed not from following him, but kept his commandments. . . ." In this he reminds us of King Josiah, of whom it was said: "And like unto him was there no king before him, that turned to the Lord with all his heart, and with all his soul, and with all his might .... neither after him arose there any like him" (2 Kings 23:25). Many years later Nehemiah said of his own activities rebuilding the ruined walls of Jerusalem: "Remember me, O my God, concerning this, and wipe not out my good deeds. . . ." (13:14). Chapters 36—39 of Isaiah record for us more of Hezekiah's exploits, in addition to what is set forth in Chronicles. No, Hezekiah was not a perfect man, and he made many and serious mistakes—but God called him a good man because of his faith, just as He called David "a man after mine own heart." As D. L. Moody succinctly said: "A little faith will bring your soul to heaven, but a lot of faith will bring heaven to your soul!"

**6**

*Now the rest of the acts of Josiah, and his goodness. . . . are written in the book of the kings of Israel and Judah. —2 Chronicles 35:26*

We've already mentioned "good King Josiah" in our meditation on Hezekiah, but he deserves another look.

J. G. Greenhough says of this unusual king: "Josiah breaks a long, monotonous series of absolutely worthless monarchs. Before and behind him are moral waste and darkness. He stands out as a figure worth looking at and loving ... Josiah's good reign was like a burst of brilliant sunset, before the final darkness comes on." Josiah was good despite his antecedents, and other strikes against him: left parentless at the age of eight; surrounded by violence and murder from his earliest impressionable years. Despite these drawbacks, he found God at the age of sixteen, choosing to follow his ancient ancestor David in goodness, rather than his wicked father and grandfather, Amon and Manasseh. He led his people back to God at the age of twenty, and rebuilt the temple at the age of twenty-six. He died at the age of thirty-nine after reigning for thirty-one years, leaving a legacy of goodness. "All Jerusalem and Judah mourned for Josiah." And Jeremiah lamented for Josiah (35:24–25). In Josiah's case, doing good was being a good king. In your case, be a good—whatever you are—for God!

*They did eat, and were filled. . . and delighted* **7**
*themselves in thy great goodness.*
—Nehemiah 9:25

This interesting comment comes in the midst of Ezra's penitential psalm in which he traces the experience of God's people as they moved into the Promised Land on God's command. As you will remember, God's people had a very "up-and-down" relationship with their God. They wavered between disobedience and rebellion, and obedience and blessing. Aren't we Christians like that today? God through Moses promised them "houses full of good things, which thou filledst not, and wells digged, which thou diggedst not, vineyards and olive trees, which thou plantedst not," but at the same time he warned them, "Beware lest thou forget the Lord, which brought thee forth

out of the land of Egypt, from the house of bondage"
(Deut. 6:11-12). God well knew their nature, and our na-
tures as well. We rebellious children need to remember
that God's spiritual blessings are, in a sense, conditional.
As Willie Loman said in "Death of a Salesman" (albeit in
an entirely different context), "They come with the territory." If we are in the place of obedience, the place where
He wants us, He will bless and benefit us. If not, and we
experience difficulties, perhaps our heavenly Father is trying to tell us something!

**8** *For they have not served thee in their kingdom, and
in thy great goodness that thou gavest them, and in
the large and fat land which thou gavest them, neither turned they from their wicked works.*
—Nehemiah 9:35

It seems that down through the ages man's pattern of
behavior has been to answer God's goodness to him by
wickedness. In Deuteronomy 28, Moses warned the Israelites about that very tendency in their past: "Because thou
servest not the Lord thy God with joyfulness, and with
gladness of heart . . . therefore shalt thou serve thine enemies . . . in hunger, and in thirst, and in nakedness . . . and
he shall put a yoke of iron upon thy neck. . . ." (vv. 47-49).
What a contrast! "Joy—hunger; gladness—thirst." In his
song recorded in Deuteronomy 32 Moses also recorded:
"But Jeshurun [Israel] waxed fat, and kicked: thou art
waxen fat, thou art grown thick . . . then he forsook God
which made him, and lightly esteemed the Rock of his salvation" (v. 15). As we contemplate God's goodness to us,
we can't help wondering "why?" Why is He so good to
me? When I compare my lot with that of others, I cannot
grasp or comprehend His great goodness to me. But I do
know this: He is looking for the fruit of goodness in my
life, as a reflection of His own majesty. What a solemn re-

sponsibility I have: "To whom much is given, will much be required." We have received so much from God, we must in turn give out His goodness to those around us who have never heard.

*Preserve me, O God; for in thee do I put my trust [take refuge]. O my soul, thou hast said unto the Lord, Thou art my Lord; I have no good apart from thee.* —Psalm 16:1-2, RSV

**9**

God is the Source of all good. Goodness is to be a natural quality of life for the Christian according to the apostle Paul's catalog in Galatians 5:22—and this goodness must stem from its Source, God Himself. In Psalm 73:24-26, Asaph says: "Thou shalt guide me with thy counsel. . . . Whom have I in heaven but thee? and there is none upon earth that I desire beside thee. My flesh and my heart faileth: but God is the strength of my heart, and my portion for ever." A childhood mealtime prayer reads, "God is great, God is good. . . ." and this pretty well sums it up. We must depend upon His grace for the goodness that is supposed to characterize the Christian life. Bishop Hugh Latimer, who greatly influenced the sixteenth century English Protestant church, and was martyred for his outspoken faith, said, "We must first be made good, before we can do good. We must first be made just, before our works can please God. . . for when we are justified by faith in Christ, then come good works." Put your trust in God, take refuge in Him, and do His works!

*Surely goodness and mercy shall follow me all the days of my life.* —Psalm 23:6

**10**

These words are so familiar to us as to be almost meaningless. What is David really saying here? As he did in

# June

Psalm 16, David is tracing goodness back to its essential Source—God. What a gracious picture David paints of that God as a Shepherd, a Restorer, a Leader, a Protector, here in Psalm 23. In Psalm 25 he further extolls God's goodness: "Remember not the sins of my youth, nor my transgressions: according to thy mercy remember thou me for thy goodness' sake, O Lord. Good and upright is the Lord: therefore will he teach sinners in the way. The meek will he guide in judgment, and the meek will he teach his way" (vv. 7-9). Another Bishop, George Horne, who ministered in the nineteenth century, said of the quality of godly goodness: "In the heraldry of heaven goodness precedes greatness, and so on earth it is more powerful. . . .The lowly and lovely may often do more good in their limited spheres than the gifted." J. H. Jowett put it this way: "God comes after us to forgive us and blot out—like the tide—our sins, and to pick up the good deeds we have left behind."

**11** I had fainted, *unless I had believed to see the good-ness of the Lord in the land of the living.*
—Psalm 27:13

The more modern translations of this verse leave out the phrase, "I had fainted," and even the King James translator put these words in italics, meaning that they were added by the translator to make the verse more mean-ingful to him personally. And I can identify with him. If I didn't have the hope of God's goodness eternally prevail-ing, I don't know whether I could cope with life as it is today! In a later psalm David expresses a similar senti-ment: "Oh, how great is thy goodness, which thou hast laid up for them that fear thee; which thou hast wrought for them that trust in thee before the sons of men" (31:19). David's concluding comment is: "Wait on the Lord: be of good courage, and he shall strengthen thine heart: wait, I say, on the Lord" (Ps. 27:14). Thus David puts an eternal perspective on this matter of goodness. Daniel Webster, American statesman and orator of the early nineteenth century, urged this same perspective when he said, "Real goodness does not attach itself merely to this life—it points to another world. Political or professional reputation cannot last forever, but a conscience void of offense before God is an inheritance for eternity."

*Oh, how great is thy goodness, which thou hast laid up for them that fear thee; which thou hast wrought for them that trust in thee before the sons of men!*
—Psalm 31:19

**12**

How great, how abundant is God's goodness, says David. I couldn't resist expanding on this verse from yesterday's meditation. Looking back at one of David's early psalms, we are reminded of more reasons for rejoicing in God's goodness: "Let all those who put their trust in thee rejoice: let them ever shout for joy, because thou defendest them: let them also that love thy name be joyful in thee" (5:11). If our refuge is in Him, if our trust lies in our great and good God, if He is our Defender and Protector, what better cause for rejoicing could we have? Isaiah was praising this same attribute of God when he wrote; "For since the beginning of the world men have not heard, nor perceived by the ear, neither hath the eye seen, O God, beside thee, what he hath prepared for him that waiteth for him" (64:4). There is a great spiritual principle taught in these verses—the promise that God will reward faithfulness and obedience, but will punish unfaithfulness and disobedience. In Romans 11:22, Paul transfers this premise from Israel to Abraham's followers in faith. May we be counted among the faithful!

# June

**13**    *He loveth righteousness and judgment: the earth is full of the goodness of the Lord.*   —Psalm 33:5

In these meditations we have been looking at God's goodness, and pondering on the fact that His goodness should be reflected in our lives. In fact, David tells us that this practice on our part will delight the Lord: "For the righteous Lord loveth righteousness; his countenance doth behold the upright" (Ps. 11:7). In Psalm 119:64 the psalmist says, "The earth, O Lord, is full of thy mercy: teach me thy statutes." Both here and in Psalm 33:5, the RSV translates the concept of God's goodness as "steadfast love," and this quality in a sense is to characterize our goodness as His children. Our attitude toward others is to mirror this quality of steadfastness and consistency. In Matthew 5:16 Jesus told us to "Let your light so shine before men, that they may see your good works, and glorify your Father which is in heaven." The sixteenth century English poet, Edmund Spencer, said:

> Good is no good, but if it be spend;
> God giveth good for none other end.

In your godly goodness, you glorify God!

**14**    *Why boasteth thou thyself in mischief, O mighty man? the goodness of God endureth continually.*
                                                    —Psalm 52:1

I've often been struck by David's sense of humor, his sense of the incongruous, his penchant for comparing the sublime to the ridiculous in his Psalms. Here he contrasts "mighty man" and his mischief with the goodness of God. Left to his own devices, man *is* mischievous, corrupt, downright evil and sinful. But the goodness of God just shines more brilliantly by contrast with man's wickedness. And man is boastful, David points out. I wonder if he was thinking of evil Doeg in this connection (read 1 Sam. 22). Don't David's next words describe Doeg perfectly: "Thy tongue deviseth mischiefs; like a sharp razor, working deceitfully. Thou lovest evil more than good . . ." (52:2–3)? In Psalm 94:4 David asks, "How long shall they utter and speak hard things? and all the workers of iniquity boast themselves?" Sounds like Doeg again, doesn't it? It is evident here that the natural man, left in his natural state, is evil and far from God. But when he is indwelt by the love and goodness of God, that quality must show through. Back in the nineteenth century, an Englishman named Edwin Hubbell Chapin pointed out: "Goodness consists not in the outward things we do, but in the inward things we are." What are you?

*The steps of a good man are ordered by the Lord: and he delighteth in his way.* —Psalm 37:23 **15**

More recent translations of this verse leave out the word "good," but somehow the passage seems "flat" to me without that adjective. And certainly the man who "delighteth" in God's way will be good, not in himself, of course, but because the Spirit of God indwells him. In 147:11 the psalmist expresses a similar sentiment: "The Lord taketh pleasure in them that fear him, in those that hope in his mercy." Living in this light will result in goodness prevailing in a man's steps or his walk, the way he lives. After her son Samuel was born, Hannah sang a song of praise to God for His goodness and greatness expressed to her. A line from that song echoes the psalmist's thought: "He will keep [guard, RSV] the feet of his saints, and the wicked shall be silent in darkness" (1 Sam. 2:9).* Let us

---

*The Living Bible gives this phrase a beautiful turn: "He will protect his godly ones."

# June

join Hannah in her worship, so that of our lives it might be said:

> Be such a man, and live such a life,
> That if every man were such as you,
> And every life a life like yours,
> This earth would be God's paradise.
> —PHILLIPS BROOKS

## 16

*We shall be satisfied with the goodness of thy house, even of thy holy temple.* —Psalm 65:4

One of the most important aspects of God's goodness to us, from which our goodness must stem, is this "goodness of thy house." If we Christians do not avail ourselves of the blessing of worship together, inevitably we must become weaker because of it. Just as our physical bodies need food for sustenance and growth, so we need the spiritual food that Christian fellowship provides, and the deep spiritual blessing that the worship experience engenders. In Psalm 36:8 David tells us, "They shall be abundantly satisfied with the fatness of thy house; and thou shalt make them drink of the river of thy pleasures." And in Psalm 4:3 he expresses the importance of setting a special time and place for worship and fellowship with God: "Know that the Lord hath set apart him that is godly for himself: the Lord will hear when I call unto him." There is a direct relationship between our habit of giving praise to God, of worshiping at His feet, and the spirit of goodness that will radiate from our lives if we do so. As one of my favorite devotional writers, the late Oliver G. Wilson, used to say,

"He who sincerely praises God will soon discover within his own soul an inclination to praise goodness in his fellow men. Goodness is one of the links in the chain of God's will for His children. We receive it as a gift from the Holy Spirit as we walk with God and fellowship with His Son, Jesus Christ."

*Thou crownest the year with thy goodness; and thy paths drop fatness.* —Psalm 65:11

**17**

This would be an excellent note on which to end our year together—but it is an equally excellent verse as we near the halfway mark in the year. Those of us who live in the Northern Hemisphere are thrilled by the new life so apparent around us in the month of June. Following a long winter, and a sometimes reluctant spring, it is reassuring to see once again the evidence of God's blessing as He clothes His creation with beautiful blossoms and succulent fruit. As a boy growing up on the farm, I well remember how June was the month when we began to reap the bounties of God's blessing—and we continued to do so well into the fall months. Think of the fruit of goodness as one of the benefits God lavishes upon His people. As we join together in worship, this fruit is shared and characterizes our fellowship. The great missionary, Hudson Taylor, perceptively pointed out, "I used to ask God to help me. Then I asked if I might help Him. I ended up by asking Him to do His work through me." Let that be our prayer as we contemplate His goodness!

*Thou, O God, hast prepared of thy goodness for the poor.* —Psalm 68:10

**18**

God's goodness provides for the poor! I like the word the RSV uses even more; instead of using *poor*, it uses

# June

needy! Not one of us is missed by the blanket coverage of that word. Our physical needs are varied, but our spiritual need is a constant and common one. All of us, rich and poor alike, have one uniform spiritual need: we are lost and need a Savior. In Psalm 74:19, Asaph made an observation similar to David's when he prayed: "Forget not the congregation of thy poor for ever." Eliphaz, Job's friend, also describes this aspect of God's care: "He saveth the poor from the sword . . . and from the hand of the mighty. So the poor hath hope. . ." (Job 5:15-16). In perhaps his most famous Psalm of all, David exults: "Thou preparest a table before me . . ." (23:5), also extolling God's goodness to the needy, the poor. "Surely," says David, "goodness and mercy shall follow me all the days of my life" (v. 6). One of the most difficult confessions for the natural man to make is this: "I am poor and needy." Yet it is upon this confession, this realization and recognition, that our very salvation rests. We would not need a Savior were we not lost! Plato, the great Greek philosopher, who lived centuries before the time of Christ, recognized man's need and God's ability to save when he wrote: "All men are by nature equal, made, all of the same earth by the same Creator, and however we deceive ourselves, as dear to God is the poor peasant as the mighty prince." Aren't you glad you're needy?

## 19

*Oh that men would praise the Lord for his goodness, and for his wonderful works. . . .*

—Psalm 107:8

This thankful refrain is repeated three more times in this Psalm—in verses 15, 21, 31. Usually we reserve our thanksgiving for a particular day or a particular season of the year. But have you ever considered that thankfulness is to be a daily habit? As we contemplate God's goodness to us, as evidenced by His "wonderful works to the children of men," our lives should show forth His goodness. And keep in mind this virtue is not something we dredge up from our innermost beings; it is a fruit implanted within us by the Divine Hand; it is a Divine Nature engrafted into us at the time of our conversion. We simply need to yield control of our lives to that Spirit within us. Psalm 25:8 reflects upon this aspect of God's nature: "Good and upright is the Lord: therefore will he teach sinners in the way." This is one way we can thank the Lord for His wonderful works *to* us—and *in* us! The psalmist also says, "It is a good thing to give thanks unto the Lord. . . ." (Ps. 92:1). How are you living?

*Who satisfieth thy mouth with good things.*
—Psalm 103:5

## 20

I like the Living Bible's presentation of this rich spiritual truth: "He fills my life with good things!" In this same verse David goes on to exult: "My youth is renewed like the eagle's!" It seems that one of the primary concerns of people in the twentieth century is this matter of retaining or regaining youth. Vast industries have sprung up to service this deep-seated desire for eternal youth: cosmetics, personal grooming, and athletics, to name just a few. Even the clothing industry reaps vast profits for catering to this urge that people have to look and act younger—even if they must use artificial means to do it. But God's recipe for eternal youth calls for an inner serenity based on a right relationship to Him. The entire range of spiritual fruit listed by Paul in Galatians 5:22–23 will contribute to a youthful spirit. As a wise man once said, "Youth is a state of mind." And our mind-set grows out of our attitude toward God. If we can say with the psalmist, "I will remember the works of the Lord" (Ps. 77:11), we will find this attitude a source of renewal, a reviving of our flagging spirits. Thomas á Kempis said it better than I: "Be thankful for

the least gift, so shalt thou be worthy to receive greater."
Is that your lifestyle?

**21** *For he satisfieth the longing soul, and filleth the hungry soul with goodness.* —Psalm 107:9

This Psalm is a poem of praise to God for His deliverance of His people who are in need, with the clear-cut contrast between man's need and God's deliverance being the underlying theme throughout. Verse 9 is the concluding verse of that portion of the Psalm having to do with Israel's suffering in the desert. In Psalm 22:26, David gives it another slant, "The afflicted (poor) shall eat and be satisfied." In her song recorded in Luke 1, Mary, the mother of Jesus, sings: "He hath filled the hungry with good things," and by contrast, "the rich he hath sent empty away" (v. 53). Jesus said, "Blessed are those who hunger and thirst for righteousness, for they shall be satisfied ["filled," KJV] " (Matt. 5:6 RSV). The key to satisfaction seems to lie, in a sense, in our attitude. If we are self-satisfied and complacent, unaware of our need, we will go on empty and unfulfilled. On the other hand, if we are "longing," if we admit our need, our hunger and thirst, then God will fill us. Come to Him with the empty cup of your lives, whether you are at the very threshhold of your marriage or well settled in it; let Him fill your "cup" with His fullness, His "good things" (RSV). With His generous provision, you will have more than enough for your whole "trip"!

**22** *They shall abundantly utter the memory of thy great goodness, and shall sing of thy righteousness.*
—Psalm 145:7

The Psalms are full of praise to God for His goodness, and we have looked at many of these. This is the last "goodness" verse from the Psalms we will be considering in this series of meditations. Here David parallels somewhat the sentiment of Isaiah: "I will mention the loving kindnesses of the Lord, and the praises of the Lord, according to all that the Lord hath bestowed on us, and the great goodness toward the house of Israel, which he hath bestowed on them according to his mercies, and according to the multitude of his loving-kindnesses" (63:7). Both Isaiah and David remind us that God's goodness is unalterably linked with another of His divine attributes—righteousness. And David reminds us that God's goodness is "abundant" (RSV). The Living Bible puts it in a way I really appreciate: "Your awe-inspiring deeds shall be on every tongue; I will proclaim your greatness. Everyone will tell about how good you are, and sing about your righteousness." If we thus exult in God's goodness and righteousness, our lives will inevitably verbalize this joy. God's goodness will show through us. As Henry Ward Beecher once said: "No man can tell whether he is rich or poor by turning to his ledger. It is the heart that makes a man rich. He is rich according to what he is, not according to what he has." Do you talk about His great goodness— and show it in your life?

*Righteousness exalteth a nation, but sin is a reproach to any people.* —Proverbs 14:34

**23**

Our nations are in trouble today. All over the world we see evidences of once-righteous nations, formerly-God-fearing governments, "going down the drain" and giving way to the dominance of godless communism and sweeping socialism. What is the problem? I believe it begins in our homes. If our homes are righteous, our nation will reflect that righteousness. The fabric of our national life is made up of the sum total of our homes and their strength

# June

or weakness. Throughout the Scriptures, the concept of individual and national righteousness is upheld as the "secret of success," spiritually speaking, of our nations. In Isaiah 32:17 the prophet says: "The work of righteousness shall be peace; and the effect of righteousness quietness and assurance forever." What a blessed benediction! Harry Lathrop Reed says: "Righteousness is just rightness. Sometimes we make it too theological as a biblical word. Rightness is not easy of definition, but everybody knows what it is. We are conscious of rightness even if we cannot adequately define it." Where does that "rightness" come from? Paul gives us the source in Ephesians 5:9, where he says, "For the fruit of Spirit is in all goodness and righteousness and truth." If the Holy Spirit held sway in our lives, righteousness would prevail!

**24** *Most men will proclaim every one his own goodness: but a faithful man who can find?*
—Proverbs 20:6

Here the wise writer of Proverbs is contrasting the shallowness of man's goodness in comparison to the steadfast love (goodness) of God. The same wise man talks picturesquely about the empty boasting of man in Proverbs 25:14, "Who so boasteth himself of a false gift is like clouds and wind without rain." Jesus talked about this sort of attitude in Matthew 6:2, "Therefore when thou doest thine alms, do not sound a trumpet before thee, as the hypocrites do in the synagogues and the streets, that they may have glory of men. Verily, I say unto you, they have their reward." The psalmist, too, bemoaned the fact that "there is no longer any that is godly; for the faithful have vanished from among the sons of men. Every one utters lies to his neighbor; with flattering lips and a double heart they speak" (Ps. 12:1–2 RSV). Later in the New Testament, James also decried the "double-mindedness" that plagues the human race. How, then, do we reconcile man's natural bent to evil with God's demand that we be good? We inject into him a new nature—and that nature comes from God! It is, in effect, God's very own nature which takes up residence in His child—and makes it possible for the fruit of goodness to flow from him and through him to others. Wise old Plato once said: "To escape from evil we must be made, as far as possible, like God; and this resemblance consists in becoming just, and holy, and wise." Christians are to become "small Christs" because His Spirit indwells them. The purpose of this infilling is not so that they can glorify themselves ("Look at how fruitful my life is!"), but it is to glorify Him!

*And he [Jesus] said unto him, Why callest thou me* **25**
*good? There is none good but one, that is God. . . .*
—Matthew 19:17

Robert Louis Stevenson once opined: "There is only one person you are to make good—yourself; the others you are to make happy, if you can." Unfortunately, most of us transpose the sentiment in our practice. We feel we deserve to be made happy ourselves, and we are equally sure we could be if only other people would be good! Instead of concentrating on our own shortcomings and weakness, we concentrate on the problems of those around us. We devote most of our energy to trying to force goodness upon them. Whatever energy we have left, we use to complain about our own unhappiness and lack of success. Someone has said, "The real mark of a saint is that he makes it easier for others to believe in God." That, to me, epitomizes goodness in the life of the Christian. Can it be said of your life—and mine? True goodness comes from God alone. Some anonymous wise man has said: "God is great, and therefore He will be sought; He is good, and therefore He will be *found*."

# June

**26**

*See that none render evil for evil unto any man; but ever follow that which is good, both among yourselves, and to all men.* —1 Thessalonians 5:15

Some of Paul's commandments are just plain difficult! I sometimes think of how fascinating it would have been to walk with Paul and learn at his feet. The only better schoolmaster would have been the Lord Jesus Himself; what an experience it would have been to join the other disciples during the three-year seminar he taught! But Paul would at least have been my second choice, if I could have chosen a teacher. He certainly didn't contradict his Teacher and Master, and he often amplified His teachings. This admonition to goodness is one of those situations. And Paul echoed that teaching elsewhere in his Epistles: "Recompense to no man evil for evil. Provide things honest in the sight of all men"; "Let us do good unto all men, especially unto them who are of the household of faith" (Rom. 12:17; Gal. 6:10). William Penn, founder of the state of Pennsylvania and prominent Quaker, said on the subject: "He that does good for good's sake seeks neither praise nor reward, though sure of both at last." What's your motivation?

**27**

*Jesus saith unto them, Fill the waterpots with water.* —John 2:7

Our Lord calls His people always to be helpers in blessing this world. We cannot do much. The best we can bring is a little of the common water of earth; but if we bring that to Him, He can change it into the rich wine of heaven, which will bless weary and fainting ones. If we take simply what we have and use it as He commands, it will do good. Moses had only a rod in his hand, but with this he did great wonders empowered by God. The disciples had only five barley-loaves, but these, touched by

Christ's hand, made a feast for thousands. The common water, carried by the servants, under the Master's blessing became wine for the wedding.   —J. R. MILLER

*And God is able to make all grace abound toward you; that ye, always having all sufficiency in all things, may abound to every good work.*
—2 Corinthians 9:8

**28**

The words *good* and *work* seem to go together. We cannot think of "doing good" without linking this with some kind of active accomplishment. Paul calls for it here in 2 Corinthians, and he also links it to God Himself in Ephesians 3:20: "Now unto him that is able to do exceeding abundantly above all that we ask or think, according to the power that *worketh* in us." In Philippians 4:19 he also links our supply of good with the Savior: "My God shall supply all your need according to his riches in glory." Notice that here in Corinthians Paul makes it abundantly clear that we aren't about to exhaust God's supply. The key word in this passage is abundance—and it applies to the quantity of fruit of the Spirit as well, with goodness being no exception: "And God is able to make all grace *abound* toward you; that ye, always having all sufficiency in all things, may *abound* to every good work. . . . For the administration of this service not only supplieth the want of the saints, but is abundant also" (2 Cor. 9:8, 12). Victor Hugo, the French poet, novelist, and dramatist, expressed it this way:

> God whose gifts in gracious flood
>   Unto all who seek are sent,
> Only asks you to be good
>   And is content.

Are you abounding in good works?

# June

## 29

*As we have therefore opportunity, let us do good unto all men, especially unto them who are of the household of faith.* —Galatians 6:10

It is not *having* that makes men great. A man may have the largest abundance of God's gifts—of money, of mental acquirements, of power, of heart-possessions and qualities —yet if he only holds and hoards what he has for himself, he is not great. Men are great only in the measure in which they use what they have to bless others. We are God's stewards, and the gifts that come to us are His, not ours. They are to be used for Him as He would use them. When we come to Christ's feet in consecration, we lay all we have before Him. He accepts our gifts; and then, putting them back into our hands, He says, "Go now and use them in my name among my people."   —J. R. MILLER

## 30

*And let us consider one another to provoke unto love and to good works.* —Hebrews 10:24

Our errand in the world is in a small way the same that Christ's errand was. He does not now Himself, in person, go about doing good; we are to go for Him. The only hands Christ has for doing kindnesses are our hands. The only feet He has to run errands of love are our feet. The only voice He has to speak cheer to the troubled is our voice. A little child had been put to bed in a dark room. She disliked being alone, so her mother brought her doll, Happy, to be with her. This did not satisfy the child, and she begged her mother to stay in the room with her. The mother reminded her that she had Happy and God, and need not be afraid. Soon the child was sobbing again. When the mother returned and scolded her, she said, "Oh Mother, I didn't want Happy and I don't want God—I want someone with skin on." We are all very much like that child. In our loneliness and heart hunger, in our sorrow and suffering, even Christ in His spiritual presence does not meet all our need. We crave the human touch, the human voice, the human love. Thus it comes that He sends us out to represent Him, and we are to be hands and face and voice and heart to Him who says, "As the Father hath sent me, so send I you."  —J. R. MILLER

# July

*The fruit of the Spirit is . . . kindness. . . .*
　　　　　　　—Galatians 5:22

**1**

This expression of certainty from the pen of the apostle Paul reminds me of a story in the Old Testament recorded in Joshua. You recall it: Joshua had sent two spies into Jericho, and Rahab agreed to hide them from the king of Jericho. In so doing, she put this claim upon them: "Swear unto me by the Lord, since I have shewed you kindness, that ye will also shew kindness unto my father's house. . . . And the men answered her, . . . And it shall be, when the Lord hath given us the land, that we will deal kindly . . . with thee" (Josh. 2:12, 14). Rahab of Jericho is teaching a valid and valuable spiritual lesson here. When you receive an act of kindness, pass it on! Someone has even written a song about it. If the world today (or in any day, for that matter) would operate on this principle of repaying kindness with kindness, ours would be a different world indeed! Instead, our world seems out to get all it can for itself—taking advantage of any kindness it can get without repaying it *in kind.*

Think of the home where this principle of repaying kindness with kindness is applied. What a pyramid of blessing awaits those who begin with just one little act of kindness. Jesus was putting His finger on a vital truth when He urged His followers to "do unto others as you would have them do unto you."

J. R. Miller says: "The first thing the love of Christ does is to sweeten all the life, the disposition, the spirit, temper, the manners. One writes of a sweetbrier life. A little group

# July

of girls were together one rainy afternoon. One of them opened the door for a moment, and a wave of wet, green, growing things poured into the room. The girl at the door turned and said to the others, 'Do you smell the sweetbrier down by the gate? It is always fragrant, but never so fragrant as in the rain.' One of the other girls said impulsively that this reminded her of her aunt. When asked to explain, she said, 'Why, you see, there are ever so many roses that are fragrant—the roses themselves, I mean—but the sweetbrier is the only one whose leaves also are fragrant. That is why it makes me think of my aunt, because everything she does, not the large things only, but all the common, everyday things—the leaves as well as the blossoms—have something beautiful in them. There is something in her spirit, a gentleness, a thoughtfulness, a kindliness, a graciousness, that goes out in everything she does, in every word she speaks, in every influence that breathes from her life.'"

**2**      *My little children, let us not love in word, neither in tongue; but in deed and in truth.* —1 John 3:1

In his helpful study Bible, Dr. Harold Lindsell captions this section of 1 John, "Love in Action." That is a good definition of kindness. It would be difficult to show love without an expression of kindness. Try it sometime! Every home would be a heaven if we husbands and wives, and children, too, would put John's admonition into practice. James put it even more strongly: "Be ye doers of the word, and not hearers only, deceiving your own selves" (1:22). James is saying, "Put your money where your mouth is!" Paul put it more gently, but nonetheless firmly: "Let love be genuine; hate what is evil, hold fast to what is good; love one another with brotherly affection; outdo one another in showing honor" (Rom. 12:9–10, RSV). Martin Luther put his finger on the pulse of life and love when he said: "Love is an image of God, and not a lifeless image, but the living essence of the divine nature which beams full of all goodness." Let *kindness* have her perfect work in you!

*And [Joseph] comforted [his brothers], and spake kindly unto them.* —Genesis 50:21 **3**

If ever anyone had cause to treat others unkindly, Joseph was that one! These same brothers, whom he now treated with kindness and even affection, had many years before, out of jealousy and hatred for him, sold him into slavery, into a life of bondage and misery. Kindness was his response. Of whom does Joseph remind you in this instance? He is an outstanding and clear-cut type of Christ as we see him responding in love to the evil acts of his brothers. His reason: "You meant evil against me, but God meant it for good" (Gen. 50:20 RSV). This is how Jesus reacted to His tormentors, those who took His life. While He was much more than an example of kindness in this situation, Jesus does exemplify that fruit of the Spirit in His attitude toward others. In this He is our example, and He is a reflection for us of His Father's love and kindness. As the old Danish proverb puts it, "Father and mother are kind, but God is kinder." And F. W. Faber applied it: "Kindness has converted more sinners than zeal, eloquence, or learning." Follow Joseph's example; speak and act "kindly unto them."

*But the stranger that dwelleth with you shall be unto you as one born among you, and thou shalt love him as thyself.* —Leviticus 19:34 **4**

Kind thoughts must be of immense consequence. If a man habitually has kind thoughts of others, and that be-

# July

cause of spiritual motives, he is not far from being a saint. Such men are rare. Kind thoughts are rarer than either kind words or kind deeds. They imply a great deal of thinking about others, of putting others first. This in itself is rare. But they imply also a great deal of thinking about others without the thoughts being criticisms. Kind thoughts also imply contact with God, and a divine ideal in our minds. Their origin cannot be anything short of divine. It must be from God's touch that such water springs. Thus by cultivating kind thoughts, as urged here by Moses, we are in a very special way rehearsing for heaven.   —E. Matheson

Paradise is open to all kind hearts.
   —Pierre Jean de Béranger

**5**   *And the king David said, Is there not yet any of the house of Saul, that I may show the kindness of God unto him?*   —2 Samuel 9:3

Without love and kindness, life is cold, selfish, and uninteresting, and finally leads to distaste for everything. With kindness, the difficult becomes easy, the obscure clear; life assumes a charm and its miseries are softened. If we knew the power of kindness, we should transform this world into a paradise.   —Charles Wagner

The greatest thing, says someone, a man can do for his heavenly Father is to be kind to some of His other children. I wonder why it is we are not all kinder than we are? How much the world needs it. How easily it is done. How instantaneously it acts. How infallibly it is remembered. How superabundantly it pays itself back—for there is no debtor in the world so honorable, so superbly honorable, as love.   —Henry Drummond

*How excellent is thy lovingkindness, O God! therefore the children of men put their trust under the shadow of thy wings.* —Psalm 36:7

Our God Himself is the epitome of kindness—and the picture we have of Him here is that of a great and protective pair of wings under which we may take refuge. In Ruth 2:12, Boaz is commending faithful Ruth for her loyalty to Naomi, and he uses the same picture: "The Lord recompense thy work, and a full reward be given thee of the Lord God of Israel, under whose wings thou art come to trust." Kindness is not a prominent Christian virtue today, when all of us seem so intent on our own courses and accomplishments. It's an almost forgotten art to put others before self—just to be kind. But in every fellowship of believers, we encounter the individual (or individuals) who goes out of his way to show love, who shows his Christianity by his kindness or consideration for others, reflecting as in a mirror that marvelous Christlike spirit which is to be our pattern. It is God who is the Source of this, our kindness.

*I will mention the lovingkindnesses of the Lord . . . the great goodness . . . which he hath bestowed on them . . . according to the multitude of his lovingkindnesses.* —Isaiah 63:7

Our God's lovingkindness is not an isolated instance of "steadfast love." No, it is plural here, and it means that love is God's way of acting toward His children, over and over again, regardless of their behavior and rebellion. And our kindness may go unrequited as well. That should not deter us from giving unselfishly of ourselves to others, for our pattern is God Himself, of whom David said in Psalm 51:1, "Have mercy upon me, O God, according to thy

# July

lovingkindness: according unto the multitude of thy tender mercies blot out my transgressions." David was a realist. He knew that he didn't deserve God's great goodness to him, but he also recognized the principle of God's grace which has been in operation toward man since the dramatic fall in Eden. We are recipients of God's love not because of who we are—but because of who He is! And the same is true of His lovingkindness to us. Let us recognize this truth with Isaiah, and join him in dedicating ourselves to the service of this great and kind God.

## 8

*He that despiseth his neighbor sinneth: but he that hath mercy on the poor, happy is he.*
—Proverbs 14:21

An anonymous wise man has said; "The ministry of kindness is a ministry which may be achieved by all men, rich and poor, learned and illiterate. Brilliance of mind and capacity for deep thinking have rendered great service to humanity, but by themselves they are impotent to dry a tear or mend a broken heart."

In John 13:34 Jesus said, "A new commandment I give unto you, That ye love one another." And yet the commandment to "love thy neighbor" is as old as the Bible, and was prescribed upon the Israelites almost as soon as they were freed from the yoke of bondage in Egypt. In what sense then is it new? Human selfishness and pride had hidden it and buried it. The Jews had ostracized all who were not of their race and faith; they had distorted this commandment, made it ineffectual by their tradition. In effect, they had changed it to read: "Thou shalt love thy neighbor and hate thy enemy." Even that mutilated form of it was the deadest of dead letters because the proud and selfish Pharisees left no room for the existence of real kindness and generosity in the social life. Jesus unburied the divine jewel, raised it from the grave which man's immorality had dug for it, and cleansed it from the thick crust of self-worship with which tradition and self-centeredness had surrounded it. He commands His disciples to wear this spirit of kindness and generosity as a badge of their love and loyalty to Himself: "By this shall all men know that ye are my disciples, if ye have love one to another."

*Thus saith the Lord, Execute true judgment, and shew mercy and compassions every man to his brother.* —Zechariah 7:9

**9**

The divinest ministries of each day are the things of love which God sends across our way. The half-hour the busy man takes from his business to comfort a sorrow, to help a discouraged brother to start again, to lift up one who has fainted by the way, to visit a sick neighbor and minister to his need, is the half-hour of the day that will shine most brightly when the records of life are unrolled before God.

A writer tells of an English nobleman who, when he went over his estate, always carried acorns in his pocket, and when he found a bare spot, he would plant one of them. By and by there would be a tree growing on the place, adorning it. So we may plant on every space of time a seed of something beautiful, which will be not only an ornament, but also a blessing to others. It is one of the finest secrets of life to know how to redeem the minutes from waste, to make them bearers of blessing, of cheer, of encouragement, of good to others. —F. B. MEYER

*A new commandment I give unto you, That ye love one another; as I have loved you, that ye also love one another.* —John 13:34

**10**

Let love and kindness have their way. So many tired hearts might go on their way singing at the mere price of a

# July

handclasp, a whisper of encouragement, or a look which told that some loving service had not come and gone without notice. Let us send to the starving peoples of the world, by all means; but let us also give a thought to the starving hearts in our own household.

—GREAT THOUGHTS

"Kind words are music to the world"; they have a power which seems to come from outside the world—and indeed it does. One of the most blessed possessions we Christians can have is the memory of the kind and loving deeds we have done for others.  —E. MATHESON

**11** *She openeth her mouth with wisdom; and in her tongue is the law of kindness.*  —Proverbs 31:26

"But the tongue can no man tame" (James 3:8). The man who wrote this wrote out of the depths of experience. The terror of the tongue. Surely James is remembering the things his own unguarded tongue had said about his brother Jesus in the old days. We can never know what passed between Jesus and James when Jesus appeared to him in the glory of His risen presence, but we do know that from that day James became the pledge servant of the brother he had despised.

One of the most notable things about the letter of James is the stress it lays on the dangers of the tongue and the harm the tongue can do. It is probable that James realized the dangers of the tongue so well because he remembered with pain the things he had said to Jesus.

"Speak evil of no man" (Titus 3:2). This is a direct command of God, and should be meditated upon and obeyed. We wrong our own souls by wrong speaking. It destroys all generous and kindly thoughts in us, and quenches love.

It prevents us from praying in faith and love for the person, which would be infinitely better than speaking evil of him. Try this motto in your home, and see if it doesn't work wonders!   —Adapted from E. MATHESON

*Whatsoever he saith unto you, do it.*  —John 2:5

**12**

We often imagine that it was a great deal easier for our Lord's first disciples to do things for Him than it is for us. They could see Him and hear His voice, and do errands really for Him. Coming back, they would hear His approval or His thanks, but we cannot hear Him telling us what to do, nor can we see His pleased look when we have done something for Him. So we find ourselves wishing He were here again, that we might get our orders right from His very lips. We sometimes ask how we can do things for Him when He is not here. But we have only to remember His promise: "I am with you all the days." He is here, though unseen, just as really as He was with His first disciples. We can do things for Him all the time. Every loving obedience is something done for Christ. Every lovingkindness shown to another in His name and for His sake is shown to Him. Every piece of common, routine housework or business activity, if done through Him, becomes something done for Christ. So we can make all our dull lives radiant as angels' ministry by doing all for Christ.

—J. R. MILLER

*Kindness should begin at home.*  —1 Timothy 5:4, TLB

**13**

Keep the lamp of love shining day after day amid the multitude of home cares and home duties, amid the criticisms of teasing and thoughtlessness, amid the thousand little irritations and provocations of home life which so tend

# July

to break peace and mar sweet temper. Let home love be of the kind that never fails. Wherever else, far away or near, you pour the bright beams of your Christian life, be sure you brighten the space close about you in your own home. No goodness and gentleness outside will make up for lack of love and irritability at home.   —J. R. Miller

A Chinese proverb says: Better do a good deed at home than go far away to burn incense.

**14**

*Blessed are the merciful: for they shall obtain mercy. . . . Give to him that asketh thee, and from him that would borrow of thee turn thou not away.*
—Matthew 5:7, 42

Worker for God, does the Lord Jesus Christ make you kind and gentle, loving, faithful and unselfish at home? The New Testament Christian is "sweet at home." Before he thinks of the evangelization of that neglected street, or that underprivileged section of town, or that distant land, he remembers that his duty is within the walls of his own home. Here is the Lord's first will for him, that he may glorify God there. No activities out of doors can compensate to the New Testament Christian for failure to show indoors the life of the Lord Jesus Christ in his life.
—H. C. G. Moule

Kind words are the music of the world. They have a power which seems to be beyond natural causes, as if they were some angel's song which had lost its way and come on earth. It seems as if they could almost do what in reality God alone can do—soften the hard and angry hearts of men. No one was ever corrected by a sarcasm—crushed perhaps, if the sarcasm was clever enough, but drawn nearer to God, never.   —F. W. Faber

*Judge not, that ye be not judged.* —Matthew 7:1

## 15

The counsel of Jesus is to abstain from judging. This sounds strange at first because the characteristic of the Holy Spirit is to reveal things that are wrong, but the strangeness is only on the surface. The Holy Spirit does reveal what is wrong in others, but His discernment is never for purposes of criticism, but for purposes of intercession. When the Holy Spirit reveals something of the nature of sin and unbelief in another, His purpose is not to make us feel smug satisfaction, but to make us lay hold of God for that one, asking God to help him overcome that evil way. Never ask God for discernment, for discernment increases your responsibility. Simply bring that one before God until God puts him right. "If any man see his brother sin a sin which is not unto death, he shall ask, and [God] shall give him life for them that sin not unto death" (1 John 5:16). Our Lord allows no room for criticism in the spiritual life, but He does allow room for discernment and discrimination. —OSWALD CHAMBERS

*The Son of man came not to be ministered unto, but to minister, and to give his life a ransom for many.* —Matthew 20:28

God sets before us work, conflict, self-denial, cross-bearing. The central law of Christian life is ministry, serving. You quote, "Man's chief end is to glorify God and to enjoy Him forever." Yes, but there is no way of glorifying God save by living to bless the world in Christ's name, to bless men by serving them, loving them, helping them, doing them good. We are debtor, therefore, to every man we meet. We owe him love; we owe him service. We are not to set ourselves up on little thrones and demand homage and service from others; rather we are to do the serving.

# July

Christ came "not to be ministered unto, but to minister," and we should be as our Lord. —J. R. MILLER

**17**

*And Jesus said. . . . She hath done what she could.*
*—Mark 14:6, 8*

What a beautiful example of acceptance we encounter in this passage. Some of those at table with Jesus criticized Mary of Bethany for her extravagance in anointing Him, and wondered aloud why the money thus spent ("wasted," they said) couldn't have gone to the poor. But Jesus knew Mary's motives and understood her heart. Indeed, He said, "She has done a beautiful thing to me" (RSV). In a marriage relationship, as in any other, we need to develop an attitude of acceptance. Often we must look beneath the surface of a situation to see the motivation underlying a particular action or statement. If we would follow the judicial injunction, "Judge one innocent until he is proven guilty," we would avoid many of the misunderstandings that can plague a marriage. Next time you are tempted to criticize, say with Jesus, "She hath done what she could." See if the positive approach isn't the best approach!

**18**

*Then said Jesus, Father, forgive them; for they know not what they do. —Luke 23:34*

In this gracious word from the cross, our Lord, in addition to showing forth His deity and divinity—epitomizes one of the fruits of the Spirit and that fruit is kindness. In spite of what His enemies could do to Him, He did not descend to their level. Rather, He replied to their cruelty with forgiveness, love in action, kindness in repayment for unkindness. Of this episode, Phillips Brooks wrote: "Close to His Father always. . . . He was hid in the secret of His Father's presence. We cannot know His peace. It must have been so absolute. There must have been such a pity in His heart when they tormented Him, when they tied Him to a column and scourged Him, when they nailed Him to the cross at last, and all the while were looking to see Him give way and tremble, and all the while the soul which they thought they were reaching and torturing was far off, beyond their reach, hid in the secret of God's presence, hid in God. It was as if men flung water at the stars and tried thus to put them out, and the stars shone on calmly and safely and took no notice of their persecutors, except to give them light." This is His spirit, and it can be ours if we draw upon our strength in Him.

*Then took Mary a pound of spikenard, very costly, and anointed the feet of Jesus. . . . And there came also Nicodemus . . . and brought a mixture of myrrh and aloes, about an hundred pound weight.*
—John 12:3; 19:39

**19**

These two scriptures are set in contrast. The first tells of the devotion of a loving heart that expressed itself when the Savior was alive; the second, of devotion that was shown to our Lord after He was dead. Mary's gift weighed one pound; Nicodemus's gift weighed one hundred pounds. (Some have wondered if he tried to make up for the lateness of his tribute by its largeness.) The one shows the helpfulness of the timely; the other, the futility of post-mortem kindness. There are heart lessons here for us all: "Do not keep the alabaster boxes of your love and tenderness sealed up until your friends are dead. Fill their lives with sweetness. Speak approving, affirming words while their hearts can be thrilled and made happier by them; the kind things you mean to say when they are gone, say before they go. The flowers you mean to send for their coffins, send to brighten and sweeten their homes before they leave them." —HENRY DURBANVILLE

# July

## 20

*Love is patient and kind.*
—1 Corinthians 13:4, RSV

We have called to your attention more than once in this series of meditations the fact that Paul frequently overlaps or closely associates the various facets of the fruit of the Spirit. Here he lumps love, patience, and kindness together, revealing once again that all three are to be an integral part of the normal Christian character. Love, God's love, is the Source of our strength to show forth that Christian life style. As Peter says, "Above all hold unfailing your love for one another, since love covers a multitude of sins" (1 Pet. 4:8, RSV). Undoubtedly he was echoing that wise writer of Proverbs who said: "Hatred [opposite of kindness] stirs up strife, but love covers all offenses" (10:12 RSV). Old Henry Burton put it well a century ago:

> Have you had a kindness shown?
>     Pass it on;
> 'Twas not given for thee alone,
>     Pass it on;
> Let it travel down the years,
> Let it wipe another's tears,
> 'Til in heaven the deed appears—
>     Pass it on!

## 21

*It is more blessed to give than to receive.*
—Acts 20:35

One aspect of kindness that is bound to evidence itself in action is a spirit of generosity. I am not saying that there is no such thing as a stingy kind man—but I am saying that his kindness will be limited by his stinginess! If to be kind will tax his billfold, that stingy spirit will force him to turn his back on human need. This is not in keeping with Jesus' admonition quoted here by the apostle

Paul. He was calling for this same attitude in Romans 15 when he urged: "We then that are strong ought to bear the infirmities of the weak, and not to please ourselves. Let every one of us please his neighbour for his good to edification" (vv. 1–2). Of that verse in Acts 20:35, Matthew Henry says: "[A generous spirit] makes me more like to God, who gives to all, and receives from none; and to the Lord Jesus, who went about doing good. It is more blessed to give our pains than to receive pay for it. It is more pleasant to do good to the grateful, but it is more honorable to do good to the ungrateful, for then we have God to be our paymaster." If a generous spirit characterizes your home, where every member gives rather than takes, your home will be a reflection of heaven!

*Bear ye one another's burdens, and so fulfil the law of Christ.* —Galatians 6:2 **22**

Kindness is a burden-bearer! A kind person will be Christlike in his attitude toward others—not judgmental. Kindness is love in action, love with a face and feet. Practical James puts it this way: "If ye fulfill the royal law according to the scripture, Thou shalt love thy neighbor as thyself, ye do well" (2:8). "We ought to lay down our lives for the brethren," says the apostle John in 1 John 3:16. A century ago, Phillips Brooks wrote: "The wayfarers come to us continually, and they do not come by chance. God sends them. And as they come . . . they are our judges. Not merely by whether we give, but by how we give and by what we give, they judge us. One sends them away unhelped. Another drops a little, easy, careless, unconcerned money into their hands. Another man washes and clothes them, and another teaches them. Thank God there are some men and women here and there, full of the power of the gospel, who cannot rest satisfied till they have opened their very hearts and given the poor person the only thing which is really their own—themselves, their faith, their energy, their hope in God." Is that how you bear another's burdens—or are you a burden?

**23** *Be ye kind one to another, tenderhearted, forgiving one another.... —Ephesians 4:32*

Kindness and forgiveness walk hand in hand in the Christian life. In Matthew 6:14-15, Jesus said: "For if ye forgive men their trespasses, your heavenly Father will also forgive you: But if ye forgive not...." This portion of the Sermon on the Mount gives the divine perspective on the subject. In writing to the Corinthians, Paul again emphasized the importance of a forgiving spirit in showing forth the fruit of the Spirit: "What I have forgiven, if I have forgiven anything, has been for your sake in the presence of Christ, to keep Satan from gaining the advantage over us" (2 Cor. 2:10-11). Early in the seventeenth century George Herbert wrote: "He who cannot forgive others, breaks the bridge over which he himself must pass if he would ever reach heaven; for every one has need to be forgiven."

**24** *For we have not an high priest which cannot be touched. —Hebrews 4:15*

The best helper is one who "has been there." If you want to know what marriage is like, don't ask a bachelor! How much more authentic sympathy seems when it comes from one who has just lost a loved one—or gone through a crisis experience. What the writer to the Hebrews is saying here in this "high priest" passage is that Jesus Christ, our Savior, has been there and really understands our needs. He's not an "ivory tower" kind of savior. No, He never married, but He did live in an ordinary home with its frustrations and its daily problems. So He understands the tensions that build up, the misunderstandings that develop, and He can solve those problem situations. The secret of a successful marriage, as with any interpersonal situation, is to give time a chance to work. And the realization that our High Priest, Jesus Christ, lives in the situation with us will do much to soften the hard blows of circumstance and give us "breathing room." Also, the realization and recognition of our partner's personhood should help us face our differences realistically— but also compassionately and empathetically.

*Since you have been chosen by God who has given you this new life, and because of his deep love and concern for you, you should practice tenderhearted mercy and kindness to others.*
— Colossians 3:12, TLB

**25**

We let our loved ones go through life without many marks of appreciation. We are stingy with our compliments. We hide our emotions and our tender feelings. We are afraid to give each other the word of praise or of encouragement for fear we would seem to flatter, afraid we will turn each other's head. Even in many of our homes there is a strange shortage of good, wholehearted, cheering words. Let us not be afraid to say appreciative and complimentary words when they are deserved and are sincere. Let us lose no opportunity to show kindness, to express sympathy, to give encouragement. Silence, in the presence of needs that words will fill, is sinful. —J. R. MILLER

*Put on therefore, as God's chosen ones, holy and beloved, compassion, kindness, lowliness, meekness, and patience.* —Colossians 3:12, ASV

**26**

Here, in miniature, is the list Paul left us in Galatians 5: 22–23. Every one of these Christian attributes involves

# July

giving, a generous and kindly attitude toward others. President Lincoln used to say that he had no difficulty in finding men who would shed their last drop of blood for America; his problem was in finding one who would shed the first drop!

A rich man once asked a preacher, "Why is it that everyone is always criticizing me for being stingy when they know I have made provision to leave everything I possess to charity when I die?"

"Well," answered the other, "let me tell you about the pig and the cow. The pig was lamenting to the cow one day about how unpopular he was. 'People are always talking about your gentleness and kindness,' said the pig. 'You give milk and cream, but I give even more. I give bacon and ham—I give bristles, and they even pickle my feet! Still, no one likes me, I'm just a pig. Why is this?" The cow thought for a minute and then said, "Well, maybe it's because I give while I'm still living!"

> I want, in this short life of mine,
> As much as can be pressed
> Of service true for God and man;
> Help me to be my best.
> —A. B. SIMPSON

**27** *You should be like one big happy family, full of sympathy toward each other, loving one another with tender hearts and humble minds.*
—1 Peter 3:8, TLB

This is the opening verse in Peter's admonition to his readers to live exemplary Christian lives as befits those who name the name of Christ. In 1 Peter 5:5, he urges them to "serve each other with humble spirits, for God gives special blessings to those who are humble" (TLB). In

Philippians 2:3, Paul urges Christians, following Christ as their model, to "in lowliness of mind (humility) let each esteem others better than themselves." This kind of an attitude is kindness in action! Thomas á Kempis wrote: "Do not consider yourself to have made any spiritual progress, unless you account yourself the least of all men. God walks with the humble; He reveals Himself to the lowly; He gives understanding to the little ones; He discloses His meaning to pure minds, but hides His grace from the curious and the proud."

*But whosoever drinketh of the water that I shall give him shall never thirst; but the water that I shall give him shall be in him a well of water springing up into everlasting life.* —John 4:14

## 28

"The well in the heart." All noble life must be an inspiration from within, a well of water, springing up, the spontaneous outflow of a full heart. We must seek to be filled with the Divine Spirit. Then self will die. Then our lives will breathe benedictions and drop blessing everywhere. Our very look will be full of kindness. We will radiate life wherever we move, chasing away the darkness of others' sorrow. Then, sharing our loaf with the hungry, our joy with the joyless, our strength with the fainting, Christ will give us more and more of comfort, joy, strength, and helpful power, and at last will share with us His own crown and glory. For the well in the heart springs up into everlasting life. —J. R. MILLER

*And whatsoever ye do in word and deed, do all in the name of the Lord Jesus.* —Colossians 3:17

## 29

If we have the true spirit of service, we will look upon every one we meet, even casually, but certainly inti-

# July

mately, as one to whom we owe a debt of love, one sent to us to receive some benediction, some cheer, some compassion, some comfort, some strength, some inspiration, some touch of beauty at our hand. We may never do one great or conspicuous thing of which men will talk, or which will be reported in the newspapers, but every word we speak, every smallest act, every influence we send out, even unconsciously, "in His name," merely our shadow falling on human need and pain and sorrow as we pass by, will prove a sweet and blessed ministry of love, and will impart strength and help. The name of Christ consecrates every smallest deed or influence, pouring it full of love.

—J. R. MILLER

**30** *Above all hold unfailing your love for one another, since love covers a multitude of sins.*
—1 Peter 4:8 RSV

An all-pervading attitude of love underlies a generous and kind spirit. Kindness illustrates love to the beholder, the onlooker, the recipient of that loving act of kindness. For Peter it is all-important—notice the "above all" in our verse for today. The unknown writer to the Hebrews held it in equally high esteem: "Let brotherly love continue" (13:1). Peter's outspoken contemporary, Paul, places this truth at the very heart of his famous "love" chapter: "[Love] beareth all things, believeth all things, hopeth all things, endureth all things" (1 Cor. 13:7). To get back to Peter, he even says that this God-given love "covers a multitude of sins." I believe that means it even makes up for some of our other shortcomings! As Henry Ward Beecher says, "Love is not a possession, but a growth. The heart is a lamp with just enough oil to burn an hour, and if there be no oil to put in again its light will go out. God's grace is the oil that fills the lamp of love." Where are you looking for oil?

*Add to godliness brotherly kindness; and to brotherly kindness charity [love].* —2 Peter 1:7

Kindness is the bridge between godliness and love! What a strategic location for such an uncommon virtue. This passage from 2 Peter is the Golden Rule put into practice: "All things whatsoever ye would that men should do unto you, do ye even so to them: for this is the law and the prophets" (Matt. 7:12). Of this Rule, Joseph Parker once said, It "would reconcile capital and labor, all political contention and uproar, all selfishness and greed." Think what it could do for your home if faithfully practiced! There is an opposite side to this coin, however, a punishment if we disobey Christ's command so clearly expressed. Phillips Brooks once wrote: "A beneficent power, if we obey it, blesses and helps us; but the same power, if we disobey it, curses and ruins us. That law runs everywhere. . . . Was not Judas cursed by the same friendship with Jesus that perfected John?" On which side of the law of love are you?

# August

*The fruit of the Spirit is . . . faith.*
—Galatians 5:22

**1**

Faith is the seventh in the series of Christian characteristics Paul gives in Galatians 5. More has been written and said on this particular aspect of the Christian walk than any other, but in spite of the spate of writing on the subject, many people are still "fuzzy" as to just what faith really is—probably because it has so many facets. Dictionary definitions are many and varied, but basically faith involves "unquestioning confidence or trust in a person or thing."

One of the most dramatic illustrations of faith in the New Testament comes early in the earthly ministry of our Lord. The disciples had been fishing all night without success. Still, in answer to the command of Jesus to "Launch out into the deep, and let down your nets," (Luke 5:4), they did so and took up a net-breaking catch of fish. Again, at the close of His ministry, following His Resurrection, Jesus commanded His disciples to cast their nets, and this time their catch was so huge they could not draw it in (John 21:6). In both cases, their faith was rewarded with success—and in both cases their faith involved commitment and confidence in Jesus. They had to obey His command before their commitment was complete.

In the Old Testament, of course, the classic example of faith is "the father of the faithful," Abraham. He, too, launched out in a commitment of faith, leaving the security of his boyhood home and the falsity of his first idolatrous faith to follow His God into the unknown.

# August

Faith *is* difficult to define, but perhaps this beautiful description from the pen of Nathaniel Hawthorne will illustrate it for you: "Christian faith is a grand cathedral, with divinely pictured windows. Standing without, you can see no glory, nor can imagine any, but standing within every ray of light reveals a harmony of unspeakable splendors." So—enter the cathedral of faith!

**2**
> *And he [Abraham] believed in the Lord; and he counted it to him for righteousness.*
> —Genesis 15:6

In three different New Testament books our attention is directed to this pivotal experience in the life of Abraham. In the simplicity of faith, he laid hold of the promise regarding the Seed through whom all the world was to be blessed. That Seed, as we are told in Galatians, was Christ. So, believing in Christ, the patriarch Abraham was justified. And in exactly the same way believers are justified today. To be justified is to be reckoned righteous. Justification is the sentence of the judge in favor of the prisoner. God justifies the ungodly—freeing them from every charge of guilt. All they must do is put their trust in the Savior He has provided, who was delivered up to death for our offenses and was raised again for, or because of, our complete justification. When God imputes righteousness, He blots out forever the record of sin and gives the believer a completely new standing before His face. This is what it means to be "accepted in the Beloved."

—H. A. IRONSIDE

God is just as generous with us today as He was with Abraham. His blessing in return for our faith—a pretty good bargain!

*I know that my Redeemer liveth, and that he shall stand at the latter day....* —Job 19:25

**3**

The poetical part of the Book of Job begins with chapter 3 and goes on to chapter 42:6. In this great drama we have Job in controversy with his three friends, who insist that God does not permit a righteous man to suffer, that affliction is the portion of the wicked only; therefore Job's case implies that God is dealing with him because of some sin or sins, open or secret, which the patriarch cannot or will not acknowledge. When the friends fail to convince him of wickedness, Elihu appears "to speak on God's behalf" and shows that suffering is not necessarily punishment for sins actually committed, but may often be chastening or discipline to bring man to a deeper realization of his own impotence, as also to emphasize man's littleness and ignorance and to magnify the greatness and wisdom of God. This the Lord Himself enlarges upon when He speaks to Job out of the storm, with the result that the heart of the sufferer is bowed in reverence and repentance before Him. During all these perplexing experiences Job maintains his faith in God and has absolute assurance that some day all will be made clear. Meantime he can say, "Though He slay me, yet will I trust in Him," for he has the sure hope of resurrection when he shall, in his flesh, see and all will be made plain. —H. A. IRONSIDE

*Because that Abraham obeyed my voice, and kept my charge, my commandments, my statutes, and my laws...* —Genesis 26:5

**4**

The life of Abraham provides the pattern spiritual biography in which the life ascends from the rational and

# August

accountable to the personally-traced footsteps of the soul's path to God. The turning points in the spiral ascent of faith are, first, obedience to the effectual call of God (Gen. 12); and second, the culmination of unreserved resignation to God (Gen. 22). Our difficulties spiritually arise from unrecognized spiritual hysterics, in which mood we unconsciously select God to watch us and our symptoms. The only cure for that is to get hold of God and have no symptoms. . . . The spirit of obedience gives more joy to God than anything else on earth. Obedience is impossible to us naturally. Even when we do obey, we do it with a pout of our moral underlip, and with the determination to scale up high enough and "boss my boss." In the spiritual domain, there is no pout to be removed because the nature of God has come into me. The nature of God is exhibited in the life of our Lord, and the great characteristic of His life is obedience. When the love of God is shed abroad in my heart by the Holy Spirit (Rom. 5:5), I am possessed by the nature of God, and I show by my obedience that I love Him. The best measure of a spiritual life is not its ecstasies, but its obedience.   —Oswald Chambers

5    *Abraham went and took the ram, and offered him up for a burnt offering in the stead of his son.*
—Genesis 22:13

Abraham did not receive a positive command to sacrifice the ram, he recognized in the ram caught by his horns in the thicket behind him a divine suggestion. Until we get into fellowship with God His suggestions are no good to us. When people are intimate with one another, suggestions convey more than words, and when God gets us into oneness with Himself, we recognize His suggestions. Abraham offers the ram as a substitute for his son; he does not withhold his son in intention, although in fact he offers a substitute. The entire system of sacrifice is an extension of the sacrifice of the ram. The spiritual sacrifice of Isaac and the physical sacrifice of the ram are made one, the natural and spiritual are blended. That Christ is the substitute of me, and therefore I go scot free, is never taught in the New Testament. If I say that Christ suffered instead for me, I knock the bottom board out of His sacrifice. *Christ died in the stead of me.* I, a guilty sinner, can never get right with God, it is impossible. I can only be brought into union with God by identification with the One who died in my stead. No sinner can get right with God on any other ground than the ground that Christ died in his stead, not instead of him.   —OSWALD CHAMBERS

*The Lord preserveth all them that love him.*
                —Psalm 145:20

**6**

It is not in our power to avert the bitter failure which earth may inflict; it is in our power to win the high success which God bestows.   —F. W. FARRAR

You may have strong, eagle-eyed faith—well, you will probably be enabled to do great things in life, to work wonders, to trample on impossibilities. You may have confident hope—well, your life will pass brightly, not gloomily. But the vision of God as He is, to see the King in His beauty, is not given to science, or talent, but only to purity and love.   —F. W. ROBERTSON

> Then shall the tossing soul find anchorage,
>     And steadfast peace;
> Thy love shall rest in His,
>     Thy weary doubts forever cease.
> Christ and His love shall be thy blessed all
>     Forevermore.
> Christ and His power shall keep thy troubled soul
>     Forevermore.
>
>                 —HORATIUS BONAR

# August

**7**   *It is better to trust in the Lord than to put confidence in man.* —Psalm 118:8

In the marriage relationship, trust is a vital ingredient. My wife and I have developed that kind of a relationship over the almost thirty years of our marriage. But both of us realize that to put our complete trust or reliance in each other would be foolish—a misplacement of our faith. The only One who deserves our unconditional trust is God Himself. As David points out in Psalm 40:4, "Blessed is that man that maketh the Lord his trust, and respecteth not the proud, nor such as turn aside to lies." Jeremiah says, "Thus saith the Lord; Cursed be the man that trusteth in man, and maketh flesh his arm, and whose heart departeth from the Lord" (17:5). We humans have "feet of clay." I have never been one who could come into God's presence as the Pharisee did, and thank God that I am not like the publican standing next to me. There, but for the grace of God, go I—when I see the drunkard, the profligate, the murderer! I have failed my wife more than once, but fortunately she has a forgiving nature—and she realizes and recognizes that she isn't perfect either. Almost, but not quite! Our trust is not in each other, though we have a wonderfully close relationship. Our trust, together, is in the Lord! We say with Thomas Benton Brooks: "We trust as we love, and where we love. . . . If we love Christ much, surely we shall trust Him much."

**8**   *And unto one he gave five talents, to another two . . .* Matthew 25:15

The man of two talents. This quiet, commonplace, unnoticed man, going his faithful way in his subdued dress which makes no mark and draws no eye, doing his duty insignificantly and thoroughly, winning so unobtrusively at last his master's praise, ought to be interesting to us all, because he represents so much the largest segment of universal human life. The average man is by far the most numerous man. The man who goes beyond the average, the man who falls short of the average—both, by their very definitions, are exceptions. They are the outskirts and fringes, the peaks and promontories, of humanity. The great continent of human life is made up of the average people, the mass of two-talented capacity and action. But he was faithful, for notice that "he that had received two, he also gained other two" (v. 17).   —PHILLIPS BROOKS

**9**

*For the Lord God is a sun and shield: the Lord will give grace and glory: No good thing will he withhold from them that walk uprightly.*
—Psalm 84:11

The first part of this striking verse speaks of the majesty and power of God. To our finite minds, describing God as a sun is to place Him at the pinnacle of the solar system, for the sun is that star around which our solar system revolves. From it we receive the light, heat, and energy we need to function. Without it, we would be literally dead! In a sense, this "sun" description for God is a picture of Him as Creator and Sustainer of His universe and all of us in it. Still, that same all-powerful Being is our "shield," a figurative expression for His protection as well as His nature, as Truth personified. Faith itself is described as a shield in Ephesians 6:16, "the shield of faith." This transcendent Being, God, cares about me! That is the marvel. In fact, our verse says that "no good thing will he withhold from them that walk uprightly." Because of His great love for us, He gave the greatest gift of all—His Son! And with His strength, we can walk uprightly; in fact, "He preserveth the way of His saints!"

# August

## 10

*Whatsoever is born of God overcometh the world: and this is the victory that overcometh the world, even our faith.* —1 John 5:4

It seems very certain that the world is to grow better and richer in the future, however it has been in the past, not by the magnificent achievements of the highly-gifted few, but by the patient faithfulness of the one-talented many. If we could draw back the curtains of the millenium and look in, we should see not a Hercules here and there standing on the world-wasting monsters he has killed; but a world full of men each with an arm of moderate muscle, but each triumphant over his own little piece of the obstinacy of earth or the ferocity of brutes. It seems as if the heroes had done almost all for the world that they can do, and not much more can come till common men awake and take their common tasks. I do believe the common man's task is the hardest. The hero has the hero's aspiration that lifts him to his labor. All great duties are easier than the little ones, though they cost far more blood and agony.

—PHILLIPS BROOKS

"Faith is the victory, we know, that overcomes the world!" What would happen if your faith were the focus of this fight?

## 11

*Mine eyes are unto thee, O God the Lord: in thee is my trust.* —Psalm 141:8

A mother and her child sit side by side in the same group. Both love Christ and are following Him. The girl is sweet and beautiful, a picture of grace. She has never known a struggle, has scarcely ever been called to make a sacrifice, has never really found it hard to do right. Her face is fair, without a line. The mother has had cares, struggles, and fights with evil, has endured wrongs, has carried burdens, has suffered, has had bitter sorrows, has been misunderstood, has poured out her life in love's sacrifice. One would say that the child is more beautiful, the fairer and lovelier in her life. But as the two appear in the eyes of Christ, while both are beautiful, the mother wears a holier loveliness. She has learned in suffering. She has grown stronger in enduring struggle. The lines of her face, which seem blemishes on her fair beauty, are the marks of Jesus Christ. The recruit who entered the ranks only yesterday, who has never seen a battle, seems by far the handsomest soldier in the regiment, with his bright uniform, clean equipment, and unscarred face. But the old soldier, who is the veteran of a score of battles, though his uniform is soiled and torn, his gun blackened with powder, his face marked with wounds and scars—is he not the more perfect soldier?  —J. R. MILLER

Faith is a battle—and Jesus is our Captain!

*They have blown the trumpet, even to make all ready.*
—Ezekiel 7:14

**12**

Conduct is the mouthpiece of character. What a man is declares itself through what he does. Character without conduct is like the lips without the trumpet, whose whispers die upon themselves and do not stir the world. Conduct without character is like the trumpet hung up in the wind, which whistles through it and means nothing. The world has a right to demand that all which claims to be character should show itself through conduct which can be seen and heard. The world has a right to disallow all claims of character which do not show themselves in conduct. "It may be real, it may be good," the world can say, "but I cannot know it or test it; and I am sure that however good and real it is, it is not shown unless there is posi-

# August

tive signs of activity." James said it another way: "What does it profit, my brethren, if a man says he has faith but has not works? Can his faith save him? If a brother or sister is ill-clad and in lack of daily food, and one of you says to them, 'Go in peace, be warmed and filled,' without giving them the things needed, . . . what does it profit? So faith by itself, if it has no works, is dead. But some one will say, 'You have faith and I have works,' Show me your faith apart from your works, and I by my works will show you my faith" (James 2:14–18).  —PHILLIPS BROOKS

**13**  *And Jesus answering saith unto them, Have faith in God.*  —Mark 11:22

You will realize the vital necessity of an increase of faith if you will but understand that faith is vastly more than an intellectual process or a mental assent to divine truth. It is vastly more than a devout emotion; and a mightily different thing is it from the pious fetish some religious quacks now employ for purposes of delusion. A genuine Christian faith is just the grappling union of the soul with the omnipotent Son of God. "I am the vine, ye are the branches: abide in me." This is the way Christ puts it, and *faith makes that very union.* The closer your connection with Jesus, the greater will be the amount of grace flowing into your soul and out into your daily life. The more abundant your faith, the fuller and more potent will be the inflow of Jesus Christ.  —THEODORE CYLER

**14**  *They took knowledge of them that they had been with Jesus.*  —Acts 4:13

One of the greatest interpreters of India, for he is one of the greatest souls in India, is a priest among the Syrians. With his long beard and flowing garments and finely chiselled face, he has the appearance of a Moses. And Moses never gave himself more for his people than this Syrian priest has done. For forty years he has poured out his life for his people, his heart going out in tenderness toward suffering, and his feet bearing him innumerable miles to human need in ministry. And his experience of Christ is rich and abundant. He walked with Him these years. When he stands to interpret no wonder the great audiences bend to catch every syllable, for his sentences scintillate with a natural eloquence. But it is not eloquence that holds them; it is the fact that forty years of beautiful Christlike living is speaking. It is not the interpretation of that hour, it is the interpretation of a whole life going into his words. The impact of forty years of unselfish living is falling upon the souls of the people. Christ becomes living and real because the interpreter is unconsciously speaking from the depths of years of intimacy with Him. This is interpreting indeed.

—E. STANLEY JONES

What kind of an interpreter are you?

*Follow after righteousness, godliness, faith ...*
—1 Timothy 6:11

**15**

Another interpreter was a youth who was a born interpreter, I could say anything and, as quick as a flash, he would run back into Sanskrit, or Arabic, or Persian, and bring the technical term. But if he was a born interpreter, he was a reborn one. He had a deep experience of Christ, and he heightened and vitalized every expression with the glow of his own soul. He more than pulled his half of the load. Again and again, I found it necessary to quicken my spiritual pace to keep up with him. One day, he was translating so beautifully and so accurately (I knew the lan-

# August

guage he was using) that I simply stopped, put my arm around his shoulder, turned to the audience, and said, "Isn't it beautiful translating?" They applauded and well they might. Calvin Singh is dead now, cut off in his youth. It may be the Master had some interpreting He needed done in some other world. I lay the tribute of my love at his feet, wherever he is. He is interpreting somewhere, I'm sure. And the hand of the Master is upon his shoulder in love and admiration. For Calvin is doing it well.

—E. STANLEY JONES

**16**
*What shall we say then that Abraham our father, as pertaining to the flesh, hath found? For if Abraham were justified by works, he hath whereof to glory; but not before God. For what saith the Scripture? Abraham believed God, and it was counted unto him for righteousness.* —Romans 4:1-3

The man who really believes in God is always able cheerfully to obey Him, because present sacrifice is set in the light of the necessity for the fulfillment of God's declared purpose. Abraham rested in God, rather than in any blessing He bestowed, even though that were Isaac. Faith, depending upon the divine purpose and the divine promises, saw beyond the sacrifice, and was able to obey.

—G. CAMPBELL MORGAN

Abraham never got to the Promised Land, though he left all to seek it. To the end of his life he journeyed on his quest; but he died a pilgrim still on the way. Yet in his heart he found a better thing than he sought; not a country but the rewards of faith and obedience. . . . Those who seem to fail often get most out of this work which they can carry with them. —D. DULLER

*By grace are ye saved through faith; and that not of yourselves; it is the gift of God.* —Ephesians 2:8

**17**

Evidence weighed and knowledge gained lead up to faith. It is true that faith in Jesus is the gift of God; but yet He usually bestows it in accordance with the laws of mind, and hence we are told that "faith cometh by hearing, and hearing by the Word of God." If you want to believe in Jesus, hear about Him, read about Him, think about Him, know about Him, and so you will find faith springing up in your heart, like the wheat which comes up through the moisture and the heat operating upon the seed which has been sown. The Bible is the window through which we may look and see the Lord. Read over the story of His suffering and death with devout attention, and before long the Lord will cause faith secretly to enter your soul. If you are anxious to give up every evil way, our Lord Jesus will enable you to do so at once. His grace has already changed the direction of your desires; in fact, your heart is renewed. Therefore, rest on Him to strengthen you to battle with temptations as they arise, and to fulfill the Lord's commands from day to day. —Charles H. Spurgeon

*Moreover it is required of stewards that they be found trustworthy.* —1 Corinthians 4:2, RSV

**18**

It is the attribute of trustworthiness that should characterize the Christian. The King James Version translates that word as "faithful." Just as God Himself is described as "faithful," to be trusted, unchangeable in His nature, so His child, the Christian, should show faithfulness in his life. Faith, or faithfulness, is the practical outgrowth of a living faith. Our very salvation depends upon God's faithfulness, and He is therefore worthy of our trust, for He keeps His promises, every one. But Christians are to evi-

# August

dence faithfulness, as well. Paul makes this very clear not only here in Corinthians, but in other places as well: "The things that thou hast heard of me among many witnesses, the same commit thou to faithful men, who shall be able to teach others also" (2 Tim. 2:2). The steward is not asked to be eloquent or a great Christian leader. It is not his *ability* that counts with God, it is his *availability*. Are you worthy of God's trust? Can God count on you? Many years ago, John Cunningham Geikie said, "An undivided heart, which worships God alone, and trusts Him as it should, is raised above all anxiety for earthly wants." On this subject, James has the final word: "[Do] not suppose that a double-minded man, unstable in all his ways, will receive anything from the Lord." Lord, let me be a single-minded steward!

## 19

*For we walk by faith, not by sight. . . .*
—2 Corinthians 5:7
*The Lord redeemeth the soul of his servants: and none of them that trust in him shall be desolate.*
—Psalm 34:22

Faith is totally distinct from trust. By faith we claim; by trust we prove that we have taken, and that the gifts of God have become to us what God in His omnipotence intended them to be.

Faith takes into our soul what God in His mercy reveals, and believes God against all comers. Trust hands over to God what God has given us, and says, "Keep, Lord, and use, for I cannot." Then comes a holy confidence and assurance which prevents us from being disturbed under any circumstances whatever, and out of which comes a boldness which enables us to act for the glory of God. Faith when it has conceived brings forth trust, and trust when it is finished brings forth confidence and boldness. —H. W. Webb-Peploe

*Stand fast in the faith. . . . The fruit of the Spirit is faith.* —1 Corinthians 16:13; Galatians 5:22

Should we not try to learn the secret of power in Christian life and Christian work? We can do a great deal more for Christ and to bless the world than most of us are doing. It is more faith that we need. Faith links us to Christ, so that wherever we go in His name He goes with us, and whatever we do for Him His power rests upon us. Every Christian life ought to be a force among men, a witness for Christ, an influence for blessing and good. Let us get nearer to Christ, that He can use us for doing the greater things.

The highest reach of faith is loving, intelligent consecration of all our life to the will of God. We are to have desires, but they should be held in subordination to God's desires and thoughts for us. We are to have plans, but they should be laid at God's feet, that He may either let us work them out for Him or show us His plan for us instead of our own. Complete consecration of our wills to God's— that is the standard of Christian living at which we are to aim. —J. R. MILLER

*So whether we are at home or away, we make it our aim to please him.* —2 Corinthians 5:9, RSV

In these words, Paul is defending his apostleship—but the truth he expresses is an excellent motto for any Christian, and particularly for a Christian couple. "At home or away" pretty well covers every area of life, all our activities—and both aspects (home and away) are equally important. If one is a saint at work, but a devil at home, he is nothing but a hypocrite putting up a good front "to be seen of men." He should be the same "at home or away," and if he is truly God's man, he will be. Charles Haddon Spurgeon once shared a rule for happy home life: "When

# August

home is ruled by God's Word, angels might be asked to stay with us, and they would not find themselves out of their element." Let God's Word control every aspect of your life, and you'll discover that His blessing will overshadow your way. "Make it your aim to please Him," and "all these things will be added unto you."

**22** *I live by the faith of the Son of God, who loved me and gave himself for me.* —Galatians 2:20

These words, "who loved me," are full of faith, and he who can say this word, "me," and apply that love to himself with a true and constant faith, as Paul did, shall be a good disputer with Paul against the law. For Christ delivered neither sheep, ox, gold or silver, but He gave Himself for me. —MARTIN LUTHER

Love is its own perennial fount of strength. The strength of affection is a proof not of the worthiness of the object, but of the largeness of the soul which loves. Love descends, not ascends. The Saviour loved His disciples infinitely more than His disciples loved Him, because His capacity to love was infinitely larger. —F. W. ROBERTSON

**23** *In whom we have boldness and access with confidence by the faith of him. . . . That Christ may dwell in your hearts by faith.* —Ephesians 3:12,17

God has made us with two eyes, both intended to be used so as to see one object. Binocular vision is the perfection of sight. There is a corresponding truth in the spiritual sphere. We have two faculties for the discovery of spiritual truth—*reason* and *faith*. The former is intellectual, the latter is largely intuitive, emotional. Reason asks: How? Why? Faith accepts testimony, and rests upon the person who bears witness.

Now reason and faith often seem in conflict, but are not. Reason prepares the way for faith, and then both act jointly. We are not called to exercise blind faith, but to be ready always to give answer to every man who asks a reason for our faith.

There are three questions which reason must answer: First, is the Bible the Book of God? Second, what does it teach? Third, what relation has its teaching to my life?

When these are settled, faith accepts the Word as authoritative, and no longer stumbles at its mysteries, but rather expects that God's thoughts will be above our thoughts. Thus, where reason's province ends, faith's begins. —ARTHUR T. PIERSON

*Whatsoever ye do, do it heartily, as to the Lord.*
—Colossians 3:23

# 24

Christ never asks for anything we cannot do. But let us not forget that He always does expect and require of each of us the best we can do. The faithfulness Christ wants and approves implies the doing of all our work, our business, our trade, our daily toil, as well as we can. Let no one think that the Christian faith does not apply to private life, the life between Sundays. Whatever your job is, you cannot be altogether faithful to God unless you do your best. To slur any task is to do God's work badly; to neglect it is to rob God. The universe is not quite complete without your work well done, however small that work may be. —J. R. MILLER

# August

## 25

*Let no man despise thy youth; but be thou an example of [to] the believers, in word, in conversation, ["in speech and conduct," RSV], in charity, in spirit, in faith, in purity.* —1 Timothy 4:12

In these words with which Paul is admonishing his spiritual son, Timothy, we find a miniature list of the fruits of the Spirit. And these are attributes which might well characterize a good marriage as well as a good person. Those who work with young people tell us that the best way to keep young people out of trouble is to offer them a challenge. They are not looking for an easy path to accomplishment, but welcome the higher goal, if it is presented to them. The generation of the '60s, with all their problems and rebellions, revealed that fact. They weren't necessarily looking for ease; they were looking for excitement. What greater challenge could there be than Paul's call here for excellence in personal faith and everyday living? Paul wants his young friend, Timothy, to be an "example" of faith, and our Lord Jesus wants us, His youthful followers, to be an example as well. His would be a hopeless challenge were it not for another truth expressed elsewhere by the apostle Paul: "For when I am weak, then am I strong" (2 Cor. 12:10). Admit and face your weaknesses, then lean on your heavenly Father for strength to be "an example" in all these areas of daily living: "love, faith, and purity."

## 26

*Brethren, be not weary in well doing.*
—2 Thessalonians 3:13

We need never be anxious about our mission. We need never perplex ourselves in the least in trying to know what God wants us to do, what place He wants us to fill. Our whole duty is to do well the work of the present. There are some people who waste entire years wondering what God would have them do, and expecting their life-work to be pointed out to them. But that is not the divine way. If you want to know God's plan for you, do God's will each day; that is God's plan for you today. If He has a wider sphere, a larger place for you, He will bring you to it at the right time, and then *that* will be God's plan for you and your mission.   —J. R. MILLER

> Our lives we cut on a curious plan,
> Shaping them, as it were, for man;
> But God, with better art than we,
> Shapes them for eternity.

*Who are kept by the power of God through faith unto salvation ready to be revealed in the last times.* —1 Peter 1:5

**27**

Three key thoughts jump out at me as I ponder this verse. "Kept by the power of God" reminds me of that blessed promise from the lips of Jesus recorded in John 10: 28, "And I give unto them eternal life; and they shall never perish, neither shall any man pluck them out of my hand." And this solid sense of security as a believer is reinforced by the psalmist: "For he shall give his angels charge over thee, to keep thee in all thy ways" (Ps. 91:11). The keeping power of God is unlimited and unending! Not only does it apply to our past, but to our future as well.

"Through faith unto salvation" in a sense pinpoints our part in this divine transaction. We tap into the inexhaustible divine resources by our faith, which in itself is a gift from God, one of that cluster of spiritual fruit listed by Paul in Galatians 5:22 (around which we have constructed this book). Faith is a product of the Divine Mind, as Jeremy Taylor says: "What can be more foolish than to think that all this rare fabric of heaven and earth could come by chance, when all the skill of science is not able to make an oyster!"

The third thought looks to the future: "ready to be revealed in the last time." God is keeping me through the present, whatever it may bring, to show me a glorious future.

## 28

*For as the body without the spirit is dead, so faith without works is dead also.* —James 2:26

Faith links a man to Christ, so that he is no more a mere common man, with only his own poor feeble strength, but is more than a man—a man whom Christ is using, behind whom Christ's omnipotent energy is working. We must yield ourselves altogether to God and let Him use us. Thus His power, His wisdom, His skill, His thoughts, His love will flow through our souls, our brains, our hearts, and our fingers. That is working by faith. It is simply putting our lives into God's hand to be used, as one uses a pen to write or a brush to paint, or a chisel to carve a statue. "I must work the works of him that sent me, while it is day: the night cometh, when no man can work" (John 9:4).

—J. R. MILLER

## 29

*Casting all your care upon him; for he careth for you.* —1 Peter 5:7

How do you handle worry—and that accompanying burden of discouragement? Worry is undoubtedly one of the worst enemies of a happy home—and a healthy body as well. Charles M. Mayo in *American Mercury* says; "Worry affects circulation, the heart, the glands, the whole nervous system. I have never known a man who died from overwork, but many who died from doubt." This certainly identifies the physical results of worry. We often speak of "doubting Thomas," but most of us forget that Peter was just as guilty, if not more so, of doubt and its accompanying anxiety as was Thomas. In his perceptive way, Bishop Fulton J. Sheen has isolated our problem: "All worry is atheism, because it is want of trust in God." An anxious, worried Christian is a contradiction in terms, an incongruity. The truly practicing Christian can say with the anonymous writer, "Leave tomorrow's trouble to tomorrow's strength; tomorrow's work to tomorrow's time; tomorrow's trial to tomorrow's grace and tomorrow's God." Earl Riney's contemporary beatitude quoted from *Christian Herald* fittingly concludes these thoughts on worry: "Blessed is the man who is too busy to worry in the daytime, and too sleepy at night." Try freedom from worry—you'll like it!

*And the grace of our Lord was exceeding abundant with faith and love which is in Christ Jesus.*
—1 Timothy 1:14

# 30

Be satisfied to have a faith that can hold in its hand this one truth: "While we were yet without strength, in due time Christ died for the ungodly." He laid down His life for men while as yet they were not believing in Him, nor were *able* to believe in Him. He died for men—not as believers, but as sinners. He came to make these sinners into believers and saints; but when He died for them He viewed them as utterly without strength. If you hold to the truth that Christ died for the ungodly, and believe it, your faith will save you, and you may go in peace. If you will trust your soul with Jesus, who died for the ungodly, even though you cannot believe all things, nor move mountains, nor do any other wonderful works, yet you are saved. It is not great faith, but true faith that saves; and the salvation lies, not in the faith, but in the Christ in whom faith trusts. Faith as a grain of mustard seed will bring salvation. It is not the measure of faith, but the sincerity of faith, which is the point to be considered. Surely a man can believe what he knows to be true; and as you know Jesus to be true, you can believe in Him.

Faith has specially to believe in Him who is the sum and substance of all this revelation, even Jesus Christ, who became God in human flesh that He might redeem our fallen nature from all the evils of sin, and raise it to eternal blessedness. We believe *in* Christ, *on* Christ, and *upon* Christ, accepting Him because of the record which God has given to us concerning His Son—that He is the propitiation for our sins. We accept God's unspeakable gift, and receive Jesus as our all in all.

If I wanted to describe saving faith in one word, I should say that it is *trust*. It is so believing God and so believing in Christ that we trust ourselves and our eternal destinies in the hands of a reconciled God.   —C. H. SPURGEON

**31**    *Be thou faithful unto death, and I will give thee a crown of life.* —Revelation 2:10

These words are taken from the very last message Christ uttered directly to His people. They are most precious, for they are spoken to a church persecuted unto death, yet holy in the midst of tribulation.

Nothing is said of any special works or achievements credited to the praise of this church, yet a poor persecuted church suffering for Christ cannot be expected to do much. To endure steadfastly, then, is all that can be expected, and such perseverance is worthy of highest commendation.

# August

Look carefully at the words of Christ: "I know thy works, and tribulation, and poverty." No one else may think you are doing anything. All may think your life a failure so far as spiritual accomplishments are concerned. But the Master knows the pressure under which you live, the day-by-day irritations and frustrations you must endure. He knows it all, and He rewards your faithfulness. Note what He says: "Fear none of these things"—verse 10 —but "Be thou faithful...."

Note it carefully: He did not say, "Be brilliant." No, "Be faithful." Not "Be popular." But "Be faithful"—knowing you will be anything but popular. He did not say, "Be successful. Produce a large harvest. Greatly impress your generation." No, He said, "Be faithful."

In Luke 16:10, the Master said, "He that is faithful in that which is least is faithful also in much." Our lives are made up of little things—"that which is least." Life can be a drudgery, monotonous, deadening. But the Christian course is to—

Be a faithful branch and produce only good fruit.

Be a faithful light. Your light may not dazzle the world, but keep it burning.

The crowns of this world are studded with valuable gems, but even the most valuable are of only finite worth. Only one crown is eternal and infinite in value—the crown of life.  —O. G. WILSON

# September

*Blessed are the meek: for they shall inherit the earth.* —Matthew 5:5

*The fruit of the Spirit is . . . meekness. . . .*
                                                   —Galatians 5:22

1

One of the aspects of "gentleness" most often misunderstood is this matter of meekness. It implies a submissive spirit, even undue submission in the face of insult or injury. The Modern Language Bible translates the Matthew passage, "Blessed are the gentle," which indicates the close relationship between the two attitudes of gentleness and meekness. "Gentleness" is the fifth in Paul's list in Galatians 5, and "meekness" is the eighth attribute he catalogs for us. The two concepts are almost interchangeable.

Meekness is not weakness, however. There are only two people in the Bible specifically described as meek—and neither of them is weak! In the Old Testament, Moses is described as " very meek, above all the men which were upon the face of earth" (Num. 12:3). But this does not mean that Moses was a doormat. No man could lead thousands of people as he did, and be weak. It was his nature, however, to put others and their interests before himself. Indeed, the Living Bible says that he was "the humblest man on earth."

In the New Testament, Jesus Christ described *Himself* as "meek and lowly in heart" (Matt. 11:29). He, too, put others and their interests before His own personal needs— but He was anything but a doormat! Read about His temple cleansing if you want to see how righteous wrath can be expressed by a meek man.

# September

Meekness and humility have been variously described down the ages, and some of the best definitions come from anonymous sources:

"The man who is to take a high place before his fellows must take a low place before his God."

"It is the laden bough that hangs low, and the most fruitful Christian who is most humble."

A contemporary writer, Estelle Smith, has summarized the concept for us:

> "Humility is strong—not bold;
> quiet—not speechless;
> sure—not arrogant."

This eighth virtue can make your home a heaven—and marriage a delight!

**2** *But the wisdom that is from above is first pure, then peaceable, gentle, and easy to be entreated, full of mercy and good fruits, without partiality, and without hypocrisy.* —James 3:17

What an apt description of the Christian spirit the writer, James, gives us here! He pretty well covers all the bases. J. R. Miller points out, "The things that hurt and sear our lives are resentment, unforgiveness, bitter feeling, desire for revenge. Men may beat us until our bones are broken, but if love fails not in our hearts meanwhile, we have come through the experience unharmed, with no marks of injury upon us. One writing of a friend who was terribly hurt in a hit-and-run accident said that the woman would probably be scarred for life, and then went on to speak of the wonderful patience of her suffering, and that the peace of God had not failed in her heart for a moment. The world may hurt our bodies, but if we suffer as Christ suffered, there will be no trace of scarring or wounding in our inner life." This is one of the fruits of gentleness in our lives. And it is apparent immediately to those with whom we come into contact. Take Jesus as your Pattern as well as your Savior—and your life will be a reflection of His!

*He shall feed his flock like a shepherd: he shall gather the lambs with his arm, and carry them in his bosom, and shall gently lead those that are with young.* —Isaiah 40:11

**3**

"Now may the God of peace who brought again from the dead our Lord Jesus, the great shepherd of the sheep, by the blood of the eternal covenant, equip you with everything good that you may do his will, working in you that which is pleasing in his sight . . ." (Heb. 13:20–21). Here, once again, we are reminded of how interwoven within the Christian spirit are those sparkling gifts of the Spirit. Love, joy, peace, patience, goodness, kindness, faithfulness, and now gentleness (rsv) are to evidence themselves equally in the life of the Christian. J. R. Miller gives this illustration: "Sometimes beside the brackish sea you will find a spring of water gushing up, as sweet as any that bursts from the hillside. When the tide is low you dig up its clear water and drink it, and it refreshes you. A few moments later you come again and find the tide covering the place, its bitter waters rolling over the spring; but in a little while you pass again, and now the tide is rolled out to sea. You find the spring again, and its clear streams are pouring forth as sweet as before, without a trace of the brackishness of the sea in which the spring has been folded so long. So should it be with the love of the Christian heart. No wrong, no ingratitude, no cruelty, should ever embitter it. We should never cease to pray for others because they have been unkind to us." Doesn't this speak of the Christlike spirit which should shine forth from the

# September

Christian life? If your life and mine were like this, what heavens our homes would be!

**4**

*God hath dealt graciously with me . . .*
—Genesis 33:11

The word "providential" should be associated more in its interpretation with the world of grace than with the world of law. We are in a world of laws, God's laws, living between the two old mountains, Ebal and Gerizim. Obedience and blessing go hand in hand. Disobedience and trouble are indissolubly linked. We must not interpret providences so that the consequences of our mistakes and sins are thought of as original choices of God, then and there; that death, for example, from pneumonia, is a "mysterious dispensation of providence." It is not to be thought that God is constantly interfering with the processes of law. But this is the thought, and is blessedly true, that this is God's world and our schoolhouse, our training ground; that all things are providential in the sense that they are in the scope of God's immediate knowledge—from the fall of the sparrow to the building of a temple; and, best of all, that all things can become "means of grace" and lead us toward God-likeness. —MALTBIE D. BABCOCK

As we attend the school of God, we grow in His likeness.

**5**

*Thou didst hide these things from the wise and understanding.* —Matthew 11:25

How grateful we should be that our faith does not depend upon our intellect! If it did, most of us would be "frozen out" because we could not understand all the ramifications of faith. G. Campbell Morgan wrote: "The keenest

# September

intellect and most cultured mind are unable to understand the mystery of redemption, and therefore cannot explain it to others. Whoever can say light has broken upon the cross, and the eternal morning has dawned, is able to do so through the direct illumination of the Holy Spirit; and apart from that, there can be no witness and no service." It is this same illuminating power of the Holy Spirit that enables us to show spiritual fruit in our lives, such as the gentleness we are currently considering. Morgan also said, "If you cannot be a Christian where you are, you cannot be a Christian anywhere. It is not place, but grace."

*The Lord reigneth.* —1 Chronicles 16:31
*Thy throne, O God, is for ever and for ever.*
—Psalm 45:6

**6**

These and kindred phrases tell the character of the music of God. When the song is of human experience at its best, it is ever the joy and peace to be found in the law of God. . . .When the music becomes a dirge, it is because in individual or national life God has been forgotten. . . .

When man, God's crowning work, first sinned, he dragged down all creation in his fall; but when Jesus shall come again, to reign in the power of His cross, passion, and atonement (for that is to be the strength of His rule), then the whole creation shall feel the touch of His presence, and shall respond to His redemptive work. "By one man sin entered into the world, and death by sin; and so death passed upon all men" (Rom. 5:12). Not until Christ shall have banished evil, brought in the new heavens and the new earth, will our Lord's work be complete and His glory at the highest. "I saw a new heaven and a new earth" (Rev. 21:1). —G. Campbell Morgan

As reflectors of God's sublime character, we Christians are to show forth "his death until he come." One of the

# September

ways we can do this is by revealing the fruit of the Spirit daily and consistently in our lives.

**7**
*We were gentle among you, even as a nurse cherisheth her children.* —1 Thessalonians 2:7

What a picture of Paul we receive in this brief description from his own pen. In verse 11 he says of his efforts to comfort and exhort the Thessalonian Christians, that he "exhorted and comforted and charged every one of you, as a *father* doth his children." The Living Bible gives verse 7 this same parental touch: "We were as gentle among you as a *mother* feeding and caring for her own children." In this same version, verse 8 reads: "We loved you dearly—so dearly that we gave you not only God's message, but our own lives too." This is the thrust of what it means to be a fruitful Christian—one who dares make himself vulnerable to others, who puts others before himself. This is what it means to be "gentle" in our attitude toward and treatment of others—as modeled for us by the Lord Jesus Himself!

**8**
*I Paul myself beseech you by the meekness and gentleness of Christ.* —2 Corinthians 10:1

Hypersensitiveness may come from overwork or illness, or from plain selfishness. To be easily annoyed is to be sick or selfish. When we are played out, or worked out, our nerves are worn to the quick, and writhe at the touch of trifles. Then—rest for our lives! We cannot afford not to. But there is an irritability that is not physical. It is moral—or immoral. It comes from being self-centered.

# September

We live, but will not let live. We want our own way, any way. If we are interrupted, we are visibly annoyed. Interference, corrections, suggestions light our firecrackers, and we explode. Other people's pleasures and pains, their children, cats, dogs, and canaries are impertinences. Why? Because they do not pertain to us. This is plain selfishness. Let us beware. It is the spirit, the essence of evil. Let us go to the cross of Jesus and learn to love. We shall always be in relationship with the world. Let us make them loving relationships. Let us look out for hypersensitiveness—for touchiness. It reveals a lack of self-control, an absence of the fruit of the Spirit in our lives.   —MALTBIE D. BABCOCK

*Behold, I set before you the way of life, and the way of death.* —Jeremiah 21:8     **9**

Christ said, "I am come that ye might have life." Life is back of love, back of believing, back of hoping, back of everything. Ezekiel in his vision of the river of life, understood life; he knew what it meant—at first a little stream to the ankles, then, as he went further in, it came to the knees, then to the loins, and finally a wide, mighty river. That is life. Do you know what life is? No, neither does anyone else. Life is indefinable; life is an ultimate; life is God; life is effectiveness; life is power. Adjustment to the things around you—correspondence to environment—that is life. The plodding man does not live. He goes out in the morning and hears the birds, the heralds of spring, sweetly singing in the trees. The flowers are blooming in the fields, the whole world is full of music, it is everywhere; but the sweet rose growing on the bank does not for him contain life and beauty and music—it remains just a rose. Life is measured by the number of things you are alive to. The fulness of our life means what we are about to do. I

# September

must have a life that is more abundant than my poor nature. I must take the power of Jesus and have inside fellowship with Him. —Maltbie D. Babcock

**10** *Cast thy burden upon the Lord, and he shall sustain thee; he shall never suffer the righteous to be moved. —Psalm 55:22*

In Philippians 4:6, Paul told us: "Be careful for nothing! But in everything by prayer and supplication with thanksgiving let your requests be made known unto God." What has this to do with the gentle spirit? A gentle spirit comes when our overall spirit is at rest, at peace with God. Hudson Taylor, dealing with Philippians 4:6, wrote: "Do we fail to be anxious for nothing, and to bring everything by prayer and supplication with thanksgiving before God? We may bring nine difficulties out of ten to Him, and try to manage the tenth ourselves, and that one difficulty, like a small leak that runs a vessel dry, is fatal to the whole. Like a small breach in a city wall, it gives entrance to the power of the foe. But if we fulfil the conditions, He is certainly faithful, and instead of our having to keep our hearts and minds—our affections and thoughts—we shall find them kept for us. The peace which we can neither make nor keep will itself, as a garrison, keep and protect us, and the cares and worries which strive to enter, will strive in vain." Out of our strength in Christ will come the grace to be gentle.

**11** *Let this mind be in you, which was also in Christ Jesus. —Philippians 2:5*

The mind that was in Christ Jesus is the lowly, gentle mind. He ever sought the glory of His Father and the blessing of others. In His gracious condescension He who had every right to command became servant of all. Though in the form of God from eternity, He did not consider equality with God something to be retained, but He divested Himself of the outward semblance of *deity*, the glory that He had with the Father before the world was, and took a bondman's, a servant's form. Having become Man He humbled Himself yet further, stooping to death, and such a death, that of the cross. This is the One whose example the Spirit brings before us, that our ways may be conformed to His.

> Thou would'st like wretched man be made
>     In everything but sin;
> That we as like Thee might become
>     As we unlike had been.
>
> H. A. IRONSIDE

*Take my yoke upon you, and learn of me; for I am meek and lowly in heart: and ye shall find rest unto your souls.* —Matthew 11:29

# 12

The RSV translates the word "meek" here as "gentle," and what a picture of divine gentleness Jesus was! We could find no better pattern or model to follow than His blessed life. J. R. Miller tells the moving story: "A poor boy was drawing home one day a little wagon full of pieces of broken boards gathered from some building operation. He was tired, his feet were bare, his clothing was ragged, his face was pinched and pale, telling of poverty and hunger. He had stopped to rest and gone to sleep. His cap had fallen from his head, and his face was exposed to the sun. Then an old man carrying a lunch pail was passing by. When he saw the boy a look of pity came into his face. Taking from his pail his own scanty dinner, he laid it be-

# September

side the lad and hurried away. Others saw the act. A man walked down from his house nearby and laid a silver dollar beside the workman's dinner. A woman, living across the street, brought a good cap and placed it on the boy's head. A child came running with a pair of shoes, and another with a coat. Others stopped by, whispered, dropped silver. So from the old man's one gentle act, there had gone out this wave of influence, leading a score or more people to do likewise." This is the picture of the influence your gentle act and mine can have.

**13** *Whosoever will be great among you, let him be your minister.* —Matthew 20:26

One aspect of gentleness is a willingness to serve, to be patient with the demands and faults of those around us, in our family and among our friends. J. R. Miller had this fruit of the Spirit in mind when he wrote: "It is sometimes necessary to tell our friends or family of their faults, but we should go about it in love, with prayer, and wise and gentle tact. A gentle, loving way is better than blurting out the criticism, as some brusque people do, abruptly, calling it frankness, saying that they always say honestly what they believe. It may be honest and frank enough, but it is not the Christlike way. 'What did you preach about yesterday?' asked an old clergyman of a young minister one Monday. 'On the judgment,' replied the younger man. 'Did you do it tenderly?' asked the old pastor. We should never speak to others of their sins and faults unless we can do it tenderly. We need patience, too, and sometimes we must wait a long time for the opportunity to do our duty in this regard, to speak the right word. But the right occasion will come, if we wait for it." If this is our attitude in the home and away from home, those around us "will rise up and call us blessed."

# September

*Then spake Jesus again unto them, saying, I am the light of the world: he that followeth me shall not walk in darkness, but shall have the light of life.*
—John 8:12

# 14

As the sun shines upon a bank of snow, no two of all the myriad particles catch its light alike or give the same interpretation of its glory. Have you ever imagined such a purpose for your commonplace existence? If you have, you must have asked yourself what the quality is in a man's life which can make it *reflective* of God—capable of bearing witness of Him. There is some quality in polished brass or the calm lake to make it able to send forth again the sunlight that descends upon it. What is it in a soul that makes it able to do the same to the God who sheds Himself upon its life? The Bible has its one great name for such a transforming quality, and that name is *love*. Love in the Bible is not so much an action of the soul as it is a quality in the soul permitting God to do His divine actions through it. The love of God is the new nature, a new fiber, a new fineness and responsiveness in the soul itself, by which God is able to express Himself upon and through it as He cannot when He finds only the medium of the coarse material of an unloving heart.   —Phillips Brooks

*The Lord lifteth up the meek.*   —Psalm 147:6

# 15

Cruden defines the meek person as one who is "gentle, kind, not easily provoked, ready to yield rather than cause trouble; but not used in the Bible in the bad sense of tamely submissive and servile." The Modern Language Bible translates Psalm 37:11, "But the gentle shall inherit the land and shall delight themselves in plenty of peace." The well-known beatitude of Jesus given in Matthew 5:5 is given the translation, "Blessed are the gentle, for they shall inherit the earth," by this same version of the Bible.

# September

Meekness is gentleness, and gentleness is meekness. Both are love in action, the Christian faith with feet on it. As G. Campbell Morgan once pointed out, "There is yet to be found a man who, out of love to God, will lay his first fruits on the altar, and then oppress another man in poverty and need." That isn't the way it works! A gentle spirit shows itself in loving activity. As Morgan also said, "Men can only live the life that is in harmony with the teaching of Christ as they are possessed and energized by the Holy Spirit of God."

**16** *I obtained mercy, that in me first Jesus Christ might shew forth all longsuffering, for a pattern to them which should hereafter believe on him to life everlasting.* —1 Timothy 1:16

A life need not be great to be beautiful. There may be as much beauty in a tiny flower as in a majestic tree, in a little gem as in a great jewel. A life may be very lovely and yet be insignificant in the world's eyes. A beautiful life is one that fulfils its mission in this world, is that which God made it to be, and does what God made it do. Those with only commonplace gifts are in danger of thinking that they cannot live a beautiful life, cannot be a blessing in this world. But the smallest life that fills its place well is far lovelier in God's sight than the largest and most splendidly gifted, who yet fails of his divine mission.

—E. Matheson

And does not our Master teach us that His service consists not so much in doing as in being? May we not serve Christ in the home-duties and in the so-called "small things" of life? Is not yielding to Christ about things rendering Him a heart-service He values and loves? Truly it is the heart-service He values most.

—Laura A. Barter-Snow

*But put ye on the Lord Jesus Christ, and make not provision for the flesh, to fulfil the lusts thereof.*
—Romans 13:14

**17**

A holy and gentle Christian life is made up of a number of small things! Little words, not eloquent sermons; little deeds, not miracles of battle, nor one great heroic deed of martyrdom; the little constant sunbeam, not the lightning. The avoidance of little evils, little sins, little inconsistencies, little weaknesses, little follies and indiscretions, little indulgences of the flesh; the avoidance of such things make up the beauty of a holy and gentle life.

—Andrew Bonar

An anonymous writer said: "I expect to pass through this world but once; any good thing, therefore, that I can do, or any kindness I can show to my fellow-men, let me do it now; let me not put it off or neglect it, for I shall not pass this way again."

If this is our spirit as we "put on Jesus Christ," our lives will truly reflect His gracious and gentle nature to those around us—in the home and everywhere we go.

*For none of us liveth to himself, and none dieth to himself.* —Romans 14:7

**18**

We must all exert influence, whether we will to do so or not. You influence every man you touch by the way you look at him and speak to him, and all the time the influence you are exerting is welling up out of your actual self, and you cannot prevent it. "Ye are . . . that ye should shew forth the praises of him who hath called you out of darkness into his marvellous light" (1 Pet. 2:9). A most important principle to be perpetually kept in mind by those who would fulfill the highest function of the Christian life is

# September

that the world waits for light; and the Christian's only capacity for shedding the light is that he should live in the day which the face of Christ creates for him. "For none of us lives to himself. . . ." No church and no individual member of the church can fling across the darkness one ray or gleam of light, save as that church or that person lives in the sunshine created by the shining of His face.

—G. Campbell Morgan

**19** *Blessed are they that have not seen, and yet have believed. —John 20:29*

There are those to whom no visions come, no moments upon the mount suffused with a glory that never was on land or sea. Let such people not envy the men of vision. It may be that the vision is given to strengthen a faith that otherwise would be weak. It is to the people who can live along the line of what others call the commonplace, and yet trust, that the Master says, "Blessed."

In view of this truth, says Paul, "Present your bodies a living sacrifice, holy, acceptable unto God, which is your reasonable service" (Rom. 12:1). Such a living sacrifice will indeed cause an aura of gentleness to descend upon the believer in Christ who seeks to allow the fruit of the Spirit to be borne by his life. The divine ideal for man is that he should be spiritual, and that his spirituality should be realized by the surcharging of his whole being with the Spirit of God. —Adapted from G. Campbell Morgan

**20** *Therefore . . . be ye steadfast . . . always abounding in the work of the Lord. —1 Corinthians 15:58*

Did you ever stop to think how dull life would be if you did not have constructive work to do? Granted, some people seem to enjoy their work more than others. Indeed, the work some people must do is just not that enjoyable. But wait a minute; Paul isn't saying here, "*your* work." No, he specifically states his subject as "*the* work of the Lord." Some people are very fortunate in that their work is also the Lord's work. Others are called upon simply to work "for a living," and must draw a line between *their* work and "the Lord's work." But regardless of your occupation in life, there is one broad area where you can be doing "the Lord's work," and that is your involvement in the building of a Christian home. God instituted and blessed marriage, and He ordained it as "the cradle of Christianity," indeed, "the cradle of civilization." Were it not for the Christian home, civilization as we know it would not have survived to our present day. Actually, because of the breakdown of the Christian family, our world is in danger of extinction even now. Your home can be a haven from the chaotic world around you—or it can be a microcosm of the world's problems, depending upon your attitude toward the divine labor of building a truly Christian home—and participating in the whole area of Christian service.

*Let brotherly love continue.*   —Hebrews 13:1

# 21

Love of our neighbor is the only door out of the dungeon of self. The region of man's life is a spiritual region. God, his friends, his neighbors, his brothers all, is the wide world in which alone his spirit can find room. He has not yet learned to love his neighbor as himself whose heart sinks within him at the words, "I say unto you, Love your enemies."   —GEORGE MACDONALD

When we wish to enlarge our coasts, as it were, by taking in greater fields of faith and holiness, patience and hu-

# September

mility, we must cultivate Christian grace as we cultivate bodily strength and skill by exercise, all the while remembering that without God's help and spirit we can do nothing. We must pray for more of Christ's love and life in our daily work and warfare.   —BOYD

**22**   *I Paul myself beseech you by the meekness and gentleness of Christ.... —2 Corinthians 10:1*

Jesus Christ Himself is our Pattern, our Model for gentleness and meekness, these little understood aspects of the fruit of the Spirit. In Romans 12:1, Paul gave the supreme advice on this matter of living the Christ-life: "I appeal to you therefore, brethren, by the mercies of God, to present your bodies as a living sacrifice, holy and acceptable to God, which is your spiritual worship" (RSV). Sacrifice is to be our life style if we are living as Christ would have us live—and this sacrificial attitude does not come naturally. It is one of the fruits of the Spirit-filled life! Our Lord Jesus is often pictured for us as the Lamb of God. Can you think of any creature more gentle and meek than this one? Have you ever seen a lamb fighting for its rights? Have you ever seen a lamb bite one of its fellows in the herd or flock? No, the lamb's nature is one of meekness, gentleness. In ourselves, we could never react this way to outside pressures and problems—but filled with the Lamb's Spirit, we can! Let us yield ourselves to Him and live the *gentle* life.

**23**   *But the wisdom from above is first pure, then peaceable, gentle, open to reason, full of mercy and good fruits, without uncertainty or insincerity.*
*—James 3:17*

These words from James sound very much like a message from Paul. Peter, too, had a way of combining the various gifts or fruits of the Spirit in some of the statements he made: "Having purified your souls by your obedience to the truth for a sincere love of the brethren, love one another earnestly from the heart" (1 Pet. 1:22, RSV). In the thinking of the New Testament writers—men like John, Paul, Peter, James, and others—love lies at the heart of the Christian walk and way of life. And love *does* lie behind the Christian virtues we have been describing in *LoveSongs*. Gentleness is no exception; gentleness finds its roots in love, and its outgrowth in actions. Gentleness is to be a way of life for the Spirit-filled Christian. It is not to be an intermittent, spasmodic kind of activity—but it is to burn steadily and quietly like a candle in a dark room. The child's prayer speaks of "Gentle Jesus, meek and mild." He is our genesis for gentleness, our mindset for meekness. "This is the way," says Jesus, "walk ye in it!"

*Behold, what manner of love the Father hath bestowed upon us, that we should be called the sons of God.* —1 John 3:1

## 24

The slender capacity of man's heart cannot comprehend, much less utter, the unsearchable depth and loving zeal of God's love toward us. He loves even enemies; yes, to the blind, hard world, He sent us a Savior, His own Son.  —MARTIN LUTHER

O Christ, our true and only light,
Illumine them who sit in night!

It is only through our human relationships, through the love and tenderness and purity of mothers, sisters and wives, through the courage, strength and wisdom of fathers and brothers, that we come to the knowledge of Him in whom alone the love and the tenderness, wisdom, strength, courage, and purity of all these dwell forever in perfect fullness.  —T. HUGHES

# September

**25**

*We are God's fellow workers; you are God's field, God's building.* —1 Corinthians 3:9, RSV

"He who labors as he prays lifts his heart to God with his hands," said Bernard of Clairvaux. The King James Version renders the verse, "We are labourers together with God." I like that word "together," and how expressive it is of the marriage bond—togetherness! Not only are we as a couple laborers together *with God*—but we are laborers *together*. It is vital that we realize this dimension of our lives together—the dimension of work. Work has a dignity well expressed by Bernard of Clairvaux in the quote that begins this thought for the day. No marriage can succeed without work. It takes work to make a marriage work! And it takes God at the helm to make a marriage go. Just as a ship without a pilot can go to its death on the rocks, so a marriage without God can be doomed to become wreckage. Put Paul's advice to work in your marriage. Consider yourselves "God's field, God's building," and let God do the planting—and the carpenter work—to make your marriage what He wants it to be.

**26**

*Look not every man on his own things, but every man also on the things of others.* —Philippians 2:4

A beautiful story is told of the Agassiz brothers. Their home was in Switzerland on the shore of a lake. One winter day the father was on the other side of the lake, and the boys wanted to join him. The lake was covered with thick ice. The mother watched as the boys set out. They got on well until they came to a wide crack in the ice. Then they stopped, and the mother became very anxious, fearing they might be drowned. The older boy jumped over easily, but the little one was afraid. Then, as she looked, she saw Louis, the older brother, get down on his face, his body stretched over the crack, making a bridge of himself, and then she saw his little brother creep over him. This story is a beautiful parable of love. We should be willing to make bridges of ourselves on which others may pass over the chasms and the streams that hinder them in their way. We have many opportunities to do this in helping our brothers over the hard places, out of temptation, through sickness, or in some other better way of living. It is not pleasant to lie down on the ice, or in the wet, and let another use us as a bridge; but Christ did it. His cross was just a laying of His own blessed self over the awful chasm of death and despair, that we might pass over Him into joy and hope and heaven. He endured the cross, despising the shame, that He might save us. We cannot call ourselves Christians if we balk or falter or hesitate to endure suffering, loss, or shame, to help others. "He that saveth his life shall lose it."   —J. R. MILLER

*Yield your members as instruments of righteousness*
*unto God.* —Romans 6:13

## 27

The very way in which we close a door or lay down a book may be a victory or a defeat; a witness to Christ's keeping, or a witness that we are not being truly kept. How can we expect that God will use this instrument of righteousness unto Him, if we yield it thus as an instrument of unrighteousness to sin? Therefore let us see to it, that it is at once yielded to Him whose right it is, and let our sorrow that it should have been for an instant desecrated to Satan's use, lead us to entrust it henceforth to our Lord, to be kept by the power of God through faith "for the Master's use." For when the gentleness of Christ dwells in us, He can use the merest touch of a finger. Have we not heard of one touch on a wayward shoulder being a turning point in a life?   —E. MATHESON

# September

**28** *And the servant of the Lord must not strive; but be gentle unto all men.* —2 Tim. 2:24

In the later days of Grecian art, a prize was offered for the best statue of one of the goddesses. A youth in the country who loved this goddess set to work to compete for the prize. But he lacked the artist's gift and experience, and his statue was crude and clumsy, far from beautiful. It seemed to have no chance at all for winning the prize. But the goddess, so the heathen legend runs, knowing of the sincere devotion of this youth to her and his love for her, when the time came for the display of the statues in the competition, entered herself into the crude stone, and at once it glowed with divine beauty, by far the most beautiful of all the statues, winning the prize.

We Christians are called to show the world the beauty of Christ, to reproduce the glory of His life, not in cold marble, but in Christian character, in Christian spirit, and in Christian service. In our weakness, and faultiness, it may seem to us we cannot do anything, that our life and work are unworthy of the holy name we bear. Our best seems most unlovely, crude, faulty, imperfect; but if we truly love Christ, if we truly believe on Him, and if at His command we strive to do what seems impossible, Christ Himself, knowing our love and seeing our gentleness, will enter into our life and fill it with Himself. Then our poor efforts will become radiant and divine in their beauty.

—J. R. MILLER

**29** *Put them in mind ... To speak evil of no man, to be no brawlers, but gentle, shewing all meekness unto all men.* —Titus 3:1, 2

There are some Christians who, by reason of their beautiful life, sweet spirit, and noble faithfulness, make us instinctively think of Christ. One said of another, "You have only to shake hands with that man to feel that he is a follower of Christ." A little child, when asked if he knew about Jesus, said, "Yes, he lives on our street." There was someone the child knew who was so beautiful in spirit, so gentle, so kind, that he visioned for the child's thought of Christ. You know such a person, in whose presence you could not do anything false, or mean, or wrong.

—J. R. MILLER

What kind of a reflector of the Holy Spirit am I?

*In lowliness of mind, let each esteem other better* **30**
*than themselves.* —Philippians 2:3

Here is an excellent code of conduct for building a solid marriage. And your marriage *is* a "building," one that can be weakened by the materials you put into it. St. Augustine said: "Do you wish to be great? Then begin by being. Do you desire to construct a vast and lofty fabric? Think first about the foundations of humility. The higher your structure is to be, the deeper must be its foundation." How high do you want your marriage to go, in terms of its quality and content? If both members of the marriage bond consider the "other better" than himself or herself, the result will be pride's pitfalls missed, and love's loftiness gained. John Bunyan, noted for his *Pilgrim's Progress*, left us a wise quatrain:

> He that is down, needs fear no fall;
> He that is low, no pride;
> He that is humble ever shall
> Have God to be his Guide.

If you put humility into your marriage, you'll be able to take out happiness!

# October

*The fruit of the Spirit is ... temperance. ...*
—Galatians 5:22–23

*When he was accused of the chief priests and el-
ders, he answered nothing. Then said Pilate unto
him, Hearest thou not how many things they witness against thee? And he answered him to never a
word.* —Matthew 27:12-14

Temperance is self-control. And Jesus is the ultimate,
the epitome of self-control! He is our Pattern and Model
in this matter of spiritual fruit-bearing. In our passage for
today, Jesus did not answer when Pilate gave Him opportunity to rebut His accusers. Earlier, before Caiaphas, the
high priest, He had also refused to defend Himself or at-
tack His accusers (Matt. 26:63). John 19:9 also recounts the
silence of Jesus in the face of His accusers: "[Pilate] went
again into the judgment hall, and saith unto Jesus,
Whence art thou? But Jesus gave him no answer."

I'm Irish, and I tend to become quite voluble if I feel
someone is taking advantage of me—or of one of my loved
ones. I think Jewish men, too, tend to become rather ex-
cited and outspoken in similar situations. But Jesus, man
though He was, was God. He was in complete control of
Himself—and of every situation. How can this same selfless Spirit operate in the life of the believer today? J. R.
Miller tells of a Christian who had been wronged by another man. One day the second man came to the Christian
for help. He had appealed to others, but they had refused
to do anything for him. Even his own brothers and sisters
had turned away from him. All the world had grown tired
of helping him; no one was left. When the appeal came to

# October

the Christian man to relieve his distress, the Christian could have demanded a confession of the grievous wrong done him, an apology at the least. But he demanded nothing. Rather, quietly and at great cost to himself, he cheerfully gave the help that was needed. Said J. R. Miller of this man: "See the print of the nails in his hands!" This is Christian self-control in action!

## 2

*Let your light so shine before men...*
—Matthew 5:16

Did you ever stand at the foot of a great lighthouse at night? Through brilliant lenses splendid floods of light were poured out to sea; but not one tiny gleam of radiance did that great lamp pour on the bit of sand close around the base of its tower. Do not be like lighthouses in this regard. Wherever else, far away or near, you pour the beams of your Christian life, be sure you brighten the space close about you in your own home. Let the light of gentleness, forbearance, kindness, unselfishness, and thoughtful ministry fall on the life next to yours—parents, brothers, sisters, the husband or wife God has given you. Carry Christ home and serve Him best there.    —J. R. MILLER

## 3

*And the man said, The woman whom thou gavest me....*    —Genesis 3:12

It is hard to admit that we are wrong. How easy to say "The woman, the serpent, my temperament, my circumstances!" Few things more clearly reveal our self-love and pride than this instinctive, automatic excuse-making. We thoroughly understand the lawyer who asked the question, "And who is my neighbor?" wishing to justify himself. There is little hope for our growth in virtue, unless we make up our minds frankly to admit the truth about ourselves, no matter how it hurts. No man can afford to play ostrich. Self-deception is seldom genuine, and conscious duplicity ruins the deceiver. "We can do nothing against the truth, but for the truth." To acknowledge our mistakes is not only wise, and indicates an advance in self-knowledge, but it means self-mastery, spiritual victory. When we pull up a weed, we leave a clean place for a flower.

—MALTBIE D. BABCOCK

*All things work together for good to them that love God.* —Romans 8:28

**4**

Can we include our mistakes and sins in the "all things" that work together for good? Certainly, if we belong to God, if love and loyalty to Him are our heart's determination, if we have purposed to press toward the mark of His high calling in Christ Jesus. The pride and self-confidence of Peter were weakness, and were breaking him down as a disciple, but when he yielded himself to the Spirit of Christ, they became self-knowledge, self-distrust, self-hatred, and the occasion and demands for divine power. The lives of St. Augustine, John Newton, Jerry McAuley, and other men saved from lives of deep sin, prove that the God of transmutation, who taught us to bring brilliant dyes, healing remedies, exquisite perfumes, from waste coal-tar, can transform the character that is put in His hands and make a repudiated past thrillingly vital in the sympathy and pity, fidelity and love, of a beautiful and fruitful future. —MALTBIE D. BABCOCK

*And the king's servants said unto the king, Behold, thy servants are ready to do whatsoever my lord the king shall appoint.* —2 Samuel 15:15

**5**

What a declaration of unlimited loyalty David's servants were making here to their earthly king. No, this was more than loyalty—it was love. Do you love your heavenly

# October

King enough to make a similarly unstinting commitment to Him? Before we can become Christ's true disciples, we must reach this point of complete committal to Him, giving up all claim to directing our own lives and turning all over to Him. David's people were giving up all rights to self-government when they made this pledge to him; if we are to be Christ's true followers, we can retain no rights to ourselves. This is what Jesus was saying in Luke 14:33: "Whosoever he be of you that forsaketh not all that he hath, he cannot be my disciple." Included in discipleship are elements of learning and self-denial, even to the point of forsaking earthly loved ones if allegiance to them comes between us and our Lord. This is why it is so important in the marriage relationship for both partners to put Christ first. There is no doubt that Jesus loved His mother deeply, but when faced with following His Father's will, even He was forced to put His feelings for her aside and take the path God had for Him to tread, giving her over into the care of others. Are you willing to do that—to put your loved one second to your loving allegiance to Christ? Bernard of Clairvaux said it well: "The true measure of loving God is to love him without measure."

## 6

*My God shall be my strength.* —Isaiah 49:5

For years you have lived, it may be, a secluded and protected life. "Lead me not into temptation"—so you have prayed every morning, and every day has brought the answer to your prayer. But some day all that breaks and goes to pieces. A great temptation comes, and is not overcome. Then you cry out for the old mercy, and it is not given. . . . And then, behold what comes! A new mercy! You go into the temptation. Your old security perishes, but by-and-by out of its death comes a new strength. Not to be saved from dying, but to die and then to live again in a new security, a strong and trusty character, educated by trial, purified by fire—that is what comes as the issue of the whole. Not a victory for you from danger, but a victory in you, strengthening you by danger—that is the experience from which you go forth, strong with the strength which *nothing* can subdue.   —PHILLIPS BROOKS

*I being in the way, the Lord led me . . .*
                    —Genesis 24:27
*For the Lord knoweth the way of the right-*
*eous. . . .*   —Psalm 1:6

**7**

If a marriage, even though "made in heaven," is to succeed, there must be agreement between the partners as to the one who is to lead the way. You probably think that, being a man, I am about to recommend the man take the responsibility for leadership. After all, what do we do with the passage in Ephesians 5:22–24? "Wives, submit yourselves unto your own husbands, as unto the Lord. For the husband is the head of the wife, even as Christ is the head of the Church: and he is the saviour of the body. Therefore as the church is subject unto Christ, so let the wives be to their own husbands in everything." But look at verses 21 and 25: "Submitting yourselves one to another. . . . Husbands, love your wives, even as Christ also loved the church." It almost seems that Paul is contradicting himself, calling for the partners in the marriage relationship to submit themselves to one another, but note that we are to submit ourselves, this new entity formed by our union as man and wife, to the Lordship and leadership of our heavenly Guide. Our responsibility is to be "in the way," to be clothed in His righteousness. Our basic commitment as a couple must be to follow His leadership, both of us making Him Lord of our lives. In this "divine triangle" lies the secret of a happy marriage!

# October

**8**     *And forgive us our debts, as we forgive our debt-
ors.*   —Matthew 6:12

In the model prayer which Christ gave to His disciples,
He linked together the divine and the human forgiveness.
While we pray to God to forgive our countless and enor-
mous sins, we are taught to extend to others who harm us
in little ways the same forgiveness which we ask for ourselves. Let us keep no bitterness in our hearts for a moment. Let us put away all grudges and all ill feelings. Let
us remember the good things others do to us and forget
the bad things. Then we can pray sincerely, "Forgive us as
we forgive." If we cannot do this, I do not know how we
are going to pray at all for forgiveness.   —J. R. MILLER

**9**     *And he said unto them, Come ye yourselves apart
into a desert place, and rest a while: for there were
many coming and going, and they had no leisure so
much as to eat.*   —Mark 6:31

It is a law of nature that we get out of life pretty much
what we put into it. As Jesus said, "We reap what we
sow." In our modern day, there seems to be a tendency to
try to cram into each day as many activities as possible,
"burning the candle at both ends" today, thinking we can
catch up on our sleep tomorrow. This same problem of
overactivity was present in Jesus' day, and among His disciples at that! How ironic! In calling people to Him Jesus
had said, "Come unto me . . . and I will give you rest." Instead, because of His popularity, our text tells us there
were so many people coming and going that the disciples
didn't even have time to eat, let alone rest.

So Jesus issues another "come" invitation. Notice He
doesn't say, "Go and rest." No, He is with them in this situation and will stay with them. That is the beauty of the

Christian life, even when it gets hectic—even then He is with us. But He wants us to use good judgment, too. Control your activities and balance them with the right amount of rest and recreation. This makes for a good marriage as well!

*Or how can you say to your brother, "let me take* **10**
*the speck out of your eye," when there is the log in*
*your own eye?* —Matthew 7:4, RSV

It is strange how oblivious we can be to our own faults and to the blemishes in our own characters, and how clearly we can see the faults and blemishes of other people. Finding so much wrong in others is not a flattering indication of what our hearts contain. We ought to be quiet and hesitant in criticizing others, for in most cases we are just telling the world what our own faults are. Before we turn our microscopes on others to search out the unbeautiful things in them, we had better look in our mirrors to see whether or not we are free ourselves from the blemishes we would condemn in our neighbor. There is a wise word in the Scriptures which bids us get clear of the "beams" in our own eyes, that we may see well to pick the "motes" or specks out of the eyes of others.

—J. R. MILLER

*From this day will I bless you.* —Haggai 2:19 **11**

The Jews, having returned from their captivity, set themselves to work to build again the temple, which not only met with God's approval, but led Him to say through the prophet Haggai: "From this day will I bless you." But this is one of the gracious acts our loving Lord ever de-

# October

lights in performing. Nothing pleases Him more than creating opportunities in which He can come and bless us. If we will but comply with certain conditions, we may hear His "still, small voice" whispering in our heart every morning: "This day will I bless thee." Now, what are these conditions? Perhaps this question may be answered in one sentence—*subjection at all times to the will of God.* He knows what is best for us, and His will concerning us is our peace, joy, happiness, holiness, and usefulness. Therefore, whether our path, for the time being, be rough or smooth, difficult or easy, painful or pleasant, we must resolve, by His grace, to say: "Thy will, not mine be done." And this perfect and perpetual subjection to His will will keep us in that condition which will make it possible for God to say: "This day will I bless you."  —John Roberts

**12**    *He went out, not knowing whither. . . .*
                        —Hebrews 11:8

Abram began his journey without any knowledge of his ultimate destination. He obeyed a noble impulse without any discernment of its consequences. He took "one step," and he did not ask "to see the distant scene." And that is faith, to do God's will here and now, quietly leaving the results to Him. Faith is not concerned with the entire chain; its devoted attention is fixed upon the immediate link. Faith is not knowledge of a moral process; it is fidelity in a moral act. Faith leaves something to the Lord; it obeys His immediate commandment and leaves to Him direction and destiny. And so faith is accompanied by serenity and self-control. "He that believeth shall not make haste"—or more literally, "shall not get into a fuss." He shall not get into a panic, neither fetching fears from his yesterdays nor from his tomorrows. Concerning his tomorrows, faith says, "Thou hast beset me before." Concerning his today, faith says, "Thou hast laid Thine hand upon me." That is enough, just to feel the pressure of the guiding hand.   —J. H. JOWETT

*Master, carest thou not that we perish?*
           —Mark 4:38

# 13

Jesus is the Christ who is in control of the crisis. And everyone, Christian or not, must face crisis times in life. In this case, the disciples feared for their lives, for the waves were filling their boat. And these were seasoned fishermen, Peter among them, who knew the sea and were used to its raging. It must have been some storm! But Jesus, weary from a strenuous day of teaching the multitudes, was peacefully asleep in the stern of the ship. How could He be so unconcerned? Isn't He Master of it all? Why should Creator fear His creation? Panic and petulance combined to cause the disciples to ask almost insolently: "Carest thou not that we perish?" Momentarily, at least, they doubted Him and let that doubt creep into their reactions. But He did not rebuke them, we read; He rebuked the storm and it was stilled. *Then* He rebuked them, asking: "Why are you afraid? Have you no faith?" Petrified Peter deserved harsher rebuke than that, but the loving Savior mildly reminded His followers that He is in charge after all. As Scroggie says, "A storm with Christ is better than a calm without Him." You can face the storms of life if the Master of the storm is your Savior!

*Ye shall ask in my name . . . for the Father himself
loveth you, because ye have loved me.*
           —John 16:26–27

# 14

It is he who gives himself to let the love of God dwell in him, and in the practice of daily life to love as God loves, who will have the power to believe in the love that will

# October

hear his every prayer. It is the Lamb who is in the midst of
the throne; it is suffering and forbearing love that prevails
with God in prayer.   —ANDREW MURRAY

> He prayeth well who loveth well
>    Both man, and bird, and beast,
> He prayeth best who loveth best,
>    All things both great and small
> For the same God who loveth us,
>    He made and loveth all.
>                    —COLERIDGE

**15**   *Yea, Lord; I believe that thou art the Christ, the Son
of God, which should come into the world.*
                                        —John 11:27

The only noble sense in which we can claim to believe a
thing is when we ourselves are living in the inner spirit of
that thing. I have no right to say I believe in God unless I
order my life as under His all-seeing eye. I have no right to
say I believe that Jesus is the Son of God unless in my personal life I yield myself to that Eternal Spirit, free from all
self-seeking, which became incarnate in Jesus.

I have no right to say that I believe in forgiveness as an
attribute of God if in my own heart I cherish an unforgiv-
ing temper. The forgiveness of God is the test by which I
myself am judged. Belief is wholesale committal; it means
making things inevitable, cutting off every possible re-
treat. Belief is as irrevocable as bereavement (cf. 2 Sam.
12:21–23). Belief is abandonment of all claim to merit.
That is why it is so difficult to believe. A believer is one
whose whole being is based on the finished work of
Redemption. . . . The greatest challenge to a Christian is
to believe Matthew 28:18: "All power is given unto me in
heaven and in earth." How many of us get into a panic
when we are faced by physical desolation, death, war, in-

justice, poverty, or disease? All these in all their force will never turn to panic the one who believes in the absolute sovereignty of his Lord.  —OSWALD CHAMBERS

*What? know ye not that your body is the temple of the Holy Ghost which is in you, which ye have of God, and ye are not your own?*
—1 Corinthians 6:19

**16**

The indwelling of the Holy Spirit is the climax of Redemption. The great impelling power of the Holy Spirit is seen in its most fundamental working whenever an issue of will is pushed. It is more pleasant to listen to poetical discourses, more agreeable to have your natural likings appealed to, but it is not good enough, it leaves you exactly where you were. The gospel appeal comes with a stinging grip—"Will you?" or "Won't you?" "I will accept," or "I'll put it off"—both are decisions, remember. We have to distinguish between acquiring and receiving. We *acquire* habits of prayer and Bible reading, and we *receive* our salvation, we receive the Holy Spirit, we receive the grace of God. We give more attention to the things we acquire; all God pays attention to is what we receive. Those things we receive can never be taken from us because God holds those who receive His gifts. The fruit of "pseudo-evangelism" is different from "the fruit of the Spirit" (Gal. 5:22–23).  —OSWALD CHAMBERS

*And they took knowledge of them, that they had been with Jesus.* —Acts 4:13

**17**

Luke is writing here about two men, Peter and John. In the eyes of the beholders (the Sanhedrin, chief priests, elders and scribes), these disciples of Jesus were "uneducated, common" men, that is, unschooled in theology and un-

# October

trained in any professional or scholarly capacity. Because of their wisdom and boldness, and Peter's remarkably well-argued and logical defense of the Christian faith before the Sanhedrin, they "marvelled" ("were amazed," TLB; "wondered," RSV) and recognized that they had been with Jesus. Luke explains the phenomenal power of the apostles in Acts 4:31, "When they had prayed, the place in which they were gathered together was shaken; and they were filled with the Holy Spirit and spoke the word of God with boldness" (RSV). Paul tells us what had happened: "God chose what is foolish in the world to shame the wise, God chose what is weak in the world to shame the strong..." (1 Cor. 1:27). The secret strength of the apostles lay in their relationship to Christ, their astonishing wisdom came from the Holy Spirit who filled and controlled them. This same strength and wisdom is available to you from the same Source. Remember, the Holy Spirit can fill your marriage with His love and wisdom, so that you, too, will have the reputation of having "been with Jesus." This is practical holiness in action.

**18**     *For in him we live, and move, and have our being.* —Acts 17:28

If we are irritable, sour, easily provoked, bad-tempered, resentful, envious, rude in any way, what sort of impression of Christ do we give to those who know nothing of Him save what they learn from our lives? And what kind of fragrance do our lives have for those who are our fellow-Christians? Surely if we love Christ truly we will not dishonor Him by living a life so unworthy of His name. Whatever we may do for Christ, in gifts to His cause or work in His service, if we fail to live out His life of sweet patience and forbearance, we fail in an essential area of our duty as Christians. —J. R. MILLER

*For whom he did foreknow, he also did predestinate to be conformed to the image of his Son, that he might be the firstborn among many brethren.*
—Romans 8:29

**19**

God has a plan for our lives, for each individual life. There is something special that He made us for; He has a thought in mind for us, something He wants us to be and to do. Now we can never be what God wants us to be except by doing His will day by day. Disobedience or lack of submission at any point will mar the perfection of His plan for us. We know that whatever He wills for us is for us the highest possible good. God's will for us is always blessing. It will lead us at every step in the best way home. It will fashion in us each day a little more fully the image of Christ. —J. R. MILLER

*Every man that striveth for the mastery is temperate.* —1 Corinthians 9:25

**20**

Paul used many metaphors in his writings to the early church, and one of his favorites was likening the Christian life to a foot-race, an athletic contest. The Revised Standard Version translates the above verse, "Every *athlete* exercises self-control in all things." Have you ever considered yourself a Christian athlete? In Ephesians 6:12, Paul uses a similar metaphor, this time comparing the Christian life to a battle: "For we wrestle not against flesh and blood, but against principalities, against powers, against the rulers of the darkness of this world, against spiritual wickedness in high places." When he wrote to his spiritual son, Timothy, he urged: "Fight the good fight of faith . . ." (1 Tim. 6:12). As Maltbie D. Babcock pointed out: "Life and character tend either upward or downward, but a single act or characteristic may not indicate the tendency of life as a whole. Esau eclipsed Jacob at first, but his

# October

virtues were accidents, incidents, without roots, and they withered before the hot tests of life. Jacob outshone Esau at the last. Day by day he fought his natural badness, and won in the hard struggle with himself. The mean supplanter Jacob became the hero Israel, a prince with God. Is it thy will or my will be done? Are we living to please God or ourselves? Our answer to this question determines our life-current."

**21**
*For the love of Christ constraineth us; because we thus judge, that if one died for all, then were all dead.... —2 Corinthians 5:14*
*I am crucified with Christ: nevertheless I live; yet not I, but Christ liveth in me: and the life which I now live in the flesh I live by the faith of the Son of God, who loved me, and gave himself for me.*
*—Galatians 5:20*

There is a direct relationship between loving and living emphasized in these two excerpts from the pen of Paul. If we are truly "constrained" ("controlled," RSV) by the love of Christ, that conviction will reflect itself in the way we live. This verse comes at the end of Paul's ringing defense of his apostolic commission and ministry, just a few verses before his classic description of the conversion experience: "Therefore if any man be in Christ, he is a new creature: old things are passed away; behold, all things are become new" (2 Cor. 5:17). This "newness" should so characterize our walk that we can truly say with Paul, "For to me to live is Christ!" God has a unique plan for each of our lives as Christians, and that plan is that we should glorify Him. As the catechism tells us, our purpose in life is to "glorify God and enjoy Him forever." This is the kind of selfless, loving living that Horatius Bonar a century ago was calling for when he wrote:

> He liveth long who liveth well!
> All other life is short and vain;

He liveth longest who can tell
Of living most for heavenly gain.

Loving and living. They go together if we are living for
Christ!

*But first gave their own selves to the Lord.*
　　　—2 Corinthians 8:5

**22**

The world asks, "How much does he give?"
Christ asks, "Why does he give?"
　　　—JOHN RALEIGH MOTT

Your attitude toward God will determine your attitude
toward one another. If you as an individual can put God
first in your life, then you can also put your marriage partner ahead of yourself in your marriage. If, however, you
have difficulty putting God first in your life, then you will
find it impossible to put any other human being before
yourself.

But today's verse suggests an even greater dimension of
dedication. There is no greater joy in married life than to
kneel with the loved one God has given you and jointly
dedicate yourselves, your marriage, to His service and to
His glory. Once this dedication has genuinely taken place,
the "pressure to perform" is eased. If God is truly first, the
selfishness that sometimes crops up (and can ruin a marriage), doesn't stand a chance to survive in the rarefied atmosphere of unselfish love. First, give yourselves to the
Lord, and see what a difference dedication makes!

*They . . . first gave their own selves to the Lord.*
　　　—2 Corinthians 8:5

**23**

Consecration is not so much a step as a course; not so
much an act, as a position to which a course of action in-
separably belongs. In so far as it is a course and a position,

there must naturally be a definite entrance upon it, and a time, it may be a moment, when that entrance is made. That is when we say, "Take"; but we do not want to go on taking a first step over and over again. What we want now is to be maintained in that position, and to fulfill that course. So let us go on to another prayer. Having already said, "Take my life, for I cannot give it to thee," let us now say, with deepened conviction, that without Christ we really can do nothing—"*Keep my life, for I cannot keep it for Thee*." This is the confidence we have in Him, that if we ask anything according to His will, He hears us; and if we know that He hears us, whatever we ask, we know that we have the petitions we desired of Him. Yes, He who is able and willing to take unto Himself, is no less able and willing to keep for Himself. Our willing offering has been made by His enabling grace, and this our King has seen with joy. And now we pray, "Keep this forever in the imagination of the thoughts of the heart of thy people" (1 Chron. 29:18).   —FRANCES RIDLEY HAVERGAL

**24**   *Trust . . . in the Living God.*   —1 Timothy 6:17

What a long time it takes us to come down to the conviction, and still more to the realization that without Him we can do nothing, but that He must work all our works in us! This is the work of God, that we believe in Him whom He has sent. And no less must it be the work of God that we go on believing, and that we go on trusting. So, dear friends, longing to trust Him with unbroken and unwavering trust, cease the effort and drop the burden, and entrust your trust to Him! He is just as well able to keep that as any other part of the complex lives which we want Him to take and keep for Himself. . . . Consecration is not a religiously selfish thing. If it sinks into that, it ceases to be consecration. We want our lives kept, not that we may feel happy and be saved, and get the power with God and man, and all the other privileges linked with it. We shall have all this, because the lower is included with the higher; but our true aim, if the love of Christ constrains us, will be far beyond this. We will want . . . to be kept for Him, that He may do just what seems good to Him with me; kept that no other Lord shall have any more dominion over me, but that Jesus will have all there is to have—little enough, indeed, but not divided or diminished by any other claim.   —FRANCES RIDLEY HAVERGAL

*In whom all the building fitly framed together grow-eth unto an holy temple in the Lord.*
                                    —Ephesians 2:21

# 25

In the early days, a stage-driver had held the lines for many years, and when he grew old his hands were crooked into hooks, and his fingers were so stiffened they could not be straightened out. There is a similar process which goes on in men's souls when they continue to do the same things over and over. One who is trained from childhood to be gentle, kindly, patient, to control the temper, to speak softly, to be loving and charitable, will grow into the radiant beauty of love. One who accustoms himself to think habitually and only of noble and worthy things, who sets his affections on things above, and strives to reach "whatsoever things are true, whatsoever things are honest, . . . pure, . . . lovely," will grow continually upward toward spiritual beauty. But on the other hand, if one gives way from childhood to all ugly tempers, all resentful feelings, all bitterness and anger, his life will shape itself in the un-beauty of all these dispositions. One whose mind turns to debasing things, unholy things, unclean, will find his whole soul growing toward earth in a permanent curva-ture.   —J. R. MILLER

# October

How is your soul growing?

## 26

*The kingdom of God is within you.* —Luke 17:21

"The kingdom of God is within you," says the Lord. Turn with your whole heart unto the Lord (Joel 2:12), and forsake this evil world, and your soul shall find rest. Learn to despise outward things, and to give yourself wholly to things inward, and you will perceive the kingdom of God coming in you. "For the kingdom of God is . . . peace, and joy in the Holy Ghost" (Rom. 14:17), which is not given to the unholy. Christ will come unto you, and show you His consolation, if you make ready a place for Him in your heart. All His glory and beauty are from within (Ps. 14:13), and there He delights Himself. The inward man He often visits; and He has with Him sweet conversation, pleasant comfort, much peace, and comfortable familiarity. O faithful soul! make ready your heart for this Bridegroom, that He may condescend to come unto you and dwell within you. —Thomas à Kempis

## 27

*Let your moderation be known unto all men.*
—Philippians 4:5

This admonition from the pen of Paul follows hard on the heels of his well-known plea to "Rejoice in the Lord always: and again I say, Rejoice" (4:4). There must be some connection between rejoicing and self-control (temperance). If the crowning characteristic of our lives is an overwhelming attitude of joy in all the Savior shares with us, we will find our souls immersed in that spirit, making it much easier to cope with the frustrations and problems, the difficulties and dangers that come our way. Thus "our moderation will be made known unto all men." Matthew Henry says of this passage: "We are here exhorted to gentleness toward our brethren: *'Let your moderation be known to all men. . . . In things indifferent do not run into extremes; judge charitably concerning one another.'* Some understand it of the patient bearing of afflictions, or the sober enjoyment of worldly good." As our lives echo this moderation and self-control, it will be easier and more natural for us to share our faith with those around us. When they see by our lives that "we have been with Jesus," they will find the same desire to know Him in their hearts.

*[Add] to knowledge temperance; and to temperance patience.* —2 Peter 1:6

## 28

In this passage temperance (moderation or self-control) is surrounded by knowledge and patience. The thrust here is that self-knowledge will lead to an ability to endure whatever comes. In His Olivet discourse Jesus said, "By your endurance you will gain your lives" (Luke 21:19). And in the message to the Ephesian church recorded in Revelation 2, Jesus said, "To him who conquers I will grant to eat of the tree of life, which is in the paradise of God" (v. 7, RSV). Here again the idea of self-control is related to that quaility or ability to endure testing and to come out on top. Endurance, and self-knowledge in it, is one of the fruits of the Spirit. Dealing with John 20:28, "My Lord and my God," G. Campbell Morgan made this observation: "The Lordship of Jesus is the basis of all Christian life. The Christian graces and virtues all spring from the recognition of that Lordship, and from absolute surrender thereto." Surrender is the key to victory in the Christian life. Temperance is but another instance of this victory.

*Submitting yourselves one to another in the fear of God.* —Ephesians 5:21

## 29

The Revised Standard Version gives this verse as: "Be subject to one another out of reverence for Christ." Paul is not talking just to the early church here, he is beginning a paragraph of precepts for the Christian household—a recipe, if you will, for happy homes. There is almost the connotation of "slavery" in this word, "subject," but Jesus Himself submitted or subjected Himself to His earthly parents, Joseph and Mary. Jacques Bénigne Bossuet says: "Thirty years of our Lord's life are hidden in these words of the gospel: 'He was subject unto them.'" Jesus, the Divine Redeemer, our Creator and Sustainer, was willing to subject Himself. If it worked for Him, doesn't it make sense for your marriage as well? Daniel Wilson has said: "God is too great to be withstood, too just to do wrong, too good to delight in any one's misery; we ought, therefore, quietly to submit to His dispensations as the very best." Submit one to another, but both to God!

**30** *Put ye on the Lord Jesus Christ, and make not provision for the flesh, to fulfill the lusts thereof.*
—Romans 13:14

Fruit-bearing for the Christian, while it is the work of the Holy Spirit, is not a passive inactivity that does nothing of itself. Paul here tells us to "Put . . . . on the Lord Jesus Christ," a definite act of our own wills. This "putting on" is part of being temperate or self-controlled. In two of his other epistles, Paul calls for active, involved Christianity: "Put on the new man, which after God is created in righteousness and true holiness" (Eph. 4:24); "Walk in the Spirit, and ye shall not fulfill the lust of the flesh" (Gal. 5:16). Your life style will determine whether the flesh or the Spirit has the predominance. Maltbie D. Babcock gives us the insight: "Jesus' aim was not to get His followers out of the world, but to get them into the world. Society, not solitude, is the natural home of Christianity. The Christian is not to flee from the contagion of evil, but to meet it with the contact of health and happiness. The church is not to be built on glass posts for moral insulation, but among the homes of common men for moral transformation. What use is light under a bushel? It must shine where there is darkness. The place of need is the field of duty, and though we are not to be of the world, we are to be first and last in the world and for the world."

*The entrance of thy words giveth light; it giveth understanding unto the simple.* —Psalm 119:130

**31**

Who wouldn't opt for understanding? Solomon did, and in Proverbs 6:23 he says, "For the commandment is a lamp; and the law is light." His father, King David, pointed out: "The law of the Lord is perfect, converting the soul: the testimony of the Lord is sure, making wise the simple. The statutes of the Lord are right, rejoicing the heart: the commandment of the Lord is pure, enlightening the eyes" (Ps. 19:7-8). Earlier in Psalm 119 (v. 99) the psalmist said, "I have more understanding than all my teachers: for thy testimonies are my meditation."

Where can understanding be found? The Word of God looked at through the eyes of faith can make the most unschooled and ignorant wiser than the most learned theologian who lacks the eyes of faith. As St. Augustine said, "Understanding is the reward of faith. Therefore seek not to understand that thou mayest believe, but believe that thou mayest understand." Centuries later, Thomas à Kempis said, "Were the works of God readily understandable by human reason, they would be neither wonderful nor unspeakable."

Do you want understanding to help you cope with the complex and complicated world around you? Seek it in God and meditation upon His Word. Meditation may be a lost art—but it is discoverable if you earnestly and in faith seek after it.

# November

*And the Lord was with Joseph, and he was a prosperous man. . . . And his master saw that the Lord was with Joseph, and that the Lord made all that he did to prosper in his hand.* —Genesis 39:2-3

We hear a great deal these days about the concept of "open marriage," meaning a certain freedom in the marriage relationship not typical of the marriages of an earlier day, supposedly a freedom to realize one's full potential as a person that has not been part of the traditional concept of marriage. Well, I think I would prefer a "prosperous" marriage, comparable to Joseph's designation here as a "prosperous" man. What was the secret of Joseph's prosperity? "The Lord was with Joseph!"

I would make it my prayer today that the Lord would prosper my marriage, that He would make "all that [we do] to prosper." I'm not thinking so much of material prosperity—I am mainly concerned about our growth as persons, as members of the body of Christ doing His bidding. Earlier in Genesis (21:22), the sacred writer has King Abimelech and his captain say of Abraham, "God is with thee in all that thou doest." Later, in Genesis 26:28, this same Abimelech says of Isaac, "We saw certainly that the Lord was with thee." So a pattern emerges here. The Lord was with His children, and He is with them today as well. His is the blessing I want. That's prosperous marriage!

> If every home were an altar,
> Where hearts weighed down with care
> Could find sustaining strength and grace
> In sweet uplift of prayer,
> Then solved would be earth's problems,
> Banished sin's curse and blight;
> For God's own love would radiate
> From every altar light. —Author Unknown

# November

**2**

*He that hath clean hands, and a pure heart; who hath not lifted up his soul unto vanity, nor sworn deceitfully. He shall receive the blessing from the Lord, and righteousness from the God of his salvation.* —Psalm 24:4-5

The probing words of this Psalm might be subtitled "Prayer for a Wedding." If the positive virtues listed in verse 4 are characteristic of the couple who are saying their vows, then the benediction of verse 5 will prove out in the practical day-by-day interaction of married life. Purity and cleanliness are to be more than physical traits; they are to be spiritual attributes as well. If they operate in a marriage relationship and a home situation, then God's blessing and His righteousness will run rampant in that home. Someone has said, "To Adam paradise was home." But he lost that through his own negligence. However, the opposite side of the coin reads, "To the good among his descendants, home is paradise." If you want that kind of a home, make the Lord its head, and yourself His obedient servant. You cannot outgive God!

**3**

*The people became impatient in the way.* —Numbers 21:4, RSV

The King James Version of this verse describes the people as "discouraged" with God and Moses. You and I, too, tend toward discouragement when the way is rough and hard—and as these people did, we usually blame the other guy—God, or in this case, Moses. Into every life and every marriage, some discouragement and impatience is bound to come. How you handle it can make all the difference.

Isaiah knew about this problem. Indeed, he experienced it firsthand, and he has the answer for us from the Lord Himself: "In returning and rest shall ye be saved; in quietness and in confidence shall be your strength" (30:15). Ear-

# November

lier in his message to the Israelites Isaiah shared the Lord's counsel: "Take heed, and be quiet; fear not, neither be fainthearted . . ." (7:4). He drives home his point with quiet confidence in 32:17, "The work of righteousness shall be peace; and the effect of righteousness quietness and assurance for ever."

Discouraged and impatient with God? Or with your loved one? Take God's remedy for discouragement—a spiritual "R & R"! Return to the God of your salvation and rest in the assurance of His care and keeping. The result will be a conquering of discouragement through "trust" and a restoration of strength through quiet dependence upon *His* strength.

*It is a good thing to give thanks to the Lord, and to sing praises unto thy name, O most High. To shew forth thy lovingkindness in the morning and thy faithfulness every night.* —Psalm 92:1-2

**4**

Love includes all graces, all perfections. Love is the fulfilling of the law. Besides a host of additional excellencies, love believes all things, endures all things; so that in faith and love, and not elsewhere, faith and hope strike living root, blossom and bear fruit unto life eternal.

Love is more potent to breed faith than faith to breed love. Because there is no comparison between the two; God is love, and that which God is must rank higher and show itself mightier than anything that God is not. Nevertheless, faith is also required of us, and faith overflows with blessings.   —CHRISTINA G. ROSETTI

Nothing so expands and deepens our nature as true love of any kind. But love to God has a special power of its own for making the heart bigger and deeper for Him to come in and inhabit it and fill it out of His fulness.   —THOROLD

# November

**5**

*Let us come before his presence with thanksgiving, and make a joyful noise unto him with psalms.*
—Psalm 95:2

As we have pointed out elsewhere, while a thankful spirit is not listed among Paul's catalog of Christian virtues, it seems to underlie this whole matter of Spirit fruit. Here it is coupled with joy, and what an integral part of the spirit of joyous living is this matter of thankfulness. R. A. Torrey puts it this way: "There is no greater, nor more simple secret of a life of uninterrupted and ever-increasing joyfulness, than a heart attuned to thankfulness. Our disappointments become God's appointments, our sorrows become joys, and our tears become rainbows. There is a song on our lips, not made in synthetic melody, but welling up from the heart." If we make the spirit of Romans 8:28 our life theme, "And we know that all things work together for good to them that love God, to them who are called according to his purpose," we will find it possible to "come before his presence with thanksgiving...."

**6**

*Blessed are they that hunger, for they shall be filled.* —Matthew 5:6

Are not many of us conscious that we are living far below our privileges? Do we not understand that we are not as good Christians, as rich in character, as fruitful in life, as we might be? Do we not know that there is a possible fullness of spiritual blessedness which we have not yet attained? Why is it? Is there any want in God, from whom all good gifts come? Is not the reason in ourselves? Is it not because we cling to other things, earthly things, which fill our hearts and leave but small room for Christ? We have not the hunger for righteousness, for holiness, and though there is abundance of provision close before us, yet our souls are starving. If we would have the abundant life Christ wants to give us, we must empty out of our hearts the perishing trifles that fill them, and make room for the Holy Spirit. We must pray for spiritual hunger; for only to those who hunger comes the promise of filling and satisfying.   —J. R. MILLER

What are my priorities—physical or spiritual? Thankful living involves hunger for spiritual food as a part of my daily regimen.

*Serve the Lord with gladness: come before his presence with singing.*   —Psalm 100:2

**7**

A writer tells of a boy who was sunny and brave of disposition. He met the ills of life, which too many regard as tragedies, with courage. Nothing ever seemed to daunt him. Where most boys would have been afraid and broken into tears, he was undismayed and untroubled. But one day something serious happened. He and a playmate climbed a tree. Just when our little philosopher had reached the top, his foot slipped and he fell all the way to the ground. He lay there, evidently hurt, but he did not cry. It was his playmate who screamed. The doctor found the leg badly broken, but the boy bore the setting patiently and without a whimper. The mother slipped out of the room to hide her own tears—she couldn't stand it as well as the boy did. Outside the door she heard a faint sound and hurried back into the room, almost hoping that the boy would be crying. "My son," she said, "do you want something? I thought I heard you call."

"Oh no, mother," he replied. "I didn't call. I just thought I'd try singing a bit." And he went on with his song.

When you have a pain, or struggle, or a heavy load, or a great anguish, don't complain, don't cry out, don't sink

# November

down in despair, don't be afraid—try the boy's remedy. Try singing a bit. Trust God and praise.   —J. R. MILLER

**8**

*Giving thanks always for all things unto God and the Father in the name of our Lord Jesus Christ.*
—Ephesians 5:20

The redeemed of the Lord should ever be praising Him who has saved us in His rich grace, and who lavishes upon us evidence after evidence of His Fatherly love and care. An unthankful child of God is a strange anomaly. Praise should ever be welling up in the hearts of those who recognize their constant indebtedness to the divine mercy and compassion. We should worry less if we praised more. Thanksgiving is the enemy of discontent and dissatisfaction. When we are tempted to doubt and fear, we should begin to praise God for past mercies, and our faith will be increased.   —H. A. IRONSIDE

> Thou hast given so much to me,
> Give one thing more—a grateful heart:
> Not thankful when it pleaseth me,
> As if Thy blessings had spare days,
> But such a heart whose Pulse may be
> Thy praise.
>
> —GEORGE HERBERT

**9**

*O give thanks unto the Lord; call upon his name: make known his deeds among the people.*
—Psalm 105:1

To give to others is but sowing seed for ourselves. He who is so good a steward as to be willing to use his substance for his Lord, will be entrusted with more. Friend of Jesus, are you giving back to Him according to the bene-

# November

fits you have received from Him? Much has been given to you—where is your fruit? Have you done everything you could do? Can you not do more? To be selfish is to be wicked, to sin grievously against the grace of God from which you have drunk so deeply. God forbid that any of us should follow the ungenerous and destructive policy of living unto ourselves. Jesus did not seek to please Himself. All fullness dwells in Him, but of His fullness have we all received. O for Jesus' Spirit, that henceforth we may not live unto ourselves!   —CHARLES H. SPURGEON

> Thank God for dirty dishes,
>   They have a tale to tell;
> While others may go hungry
>   We're eating very well,
> With Home, Health, and Happiness
>   I shouldn't want to fuss;
> By the stack of Evidence,
>   God's been very good to us.
>         —AUTHOR UNKNOWN

*Greater is he that is in you, than he that is in the world.*   —1 John 4:4

**10**

The man is weak and useless who, however devoutly, looks only for the repetition of past miracles, good and great as those miracles were in their own time. Solemnly and surely—to some men terribly and awfully, to other men joyously and enthusiastically—it is becoming clear to men that the future cannot be what the past has been. The world of the days to come is to be different from the world that has been. Every interest of life is altered; government, society, business, education—all is altered, all is destined to alter more and more. Only these two elements remain the same—God and man! What then shall we expect? That God will guide man and supply him as He has in all the times which are past and gone, but that the new

# November

government and guidance will be different for the new days. He who believes that looks forward to changes of faith and changes of life without a fear, for underneath all the changes is the unchangeableness of God.

—PHILLIPS BROOKS

**11**    *His lord said unto him, Well done, thou good and faithful servant.* —Matthew 25:21

A life need not be great to be beautiful. There may be as much beauty in a tiny flower as in a majestic tree, in a little gem as in a great mountain, in the smallest creature as in a mammoth. A life may be very lovely and yet be insignificant in the world's eyes. A beautiful life is one that fulfills its mission in the world, that is what God made it to be, and does what God made it to do. Those with only commonplace gifts are in danger of thinking that they cannot live a beautiful life, cannot be a blessing in this world. But the smallest life that fills its place as well is far lovelier in God's sight than the largest and most splendidly gifted that yet fails in doing its divine mission. —J. R. MILLER

> Far better in its place the lowliest bird
>   Should sing aright to Him the lowliest song,
> Than that a seraph strayed should take the word
>   And sing His glory wrong.

**12**    *There arose a great storm . . . and he was in the boat.* —Mark 4:37–38

There are many lessons in this account of Christ's authority and power over the storm, but the one that stands out for me is this: "he was in the boat." Let's face it, life, even for the Christian, isn't necessarily stormproof. The popular song has it, "I never promised you a rose garden," and neither did Jesus promise His disciples a life exempt from problems. But . . . He's in the boat with us! Your marriage is something like the boat of life. At times it will float on calm seas, but at other times it may be rocked by raging waves, in danger of foundering. You don't need someone shouting directions at you from the shore—you need Someone you can count on right in the boat with you. If Jesus is in the boat, we know it won't sink. If He is in your marriage, you know it will survive even the toughest test. Be sure of this: there *will* be times of testing even in the best of marriages. Be even more certain of this, however: the biggest blessings follow the severest tests—if Christ is in the boat!

*A bruised reed shall he not break.* —Isaiah 42:3

## 13

Dr. J. H. Jowett says it is a common custom in Syria to cut a reed and use it for a staff to lean on when walking. As one climbs a hill, however, and places more of his weight on his staff, it sometimes gives way and the reed is cracked and broken. All a man can do then with his shattered staff is to break it altogether and throw it away as worthless. These poor reeds are symbols, Dr. Jowett suggests, of people on whom we have leaned and who have failed us. We trusted them and helped them in some time of need in their lives, but they did not prove loyal and true. We showed them kindness when they were in trouble and turned to us for help, but they forgot that kindness. They broke their word to us. The staff became a bruised reed. Now what should we do? Should we be hard on them? Should we vent our hatred on them? Should we turn our backs on them and say we will have nothing more to do with them? What would Jesus do? "A bruised reed shall he not break." We need the gentleness of Christ in dealing with those who have failed us or proved ungrateful to our kindness. This is living thankfully.

# November

**14**

*But we are bound to give thanks alway to God for you, brethren beloved of the Lord . . . God hath from the beginning chosen you to salvation through sanctification of the Spirit and belief of the truth: whereunto he called you by our gospel, to the obtaining of the glory of our Lord Jesus Christ.*

—2 Thessalonians 2:13-14

Notice the order here. Believers were chosen by God from the beginning. He foreknew all who would form part of the church, the body and bride of Christ, His Son. In bringing them to the knowledge of salvation He wrought upon their hearts by His Holy Spirit, thus separating them from the godless world around. As a result of the Spirit's working, they were led to believe the truth—"the word is the truth of the gospel"—and now they can look forward in faith to the coming glory into which they shall enter at our Lord's return.    —H. A. IRONSIDE

**15**

*But whoever would be great among you must be your servant, and whoever would be first among you must be slave of all.*  —Mark 10:43-44 RSV

If you are looking for a model of service to follow, Jesus Christ is the supreme example that the Scriptures give us, as to what a Christian servant should be. Always busy, He was also completely dependent upon His heavenly Father for every step of His way. His prayer life is an inspiration to believers, for He did not take a step without communicating to His God.

God has a plan for each of His children. If they are able-bodied, that plan includes physical work of some kind. If Jesus was willing to serve, and is our example in service, how much more should we, His followers, be willing to serve? Jesus here contrasts the spirit of the pagan with that of the Christian, and calls for Christians to react to servitude in an opposite way from the world around them. In verse 42 He described the opposing spirit of the Gentiles: "You know that those who are supposed to rule over the Gentiles lord it over them, and their great men exercise authority over them" (Mark 10:42, RSV).

If Christians today would copy Jesus' example, what a different world this would be! He came not to be ministered unto, but to minister. Let us do the same!

*We are more than conquerors through him that loved us.* —Romans 8:37
*Thanks be to God, which giveth us the victory....* —1 Corinthians 15:57

**16**

Jesus said, "If any man love me, let him take up his cross." Some say this means the troubles and persecution we bring on ourselves by confessing Jesus. But surely that is a narrow thought. The true cross of the Redeemer was the sin and sorrow of this world, that was what lay heavy on His heart, and that is the cross we must share with Him, the cup we must drink with Him, if we would have any part in that divine love, which is one with His sorrow. —GEORGE ELIOT

> Briers beset my every path
>   Which call for patient care;
> There is a cross in every lot
>   An earnest need for prayer;
> But a lowly heart that leans on Thee,
>   Is happy everywhere.
>
> In service which thy love appoints,
>   There are no bonds for me;
> My secret heart is taught "the truth"
>   That makes Thy children free,
> A life of self-renouncing love
>   Is a life at liberty.
>       —ANNA L. WARING

# November

**17** *I will sing unto the Lord, because he hath dealt bountifully with me.* —Psalm 13:6

Throughout this book we have been singing "Love-Songs," and what a theme for singing! The Psalms, particularly, return again and again to the theme of thanksgiving, and here in Psalm 13 David declares the reason he can sing in every circumstance—"because he hath dealt bountifully with me." As I think of my own married life, I cannot help echoing David's triumphant refrain. What if I had married someone with whom I was not compatible? I shudder to think how unhappy married life might then have been. Or what if I had been forced by circumstances to go through life alone? Some people do, and many seem to make a good life for themselves. But if I had my life to live over, I would choose to live it with the same lovely person at my side. Because of her, the life I have lived has been rich and full. But at an even deeper level, it has been beautiful because of the One who brought us together and now leads us day by day. The Living Bible translates this verse, "I will sing to the Lord because he has blessed me so richly." That's the refrain of my "lovesong"!

**18** *They which receive abundance of grace and of the gift of righteousness shall reign in life by one, Jesus Christ.* —Romans 5:17

Do you reign in life? If not, the reason may be that you do not distinguish between *praying* and *taking.* There is a profound difference between praying for a thing and appropriating it. You may admit God's abundant grace is near you through Jesus Christ, and yet you may not quite see the necessity of learning how to take. Some people are always telegraphing heaven for God to send a cargo of blessing to them; but they are not at the dock to unload the blessing when it comes. How many of God's richest

# November

blessings for which you have been praying for years have come right close to you, but you do not know how to lay hold and use them? Notice—"they which receive the abundance of grace shall reign." The emphasis is not on grace, not on abundance, but on receiving it. The whole grace of God may be around you today, but if you have not learned to take it in, it will do you no good.

—F. B. Meyer

*As ye have therefore received Christ Jesus the Lord, so walk ye in him: Rooted and built up in him, and stablished in the faith, as ye have been taught, abounding therein with thanksgiving.*

**19**

—Colossians 2:6,7

What a stirring motto for daily living these two verses from the pen of Paul suggest! The Living Bible gives them an even stronger thrust: "And now just as you trusted Christ to save you, trust him, too, for each day's problems; live in vital union with him. Let your roots grow down into him and draw up nourishment from him. See that you go on growing in the Lord, and become strong and vigorous. . . . Let your lives overflow with joy and thanksgiving for all he has done." We are talking about more than just a "walk," we are talking about *living*. In 1 Thessalonians Paul expands the theme: " . . . lead a life worthy of God. . . . as you learned from us how you ought to live and to please God, just as you are doing, you do so more and more" (2:12; 4:1, RSV). If this way of life Paul is calling for had to be lived in my own strength, I would give it up as a lost cause right now, but thank God for the "in him." In Christ lies the key to spiritual success. The great J. Wilbur Chapman once said: "The rule that governs my life is this: Anything that dims my vision of Christ, or takes away my taste for Bible study, or cramps my prayer life, or makes Christian work difficult, is wrong for me, and I

# November

must, as a Christian, turn away from it." Are you "rooted and grounded" in Him? If you are, your life will glow and grow with the vitality of Christ!

**20** *In everything give thanks: for this is the will of God in Christ Jesus concerning you.*
—1 Thessalonians 5:18

There cannot be, of course, always the word of thanks on our lips, but there can always be the heart going up toward God in gratitude and praise. Thanksgiving and prayer should be the atmosphere in which we live, the air we breathe, and just as a man keeps right on breathing while doing a thousand other things, so we can keep on praising and thanking, and praying to God while doing a thousand other things just as easily and naturally.

—R. A. Torrey

Do we take the blessing that the common days bring to us? Do we extract the honey from every flower that grows by our path? Should we not learn to see the goodness and the beauty in the gifts God sends to us? Their very commonness veils their blessedness. Let us seek for the good in everything. Then, though we see it not, let us never doubt that it lies hidden in every gift of God to us. Every moment brings some benediction. Even the rough hand of trial holds in its clasp for us some treasure of love.

—J. R. Miller

**21** *And let the peace of God rule in your hearts, to the which also ye are called in one body; and be ye thankful.* —Colossians 3:15

Here is another instance where the fruits of the Spirit are inextricably linked. In this case, we have peace combined with thankfulness. While Paul does not include thankfulness as such in his list of Christian virtues in Galatians 5:22-23, he says so much in his Epistles about being thankful in all things that it seems to rank with the other listed fruits of the Spirit. On this subject, F. B. Meyer says: "I have a beloved friend, who has made it the habit of her life to obey this injunction, 'Be ye thankful,' literally. When her husband's factory was in flames, when her children were seriously ill, and when other apparent disasters befell her, she went alone to her chamber, and knelt down to thank God for all, because she knew He was her Father still; that He loved her too well to give her anything but the best; and that He must love her very much to be willing to bless her at the cost of so much pain. We may not always *feel* like thanking God for all things; but let us always will and dare to do it. Let us not look at the providence, but at the Father behind it. Let us not examine the crate, but let us search within for the gift of love. Though at first sight we may be disappointed and sad, whatever the Father sends must be the very best. Dare to believe it, and you will come to find it so."

*Remembering without ceasing your work of faith, and labour of love, and patience of hope....*
—1 Thessalonians 1:3

# 22

Love for Christ in human hearts shapes itself into many forms of gentle, helpful ministry, according to the quality, the circumstances, and the relationships of each life. What we need to make sure of is that we truly have the spirit of service, "the mind that was in Christ Jesus." It is not great deeds that God expects or requires of us, unless He has endowed us with large gifts and has given us great things to do. He gives us certain talents and puts us into certain relationships, and then asks us to be faithful—nothing more. The man with the plain gifts and the small opportunities

# November

is not expected to do the great things that are required of the man with the brilliant talents and the large opportunities. "She hath done what she could" is the highest approving word that could be spoken of anyone, and it may be only for a smile of love and a crust given in Christ's name.   —J. R. MILLER

If husbands and wives could honestly express to each other the commendation Paul is sharing with the Thessalonian Christians here, what a difference it would make in each home. Honest appreciation of the efforts of others is part of thankful living.

## 23

*Be content with such things as ye have.*
—Hebrews 13:5

Your Christianity is not worth much if it encourages your discontent; for, after all, if you and the Lord keep together you will always be in good company, and you will always have something to make you glad and cheerful. What is around you will be brightened by what is above you; and today, cloudy though it may be, will be made radiant by the hopes that come from the great tomorrow.

It is when your heart is not satisfied that the nature of your environment assumes undue importance. Two rooms will do, if nothing better may be had, when love builds the home; but a palace is too small when the heart is heavy and the spirit dissatisfied.   —G. H. HEPWORTH

## 24

*Be careful to maintain good works.*   —Titus 3:8

We are so related to each other that we are continually leaving impressions on those we touch. It is easier to do harm than good to other lives. There is a quality in the human soul which makes it take more readily and retain more permanently touches of sin than touches of holiness. Among the ruins of some old temple there was found a slab which bore very faintly and dimly the image of the king, and, in deep and clear indentations, the print of a dog's foot! The king's beauty was less clear than the marks of the animal. So human lives are apt to take less readily and deeply, to retain less indelibly, the touches of spiritual beauty, and more clearly and permanently the marks and impressions of the earthly. We need to be careful, therefore, as we walk among other lives, that some word, or look, or act, or influence of ours will not hurt them irreparably.   —J. R. MILLER

---

*For every creature of God is good, and nothing to be refused, if it be received with thanksgiving: for it is sanctified by the word of God and prayer.*
—1 Timothy 4:4–5

# 25

Blessed it is to recognize in the temporal, creative mercies of each day, the evidences of a loving Father's care. "He giveth us richly all things to enjoy." To receive all as from His own hand, giving thanks in the name of our Lord Jesus, is to honor the Giver in the use of the gifts. There is a golden mean between fleshly asceticism on the one hand, which discounts many of God's gifts and thus throws discredit on Him who provides them, and carnal self-indulgence on the other hand, which uses the mercies of God with no regard to Him from whom they come, and in such a way as to turn even our blessings into curses. We should ever recognize the bounty of our Father in these things, and whether we eat or drink, do all to His glory, our hearts going out to Him in adoring gratitude.
—H. A. IRONSIDE

# November

**26**

*And Jesus said unto them, I am the bread of life; he that cometh unto me shall never hunger.*
—John 6:35

Ian Maclaren tells of once hearing a plain sermon in a little country church. A layman, a farmer, preached, but Maclaren says he never heard so impressive an ending to any sermon as he heard that day. After a fervent presentation of the gospel, the preacher said with great earnestness, "My friends, why is it that I go on preaching to you week by week? It is just this, because I can't eat my bread alone." That is our Savior's own burden—His heart is breaking to have men share with Him the blessings of life. He cannot bear to be alone in His joy. There is no surer test of love for Christ than the longing to have others love Him!

What better way for us to show our love and gratitude to God for His salvation gift to us, than to share the bread of our salvation with others!

**27**

*Seeing ye have purified your souls in obeying the truth through the Spirit unto unfeigned love of the brethren, see that ye love one another with a pure heart fervently.* —1 Peter 1:22

God employs His people to encourage one another. We should be glad that God usually works for man by man. It forms a bond of brotherhood, and being mutually dependent on one another, we are fused more completely into one family. Fellow Christians, take the text as God's message to you. Aim to comfort the sorrowful, and to cheer the despondent. Speak a word in season to him who is weary, and encourage those who are fearful to go on their way with gladness. God encourages you by His promises;

Christ encourages you as He points to the heaven He has won for you, and the Spirit encourages you as He works in you to will and to do of His own will and pleasure.

—CHARLES H. SPURGEON

> Love demands the loving deed,
>     Pass it on!
> Look upon your brother's need—
>     Pass it on!
> Live for self, you live in vain;
> Live for Christ, with Him you reign—
>     Pass it on!

AUTHOR UNKNOWN

*We love him because he first loved us.*
—1 John 4:19

**28**

John the disciple had learned from Jesus, his Master, the truth of the priority of God—the truth that before everything is God. It is as when up the morning sky, all coldly beautiful with ordered ranks of cloud on cloud, is poured the glow of sunrise, and every least cloud, still the same in place and shape, burns with the transcending splendor of the sun. So is it when the priority of existence is seen to rest in a Person, and the background of life is God. Then every new arrival instantly reports itself to Him, and is described in terms of its relationship to Him. Every activity of ours answers to some previous activity of His. Do we hope? It is because we have caught the sound of some promise of His. Do we fear? It is because we have had some glimpse of the dreadfulness of getting out of harmony with Him. Are we curious and inquiring? It is that we may learn some of His truth. Do we resist evil? We are fighting His enemies. Do we need help? We are relieving His children. Do we love Him? It is an answer of gratitude for His love to us. Do we live? It is a projection and exten-

# November

sion of His being. Do we die? It is the going home of our immortal souls to Him. Oh, the wonderful richness of life when it is all thus backed up with the priority of God. It is the great illumination of all living.   —PHILLIPS BROOKS

**29**   *For the lamb . . . shall feed them, and shall lead them.*  —Revelation 7:17

To feed on Christ is to get His strength into us to be our strength. You feed on the corn, and then go and build your house; and it is the corn in your strong arm that builds the house, that piles the stone and lifts the roof into place. You feed on Christ, and then go and live your life; and it is Christ in you that lives your life; that helps the poor, that tells the truth, that fights the battle, and that wins the crown.

But what is this strength of Christ that comes to us? It is His character, His strength, His purity, His truth, His mercifulness—in word, His holiness, the perfectness of His moral life. That is the inner strength. That is the strength of food.

Notice how this last alone is vital. It alone makes life. It lives. The prop keeps the dead wall standing, but the sap makes the live tree still more alive with growth. So compulsion and fear keep us true to duty, but love makes us larger, and fit for greater duty every day. Every vital strength must be the strength which incorporates itself with the very being of the thing it supports. Except we eat, we can have no life in us.   —PHILLIPS BROOKS

**30**   *The length and the breadth and the height of it are equal.*  —Revelation 21:16

The life which to its length and breadth adds height, which to its personal ambition and sympathy with man adds love and obedience to God, completes itself into the

# November

cube of the eternal city and is the life complete. Think for a moment of the life of the great apostle, the manly, many-sided Paul. "I press toward the mark for the prize of the high calling...," he writes to the Philippians. That is the length of life for him. "I will gladly spend and be spent for you," he writes to the Corinthians. There is the breadth of life for him. "God hath raised us up and made us sit together in heavenly places in Christ Jesus," he writes to the Ephesians. There is the height of life for him. You can add nothing to these three dimensions when you try to account to yourself for the impression of completeness which comes to you out of his simple, lofty story. Look at the Lord of Paul. See how in Christ the same symmetrical manhood shines yet more complete. See what intense ambition to complete His work, what tender sympathy with every struggling brother by His side, and at the same time what a perpetual dependence on His Father is in Him. "For this cause came I into the world." "For their sakes I sanctify myself." "Now, O Father, glorify thou me." Leave any of these dimensions out, and you have not the perfect Christ, nor the entire symmetry of manhood.

—Phillips Brooks

# December

*For without me ye can do nothing.* —John 15:5

**1**

To grasp what Jesus is saying here, one needs to digest the rest of this striking verse: "I am the vine, ye are the branches: He that abideth in me, and I in him, the same bringeth forth much fruit." Then Jesus drives home the clincher: "For without me ye can do nothing."

In this book, *LoveSongs*, we have been emphasizing the fruit that should be evident in the Christian life—and in the Christian marriage. Jesus adds a deeper aspect to this "vine-centered" life later in John 15: "Ye have not chosen me, but I have chosen you, and ordained [appointed] you, that ye should go and bring forth fruit, and that your fruit should remain: that whatsoever ye shall ask of the Father in my name, he may give it you" (v. 16). What a power source! Prayer power seems to be the secret to "people" power. And the secret source of power is Jesus Himself, who is as available to us as the vine is to the branches. There is a *direct* connection through which His power can flow into and out of us, making us useful and creative; if some obstacle interrupts that flow of divine power, we "can do nothing."

What a tragedy an unfruitful life is. Nothing gets done; no lasting good is accomplished; our days careen past us, and it makes no difference to the world whether we are alive or not. On the other hand, we have the promise that if the connection to Divine Power is open, we will "bring forth much fruit." Our prayerful attitude of expectancy assures this, for as Mark Hopkins says, "Our prayer and

# December

God's mercy are like two buckets in a well; while the one ascends, the other descends."

R. A. Torrey shares this insight with us: "The only living or doing or accomplishing in the Christian life that is acceptable to God is through union with the risen Christ. Through union with the *crucified* Christ we get our pardon, our cleansing from guilt, our justification, our perfect standing before God. Through union with the *risen* Christ, we get power for life and fruit."

**2**      *He turneth rivers into a wilderness, and the water-springs into dry ground.* —Psalm 107:33

This is one of the miracles of grace. The good Lord makes a dry experience the fountain of blessing. I pass into an apparently waste place and I find riches of consolation. Even in "the valley of the shadow" I come upon "green pastures" and "still waters." I find flowers in the ruts of the hardest roads if I am in "the way of God's commandments." God's providence is the pioneer of every faithful pilgrim. "His blessed feet have gone before." What I shall need is already foreseen, and foresight with the Lord means forethought and provision. Every hour gives the loyal disciples surprises of grace. Let me therefore not fear when the path of duty turns into the wilderness. The wilderness is as habitable with God as the crowded city, and in His fellowship my bread and water are sure. The Lord has strange manna for the children of disappointment, and He makes water to "gush forth from the rock." Duty can lead me nowhere without Him, and His provision is abundant both in "the thirsty desert and the dewy meadow." There will be a spring at the foot of every hill, and I will find "lilies of peace" even in the lonely valleys.

—J. H. JOWETT

# December

*Grow in grace, and in the knowledge of our Lord
and Savior, Jesus Christ.* —2 Peter 3:18

The Bible is a garden book. There is one at the beginning, a better one at the end, and the Gethsemane garden in between. Every man should be a gardener, and his life a garden. There's sowing and sunshine, dewfall and rain, and special watering in dry spells. Then there's weeding, watching for destructive insects, and pruning, a cutting back to get better fruit. Let us be good gardeners, with the Man of Gethsemane to help. We think evil, like weeds, grows rank and fast without cultivation—but it isn't so. There's another gardener, a special, unseen gardener for evil. He sows, and waters, and cultivates, and tries to weed out the good. He is an old hand at gardening. He began in Eden! He stays up nights, watching for chances. We must fight him. The best way is to get our crop in first; weed and work it sleeplessly. The best work in this garden is done down on our knees. —S. D. GORDON

## 4

*For we are his workmanship, created in Christ Jesus
to do those good works which God prepared before-
hand that we should walk in them.*
—Ephesians 2:10

I've just learned that I am a grandfather. This is my first time! And I learned about it second-hand. My niece, who works as a "preemie" nurse in the hospital, wandered down the hall during her break period and looked in the nursery window. There was a new "Baby Bryant." When she went home later that morning (the baby was born at 12:47 A.M., April 28, 1977) she told her mother, my sister-in-law, who called my other sister-in-law, who in turn called my wife and said: "Congratulations, grandma!" My son, the baby's father, was home asleep. It had been a

# December

pretty rough night for him and he hadn't wanted to disturb us! Anyway, it doesn't seem that long ago that I became a father for the first time. This is the chain of life, tiny links that go on and on. The first earthly father must have felt something of the same thrill that I feel now—and something of the same awe. I carry the very essence of life in me—it is something of the divine spark of creation. And I pass it along to my children and grandchildren. This first grandchild has that spark—and, if the Lord tarries, she too, will pass it along to her children. It's an awesome gift —too often ignored and mistreated by its recipients. May she treat it with the reverence it deserves. If I cannot share anything else with her, may I share my awareness of God, who He is, and who I am in the chain of His creation. May the love that keeps that chain pliable and usable melt her heart and win her to Him who alone can supply every need of life.

**5**

*When he had found one pearl of great price, [he] went and sold all that he had, and bought it.*
—Matthew 13:46

Every man who desires the pearl of great price must sacrifice his all to buy it. It is not enough to see the beauty and the glory and almost to taste the joy of this wonderful life; you must become the possessor of it. The man had found and seen, desired and rejoiced in the pearl of great price; but he did not have it until he gave up everything and bought it.

You cannot live every day in perfect fellowship with God without giving time to it. Hours, days, weeks, months, and years are gladly given by men and women to perfect themselves in some profession or accomplishment. Do you expect the Christian walk is so easy and cheap that without giving time you can find close fellowship with God? But this pearl is worth everything. If you find there is struggle in your heart, never mind. By God's grace, if you will lie at His feet, you may depend upon it— deliverance will come!   —ANDREW MURRAY

*... helpers of your joy: for by faith ye stand.*
—2 Corinthians 1:24

**6**

We ought to think of the convenience of others more than some of us do. The home is the place where this thoughtfulness ought to begin and be cultivated. One who comes late to breakfast and keeps others waiting admits that he is guilty of an amiable self-indulgence, but forgets he has marred the harmonious flow of the household life, and caused confusion and extra work. The other day an important committee of fifteen men was kept waiting for ten minutes for one tardy member, who came sauntering in at the last without even an apology for having caused fourteen men a loss of time that was to them very valuable, besides having put a sore strain on their patience and good nature. Common life is full of just such thoughtlessness, which often produces irritation and hurts the hearts of those around us. We ought to train ourselves in all our life to put others first.   —J. R. MILLER

There is a formula for life: J-O-Y—Jesus first, Others second, Yourself last. Living it out would help in the building of a happy home—and a joyous marriage relationship.

*Lo, I am with you alway, even unto the end of the world.*   —Matthew 28:20

**7**

As a well-known preacher has said, "It was a strange fact that He should, for the first time, promise to be with them always, at the very last moment before vanishing

# December

from the world; and we may be certain that words apparently so contradictory have a very deep significance . . . . The meaning of this saying . . . was, that His departure would really be the commencement of His nearer presence as a Friend than they had known while they saw Him with the bodily eye."

That presence is a special presence. God is everywhere. But the Lord speaks now of His special presence with His people. It is a spiritual presence. Jesus—the visible human but glorified nature—is in heaven. But Christ, the spiritual risen Lord of life and glory—He is in and with His church on earth, as well as on the throne in heaven.

It is a sanctifying presence. Holiness has its embodiment in Him. We are holy as we are in Him and He in us. Spiritual and moral transfiguration is the result of being brought into union and fellowship with the Holy One.
—EVAN H. HOPKINS

**8** *For he will give his angels charge over thee, to keep thee in all thy ways.* —Psalm 91:11

There is an all-inclusiveness about this Psalm of security for the believer. It seems that the psalmist has "touched all the bases" in Psalm 91. I remember that this was the Psalm written on the flyleaf of the Testament I received from my church when I went off to war—and the Psalm certainly speaks to a soldier's needs. But how blessed to see how it speaks to the needs of the civilian as well. So many of the verses capsulize God's care for His own, but none is more comforting to the believer's heart than verse 11, which has been variously translated: "For he orders his angels to *protect* you wherever you go"(TLB); "For he will give his angels . . . to *guard* you in all your ways" (RSV). John Calvin said: "The angels are the dispensers and administrators of the Divine beneficence toward us; they regard our safety, undertake our defense, direct our ways, and exercise a constant solicitude that no evil befall us." How encouraging to know that these angelic beings, fresh from their confrontation with God Himself, are delegated to "keep," "guard," and "protect" us!

*Ye also helping together by prayer for us.*
*—2 Corinthians 1:11*

**9**

Praying together strengthens marriages. I don't know that Paul had that truth particularly in mind when he urged the Corinthians to pray together, but it's a valid spiritual truth anyway. Some more recent translations of this verse leave out the word "together" which, it seems to me, somewhat weakens its impact. The Modern Language Bible, however, uses the word "cooperate" to indicate that the prayer is to be a team effort. And what team could better cooperate in prayer than a godly husband and wife? In Romans 15:30 Paul again expresses the idea of praying together. The Living Bible translates it with a lilt: "Will you be my prayer partners?" To paraphrase a popular motto, "The couple that prays together, stays together." Maltbie D. Babcock was asking for earnestness in prayer when he said nearly a hundred years ago, "Our prayers must mean something to us if they are to mean anything to God." May our prayers together as man and wife have this spirit of urgency and dedication Paul calls for among the Corinthians!

*And when he had sent the multitudes away, he went up into a mountain apart to pray: and when the evening was come, he was there alone.*
*—Matthew 14:23*

**10**

The mountains, in their majesty, seem to bring God wonderfully near to us, and us wonderfully near to God. The mountains were His "secret place" where He might be alone with God. He sought their quietude and majesty, to be alone with His God. There He poured out His soul

# December

to His Father, and there received sustaining grace. There is undoubtedly a sense in which we can find a solitary place in our crowded streets, but it is well to follow Christ's example literally, and get alone with God. If you have never known what it is to kneel down in the woods where no human voice could be heard, or beneath a tree in the silent starlight, and look up with open eyes toward the face of God, you have missed a blessing that cannot be described, but every child of God should know. If we commune with God more and more, His beauty will illumine and reflect itself in our lives. Moses' very face shone because he had been with God. So will our lives shine with heavenly glow and glory if we habitually walk and talk with God.  —R. A. TORREY

**11** *To everything there is a season, and a time to every purpose under the heaven.* —Ecclesiastes 3:1

We need a period daily for secret fellowship. Time to turn from daily occupation and search our hearts in His presence. Time to study His Word with reverence and godly fear. Time to seek His face and ask Him to make Himself known to us. Time to wait until we know that He sees and hears us so that we can make our wants and needs known to Him in words that come from the depth of our hearts. Time to let God deal with our special needs, to let His light shine in our hearts, to let ourselves be filled with His Spirit! Fellowship with God should have first claim on our time, and if we will only arrange for this brief communion with God we will learn to value it. It will not be long before we will feel ashamed that there was ever a time when we thought fifteen minutes would suffice. Everything on earth needs time. Think of the hours per day for so many years that a child spends at school gathering the rudiments of knowledge that he may cope with this life. How much longer then should we spend in learning from God for life everlasting?  —ANDREW MURRAY

*And he shall be like a tree planted by the rivers of water, that bringeth forth his fruit in his season; his leaf shall not wither; and whatsoever he doeth shall prosper.* —Psalm 1:3

**12**

Proper planting is important in this matter of fruit-bearing. No farmer plants where he does not expect to grow a good crop. He is looking for a harvest. In this passage, the gateway, as it were, to the Psalms, we are given the guidelines for good planting. The spiritual farmer is promised prosperity if he follows the formula. Joseph is probably the outstanding example in Scripture of spiritual (and material) prosperity. Genesis 39:3 says: "And his master saw that the Lord was with him, and that the Lord made all that he did to prosper in his hand." Jeremiah, too, echoes the sentiments of Psalm 1 when he says, "Blessed is the man who trusts in the Lord . . . He is like a tree planted by water, that sends out its roots by the stream, and does not fear when heat comes, for its leaves remain green, and is not anxious in the year of drought, for it does not cease to bear fruit" (Jer. 17:7–8, RSV). Another Psalm, subtitled "The God-fearing family is blessed," has this promise: "Blessed is every one who feareth the Lord; that walketh in his ways. For thou shalt eat the labour of thine hands: happy shalt thou be, and it shall be well with thee." Looking for a prosperous marriage? Be sure you are planted right—by the streams of heavenly water!

*Blessed is the nation whose God is the Lord; and the people whom he hath chosen for his own inheritance.* —Psalm 33:12

**13**

I would like to paraphrase this grand passage slightly— and show why I feel that liberty is merited. "Blessed is the

# December

home (or the marriage) whose God is the Lord. . . . " Since our nation can rise no higher spiritually than the spiritual temperature of its homes and families, I think this majestic promise applies even more specifically to our homes than it does to our nation. The late J. Edgar Hoover once pointed out in *The Christian Herald:* "There is no synthetic replacement for a decent [godly] home life. Our high crime rate, particularly among juveniles, is directly traceable to a breakdown in moral fibre—to the disintegration of home and family life. Religion and home life are supplementary. Each strengthens the other. It is seldom that a solid and wholesome home life can be found in the absence of religious inspiration." May the truth of this insightful appraisal abide upon our homes all the way from the White House on Pennsylvania Avenue right on down to the most humble dwelling on Main Street, U. S. A. James A. Garfield, twentieth president of the United States, said, "The sanctity of marriage and the family relationship make the cornerstone of our American society and civilization."

**14** *Come ye, and let us go up to the mountain of the Lord.* —Isaiah 2:3

It is very beneficial to our souls to mount up above this present world to something nobler and better. The cares of this world and the deceitfulness of riches are apt to choke everything good within us, and we grow fretful, desponding, perhaps proud and carnal. It is well for us to cut down these thorns and briers, for heavenly seed sown among them is not likely to yield a harvest; and where will we find a better sickle with which to cut them down than communion with God? May the Spirit of God assist us to leave the mists of fear and the fevers of anxiety, and all the

# December

ills which gather in this valley of earth, and to ascend the mountains of anticipated joy and blessedness. May God the Holy Spirit cut the cords that keep us here below, and assist us to mount! We sit too often like chained eagles fastened to the rock, only that, unlike the eagle, we begin to love our chain, and would perhaps, if it came really to the test, dislike having it snapped. May God now grant us grace, if we cannot escape from the chain as to our flesh, yet do so as to our spirits; and leaving the body like a servant, at the foot of the hill, may our soul, like Abraham, attain the top of the mountain, there to indulge in communion with the Most High.   —CHARLES H. SPURGEON

*He departed again into a mountain, himself alone.*
—John 6:15

## 15

Man needs to be alone with God. Without this, God cannot have the opportunity to shine into his heart, to transform his nature by His divine working, to take possession and to fill him with the fulness of God. Man needs to be alone with God, to yield to the presence and the power of his holiness, of His life and of His love. Christ on earth needed it; He could not live the life of a Son here in the flesh, without at times separating Himself entirely from His surroundings and being alone with God. How much more must this be indispensable to us! When our Lord Jesus gave us the blessed command to enter our inner chamber, shut the door, pray to our Father in secret, all alone, He gave us the promise that the Father would hear such prayers, and mightily answer them in our life before men. What a great privilege is the opportunity of daily prayer to begin every morning. Let it be the one thing our hearts are set on, seeking and finding, discovering and meeting God.   —ANDREW MURRAY

# December

**16**
*If ye abide in me, and my words abide in you, ye shall ask what ye will, and it shall be done unto you.* —John 15:7

Jesus is here expressing a principle of fruit-bearing in prayer that is related to the entire issue of the fruit of the Spirit with which we are dealing in this book. This passage in John begins with the famous Vine-and-branch analogy in which Jesus explains the vital relationship which the Christian must have in order to be a fruitful follower of Christ. As Scroggie has said, "Here is an unlimited promise resting on a limited condition." The limiting condition is our "abiding" in Christ. The evidence of abiding is divine life. Where there is no life, there will be no fruitfulness. This does not refer to *service*, but to character. "Abiding" implies the idea of "remaining." We are to stay where He has placed us. In a sense, it's as if we were in an elevator, rising from floor to floor until we consciously choose to step out of that relationship. Choosing to abide in Him, we will learn to know His mind and will naturally ask those things in prayer which He in His love is only too willing to grant. If His words are to abide in us, then our lives must be empty of self and sin, to make room for His presence and His joy. Do you want power in prayer? An anonymous disciple has given us this formula: "In the morning, prayer is the key that opens to us the treasures of God's mercies and blessings; in the evening, it is the key that shuts us up under His protection and safeguard." I'd like to live that way, wouldn't you?

**17**
*[Ruth said to Naomi]: Entreat me not to leave thee ... for whither thou goest I will go; and where thou lodgest, I will lodge; thy people shall be my people, and thy God my God.* —Ruth 1:16

This beautiful expression of commitment and dedication is often quoted in modern marriage cermonies. It is a fitting statement of faith in the sacredness of the marriage vows—even though it was expressed by a daughter-in-law to a mother-in-law. (Apparently God is not as enamored of "mother-in-law" jokes as we are! At least, the Scriptures do not reveal any lightness as far as His attitude toward the in-law relationship is concerned.) If both parties in the marriage can sincerely echo the sentiments of this beautiful pledge, then their marriage will not suffer the disillusionment and dissolution implied in this selection from the writings of William Wadsworth:

> Why do not words and kiss, and solemn pledge,
> And nature that is kind in woman's breast,
> And reason that in man is wise and good,
> And fear of Him who is righteous judge—
> Why do not these prevail in human life,
> To keep two hearts together, that began
> Their spring-time with one love.

If you want to make your marriage work, use Ruth's formula for success!

*Shew me thy ways, O Lord; teach me thy paths. Lead me in thy truth, and teach me: for thou art the God of my salvation; on thee do I wait all the day.* —Psalm 25:4-5

**18**

This Psalm of David would make an excellent "pretrip" prayer. Before starting out on any kind of journey, it would be well to pray this kind of prayer for guidance from the heart. In our family, we have always made it a practice to pray before beginning a trip of any length. Our children would as soon leave home without a map as without prayer. Marriage and the establishment of a home is a journey of a sort—it is supposed to be a life-long, "life-together" commitment. From that premise, make it your

# December

practice, wherever you are in the marital "trip," to breathe this heartfelt prayer together. Ask God to keep you as marriage partners "teachable," and willing to be led by the Lord. Be patient in your waiting for the Lord, and your patience will be rewarded with clear-cut direction, a map for the trip that you can follow without fear. Merv Rosell has an appropriate word here: "God could have kept Daniel out of the lion's den. . . . He could have kept Paul and Silas out of jail—He could have kept the three Hebrew children out of the fiery furnace. . . . But God has never promised to keep us out of hard places. . . . What He has promised is to go with us through every hard place, and to bring us through victoriously." If Jesus goes with me, I'll go—anywhere!

**19** *Spread the gospel like a sweet perfume. As far as God is concerned there is a sweet, wholesome fragrance in our lives. It is the fragrance of Christ within us, an aroma to both the saved and unsaved all around us.*  —2 Corinthians 2:14-15, TLB

It used to be just the perfume makers (and the people themselves) who were concerned about the smells emanating from the human body. The perfume trade dates back to centuries before the time of Christ, so it was a familiar industry in Jesus' day—and Paul's. Today there is a whole new industry rising and having its heyday—the deodorant business. We are daily assailed on our TV screens and radios, as well as newspapers, with advertising that tells us we can't succeed, we can't be beautiful, we won't be accepted unless we make use of the multitude of deodorant products now on the market. How on earth did our ancestors survive without this all-important product?

Our text today tells us that God, too, is concerned about

fragrance. In fact, He wants His children to have a distinct fragrance that will mark them indelibly as His own. This fragrance will glorify Him—and identify them. How is your deodorant working?

*There is a friend that sticketh closer than a brother.* —Proverbs 18:24 **20**

It is interesting to compare the opening words of this verse in the King James Version: "A man that hath friends must shew himself friendly . . ." with the Revised Standard Version rendition: "There are friends that pretend to be friends." Every marriage needs friends, but you can do without "pretend" or counterfeit friends. Believe it or not, good friends can help you build a better marriage—and poor friends can help you destroy your marriage. Good friends can help you discover new depths of meaning in your relationship with your loved one. Is there someone, a person or another couple, with whom you can share your life, someone to whom you can go when a problem situation arises, as they do in even the best of marriages? Is there someone you can trust with even some of the most intimate problems, knowing that this person has your best interests at heart, and has the wisdom necessary to give you the right practical and spiritual guidance? Elsewhere in Proverbs, Solomon says, "Where no counsel is, the people fall: but in the multitude of counsellors there is safety" (11:14), and this would seem to contradict what I am saying about "one counselor." However, in Proverbs 17:17 Solomon says, "A friend loveth at all times, and a brother is born for adversity." This bears out what I am saying about the importance of having a "best friend" to whom you can go with your needs as a married couple. But choose carefully! Remember, the best Friend of all is

# December

the Lord Jesus, whose blessing was invoked on your marriage. Let Him be "the friend that sticketh closer than a brother"!

**21**

*And he is the head of the body, the church: who is the beginning, the first-born from the dead; that in all things he might have the preeminence.*
—Colossians 1:18

What does it mean to make Christ preeminent in one's life? The dictionary defines the word *preeminence* as putting someone or something "above and before others." Is that where I put Jesus Christ in my life? There are two other interesting translations of this verse that shed additional light on the meaning of putting Christ in the place of preeminence: ". . . so that in every respect he might have *first place*" (MLB); ". . . so that he is *first in everything*" (TLB). If Christ *is* first in everything, all other aspects of my life will fall into place perfectly. If I join the psalmist, I will follow God's formula for "firstness": "[God says] Also I will make him my firstborn, higher than the kings of the earth" (Ps. 89:27). In the same context with our verse for the day, Paul describes Jesus: "Who is the image of the invisible God, the firstborn of every creature." (Col. 1:15). In Ephesians 1:22–23, Paul gives us this perspective on Christ's preeminence: "And hath put all things under his feet, and gave him to be the head over all things to the church, which is his body, the fulness of him that filleth all in all." St. Augustine put it succinctly: "Christ is not valued at all unless He is valued above all."

**22**

*For what is our hope, or joy, or crown of rejoicing? Are not even ye in the presence of the our Lord . . .?*
—1 Thessalonians 2:19

Nothing else is so cleansing as the consciousness of God's presence. Things that we have long tolerated become intolerable when we bring them into the white light of the presence of the Holy Spirit. How many things we do in the darkness of the night, even in the broad light of day, that we could not for a moment think of doing if we realized God was right there by our side—*looking*. God *is* always present, whether we realize it or not; if we cultivate the consciousness of His presence, our lives and hearts will speedily whiten, until they become as the very snow. People wonder what Jesus would do in this situation or that, but the Bible tells us plainly what He actually did do—He spent much time in prayer. He would rise a great while before day and go out into the mountain to pray alone. He spent whole nights in prayer. If we are to walk as Jesus walked we must lead a life of prayerfulness. The man who is not leading a life of prayer, no matter how many excellent things he may be doing, is not following his Lord.   —R. A. TORREY

*When thou prayest, enter into thy closet, and when thou hast shut thy door, pray to thy Father which is in secret.*   —Matthew 6:6

# 23

This shutting of the door is significant in several ways. It shuts the world out. It secures us against interruption. It ought to shut out worldly thoughts and cares and distraction, as well as worldly presences. Wandering in prayer is usually one of our biggest problems. Then it shuts us in, and this is also important and significant. It shuts us in alone with God. No ear but His hears as we pour out our heart's feelings and desires. No eye but His sees us as we bow in the secrecy. Thus we are helped to realize that with God alone have we to do, that He alone can help us. As we are shut up alone *with* God, so also are we shut up *to* God. There is precious comfort in the assurance that when we thus pray we are not talking into the air. There is an ear to hear, though we can see no presence, and it is

# December

the ear of the Father. This assures us of loving regard in heaven, also of prompt and gracious answer.

—J. R. MILLER

## 24

*Jesus also was invited to the marriage.*
—John 2:2 ASV

It is easy for me to identify with Jesus in this passage. Since my wife is a church organist, I've been invited to many weddings, and I must confess a certain weariness with the sameness of the ceremonies I've attended. But our own wedding was anything but boring to me! And I remind myself that there is excitement and thrill in every wedding—at least for the couple taking the vows. Undoubtedly, the young couple at Cana of Galilee, whose wedding Jesus graced with His presence, were just as thrilled. But Jesus was just a guest at their wedding, as He is at so many—until the wedding was in trouble. The wine ran out (v. 3) and His mother came to Jesus with the problem. Suddenly, Jesus was no longer just a guest—He was in charge! What a remarkable change in a previously hopeless situation. With Jesus in charge, the best was yet to be! As the "master of ceremonies" (see The Living Bible) said to the bridegroom, "Every man at the beginning doth set forth good wine; and when men have well drunk, then that which is worse: but thou hast kept the good wine until now" (v. 10). Is your marriage floundering —or just going slightly "flat"? Put Jesus in charge and watch it change for the better!

## 25

*Stephen said, Behold I see the heavens opened, and the Son of Man on the right hand of God.*
—Acts 7:56

The Incarnation opened the spiritual, the supernatural, the eternal. It was as if the clouds were broken above this

# December

human valley that we live in, and men saw the Alps above them, and took courage. For, remember, it was a true Incarnation. It was a real bringing of God in the flesh. It was a real assertion of the possible union of humanity with divinity; and by all its tender and familiar incidents, by the babyhood and home life, the hungerings and thirstings of the incarnate Christ, it brought the divinity that it intended to reveal close into the hearts and houses of mankind. It made the supernatural possible as a motive in the smallest acts of men. It brought God so near that no slightest action could hide away from Him; that every least activity of life should feel His presence, and men should not only lead their armies and make their laws, but rise up and go to sleep, walk in the street, play with their children, work in their shops, talk with their neighbors, all in the fear and the love of the Lord.   —PHILLIPS BROOKS

*For ever, O Lord, thy word is settled in heaven.*

## 26

—Psalm 119:89

The utterances of Jesus Christ are not outgrown; they are as precious today, as when they were first spoken. They are as perfectly applicable to present-day needs as the needs of that day. They contain the solutions to all modern individual and social problems; they have perpetual youth. There is not one single point at which the teachings of Jesus Christ have been outgrown or become antiquated. The human mind has been expanding for nearly twenty centuries since Jesus Christ spoke here on earth, but it has not outgrown Him. Words that can endure twenty centuries of growth and still prove as thoroughly adequate to meet the needs of the race and each member of it as when first given, will stand for ever.

—R. A. TORREY

# December

God be thanked for that good and perfect gift, the gift unspeakable: His life, His love, His very self in Christ Jesus. —MALTBIE D. BABCOCK

**27** *Draw nigh to God, and he will draw nigh to you.*
—James 4:8

Here is a basic biblical principle that has a special application to the marriage relationship. The formula is not limited to the New Testament, for Ezra, the probable writer of the Chronicles as well as the book that bears his name, says: "The Lord is with you, while ye be with him; and if ye seek him, he will be found of you; but if ye forsake him, he will forsake you" (2 Chron. 15:2). How does this principle apply to marriage? The best way is to picture it this way:

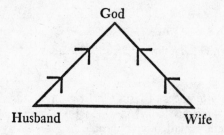

Normally, a triangle situation like this would be death to a marriage, but notice what happens in this particular geometric pattern. As husband and wife both move closer to God, they also move closer to one another. Notice, too, that as their mutual love for God draws husband and wife closer together, it also draws them higher. Hundreds of years ago, an insightful Thomas Fuller discovered: "Love is wont rather to ascend than descend." If you want your marriage to deepen and grow, apply this spiritual principle!

*Blessed be the God and Father of our Lord Jesus Christ, who hath blessed us with all spiritual blessings in heavenly places in Christ Jesus.*

**28**

—Ephesians 1:3

Men do not fly up mountains; they go up slowly, step by step. True Christian life is always mountain-climbing. Heaven is above us, and ever keeps above us. It never gets easy to go heavenward. It is a slow and painful process to grow better. No one leaps to sainthood at a bound. No one gets the victory once for all over his faults and sins. It is a struggle of years, and every day must have its victories if we are ever to be final and complete overcomers. Yet while we cannot expect to reach the radiant mountaintop at one bound, we certainly ought to be climbing at least step by step. We ought not to sit on the same little terrace, part way up the mountain, day after day. Higher and higher should be our unresting aim.   —J. R. Miller

*A land which the Lord your God careth for: the eyes of the Lord are always upon it, from the beginning of the year even unto the end of the year.*

**29**

—Deuteronomy 11:12

"A land which the Lord . . . careth for." Apply that thought to your home and your marriage. Remember this: God cares for you! And *about* you! Just as He watched over His people, the Jews, and the land He had given them, so He "watches over" and "cares for" you. This truth is borne out in countless passages throughout the Scriptures. To single out only a few:

The eyes of the Lord are upon the righteous, and his ears are open to their cry (Ps. 34:15).
He withdraweth not his eyes from the righteous . . . (Job 36:7).
For the eyes of the Lord are over the righteous, and his ears are open to their prayers . . . (1 Pet. 3:12).

# December

There is another side to this coin, as well. Amos 9:8 points out that "the eyes of the Lord God are upon the sinful kingdom, and I will destroy it from off the face of the earth. . . ." God's eyes look down upon sin in judgment, but those same eyes are upon His children to bless, guide, and protect them!

**30**    *I will instruct thee and teach thee in the way that thou shalt go: I will guide thee with mine eye.*
—Psalm 32:8

If we have absolute confidence in God's judgment, and God's willingness to guide us, and are absolutely surrendered to His will, whatever it may be, and are willing to let God choose His way of guidance, and will go on step by step as He does guide us, and are studying His Word to know His will, and are listening for the still, small voice of the Spirit, going step by step as He leads, He will guide us with His counsel to the end of our earthly pilgrimage, and afterwards receive us into glory.   —R. A. Torrey

A walk is made up of steps. Though a man circle the globe, yet he must do it one step at a time; and the character of the steps will determine the character of the walk. So life is made up, for the most part, of trifles, of commonplaces, or the reiteration of familiar and simple acts. And what we are in those, that will determine the color and value of our lives in the verdict of eternity. Life is not made by the rapturous but brief moments which we spend on the transfiguration mount but by the steps we take along the pathway of daily duty, and of sometimes monotonous routine.   —F. B. Meyer

**31** *Brethren, the time is short.* —1 Corinthians 7:29

Life as a part, life set upon the background of eternity, life recognized as the temporary form of that whose substance is everlasting, that is short; we wait for, we expect its end. And remember that to the Christian the interpretation of all this is in the incarnation of Christ: "I am He that liveth, and was dead; and behold, I am alive for ever more." The earthly life set against the eternal life, the incorporate earthly form uttering here for a time the everlasting and essential being, those years shut in out of the eternities between the birth and the ascension, that resurrection opening the prospect of the life that never was to end—these are the never failing interpretations to the man who believes in them of the temporal and eternal in his own experience. The old year is slipping behind us. We cannot stop it if we would. We must go forth and leave our past. Let us go forth nobly, as those whom greater thoughts and greater deeds await beyond. Let us go humbly, solemnly, bravely, as those must go who go to meet the Lord. With firm, quiet, serious steps, full of faith, hope, let us go to meet Him who will certainly judge us when we meet Him, but who loves us while He judges us, and who, if we are only obedient, will make us, by the discipline of all the years, fit for the everlasting world, where life shall count itself by years no longer.

—Phillips Brooks

## Scripture Index

Note: The numbers to the right of the Scripture references are keyed to the daily devotions in this book, i.e., 1 = January, 2 = February, 3 = March, 4 = April, 5 = May, 6 = June, 7 = July, 8 = August, 9 = September, 10 = October, 11 = November, and 12 = December. The number following the solidus (/) refers to the day. Thus 1/1 = January 1, 3/4 = March 4, etc.